Urban Grit

Recent Titles in
Genreflecting Advisory Series

Diana Tixier Herald, Series Editor

Urban Grit

A Guide to Street Lit

Megan Honig

Genreflecting Advisory Series

Diana Tixier Herald, Series Editor

 **LIBRARIES UNLIMITED**

AN IMPRINT OF ABC-CLIO, LLC
Santa Barbara, California • Denver, Colorado • Oxford, England

Library of Congress Cataloging-in-Publication Data

Honig, Megan.
  Urban grit : a guide to street lit / Megan Honig.
      p. cm. -- (Genreflecting advisory series)
  Includes bibliographical references and index.
  ISBN 978-1-59158-857-3 (acid-free paper) 1. Urban fiction, American--Bibliography. 2. Urban fiction, American--Stories, plots, etc. 3. Readers' advisory services--United States. 4. Fiction in libraries. I. Title.
  Z1231.U73H66 2011
  [PS374.U73]
  016.813'609358209732--dc22   2010041099

ISBN: 978-1-59158-857-3
15 14 13 12 11   1 2 3 4 5

This book is also available on the World Wide Web as an eBook.
Visit www.abc-clio.com for details.

Libraries Unlimited
An Imprint of ABC-CLIO, LLC

ABC-CLIO, LLC
130 Cremona Drive, P.O. Box 1911
Santa Barbara, California 93116-1911

This book is printed on acid-free paper ∞
Manufactured in the United States of America

Contents

Acknowledgments

This book could never have been written without the support of friends, family, and colleagues or without the tireless enthusiasm of the teens of New York Public Library. Particular thanks to Shauntee Burns, for helping me brainstorm keywords and chapter headings and for bringing in a fan's perspective; Anne Rouyer, for getting me into this project in the first place; and Jack Martin and Chris Shoemaker, for their continuing support and for the best and longest-running horse joke in library history.

Heartfelt appreciation also to my friends, family, and support network: You know who you are. Thank you.

Introduction

Street lit. Urban fiction. Hip-hop books. In the past ten to fifteen years, the resurgence of gritty, action-packed stories of street life and survival has rocked the literary landscape.

Published by independent presses, or by the authors themselves, street lit became popular through community channels and word of mouth, bypassing traditional book distributors and advertising venues. Readers' demand for the genre still takes many librarians and mainstream booksellers by surprise.

Intrigued? Confused? This guide will tell you what your readers already know: what street lit is, which books are hot for what readers, and which titles are essential for your library.

Genre Overview

Also called "urban fiction" "hip-hop lit," "hood lit," "gangsta lit," and a few other names, the set of books now called street lit is a unique genre that rose to widespread popularity in the late 1990s and has been growing ever since.

Readership

Sales figures and the growth of the street publishing industry show that street lit is a publishing phenomenon, but little data exist on who reads street novels. Anecdotal evidence suggests that many of street lit's readers are in similar demographics to the authors': young, working class, African American, often female. Many articles have also been written on urban fiction's popularity with teenagers. Without formal research, however, it is difficult to determine how broad the genre's appeal is. Do readers in rural areas find street lit meaningful? Older readers? Latino readers? Asian readers? White readers? Readers from the suburbs?

If your library is located outside a poor or working-class urban area, don't assume that street lit is not for your collection. Buy a few titles, market them, and see what happens. You may find interest you hadn't expected, or you may reach members of your community you didn't know were there.

Genre Definition and Characteristics

For the purposes of this guide, we define street lit as raw, gritty, urban stories set in the violent, dangerous, familiar, and sometimes exhilarating landscape of the streets, featuring tough African American characters and focusing on themes of interpersonal relationships and survival by any means necessary.

Although individual works of street lit can differ greatly from one another, books in the genre typically share many if not all of the characteristics listed below.

Settings and Themes

African American Authors, Characters, and Intended Audience

Contemporary street lit emerged from within African American urban communities. The books tell stories from within those communities and are intended to speak to readers familiar with the landscape and language of socioeconomically disadvantaged, urban African American neighborhoods.

Urban Settings

Most street lit is set in urban areas. New York and Philadelphia are common settings, but some street lit takes place in less prominent cities, including Gary, Indiana; Richmond, Virginia; and even Waterloo, Iowa.

Focus on Street Life

Unsurprisingly, the milieu of "the streets" is prominent in street lit. The streets are a social space, where news and rumors travel, and where crime and violence grow largely unchecked. Many subjects and themes of street lit involve the streets: drug dealing, prostitution, and robberies; friendship, betrayal, and revenge.

Hip-Hop Culture Elements

Elements of hip-hop culture, including rap music, street fashion, and an emphasis on brand name clothes and cars, play a prominent role in street lit. Many works of street lit invite the reader to take pleasure in lush descriptions of expensive, high-status material goods, such as Brianna's $1,200 weave in Wahida Clark's *Payback Is a Mutha* or drug dealer Black's iced out Bentley in Shannon Holmes's *B-More Careful*. Popular hip-hop music also plays a significant role in many works of street lit. Many street lit novels take place within the music business, and some use popular songs or lyrics as titles or themes. Erica Hilton's *10 Crack Commandments*, for example, takes its name from a Notorious B.I.G. song, and each chapter focuses on one of the rules of drug dealing named in the song.

Appeal Characteristics

Language

Street lit is often narrated in a straightforward tone that reflects casual spoken language. Many novels are narrated in the first person, and most use street slang, nonstandard grammar, and curse words in narration. Rather than being explicitly shaped or crafted for an effect of its own, the language in street lit serves as a tool for telling the story simply and directly. A glossary of common street lit terms is included in this book for readers unfamiliar with hip-hop or street slang.

Authenticity

Many street lit authors write directly from personal experience and acknowledge that their stories are personal. Some works include a preface in which the author speaks directly to the reader, saying that the novel is based on the author's own experience or the experience of friends, family, or other members of the author's community. Sometimes this statement, or the knowledge that the author has lived the life described in the book, serves to lend credence to an outlandish story. At other times, there is a cautionary note: the author is writing from prison or is no longer in the life and wants to warn readers away from making the same mistakes.

External Action

Some street lit is tightly plotted, with all events centered around one key incident or situation. Other works are episodic, following a character or a set of characters through a series of sequential events. Whether tightly plotted or episodic, however, the vast majority of action in street novels is external, happening between characters rather than within one character's mind. In the drama subgenre, one lie, infidelity, insult, or betrayal leads to another. In the players and hustlers subgenre, characters hustle, scheme, and commit heists and robberies, and further violence, turf wars, or raucous celebrations result.

Matter of Fact Treatment of Sex, Drugs, and Violence

Sexuality, drug use, drug dealing, and street violence are part of the landscape of street lit. Even in scenes that are not intended to titillate the reader, sex is discussed openly and directly. Similarly, drugs appear frequently, and characters who deal drugs, use drugs, or are addicted to drugs are common in street novels. Street violence is often described in explicit, matter of fact terms, though some novels are more graphically violent than others.

Pragmatism

Rather than reflecting a code rooted in an absolute sense of good and evil, most street lit tells stories of characters making choices based on getting their basic needs met: shelter, providing for their families, freedom from abuse or mistreatment, respite from the pain of daily life, or respect of peers and community. Drug dealing, sex work, and violent crime are frequently seen as paths to getting one's needs met. Though many works of street lit are cautionary tales, the message is not that crime is inherently morally wrong, but instead that it is unsustainable in the long term: that characters who base their lifestyles in hustling and violence will most likely end up dead or in prison.

Publication and Packaging

Book Packaging

Most street lit is published in paperback. Covers of street lit novels are often similar to covers of mainstream rap albums. They are usually photographic and often feature women in sexualized poses. Elements of street culture and crime are often present, including urban landscapes, popular fashions, and representations of wealth or money.

Independent or Self-Publication

Street lit books are often published by the author or by an independent publishing house owned by another street lit author. In recent years, some mainstream publishers have begun publishing street lit. A section explaining the history of the genre and its publication circumstances follows.

History of Street Lit

The authentic tone, flavor, and appeal of contemporary street lit are directly connected to its publishing history. Rather than conform to the standards of mainstream publishing, where tastes are dominated by whiteness and middle- and upper-class aspirations, street novelists from the beginning wrote for and marketed to their own communities. Even when mainstream publishers began to embrace street lit, they did so in ways that let street novelists maintain creative control.

Precursors to Street Lit

Conversational, plot-driven novels dealing with poverty, street crime, and the struggle for survival have been part of Western literature for centuries, but the most direct precursors to contemporary street lit arose in the 1960s and 1970s with the work of Iceberg Slim and Donald Goines. Unlike their contemporaries, Chester Himes and Ralph Ellison, who covered similar topics but received more critical praise from both African American and white audiences, Goines and Slim appealed to the masses, writing stories of pimps, hustlers, and street brutality in blunt, matter of fact prose.

Though the tones and topics of Slim and Goines's novels are similar to those of contemporary street lit, the authors' relationship to the novels' production and distribution is different. Goines, for instance, had a lifetime contract with publisher Holloway House (Horton-Stallings 2003) and received relatively small compensation for his best-selling works. Were Slim and Goines publishing today, they might be selling their books directly to consumers or operating their own urban publishing houses, allowing the writers to profit more directly from their work and maintain greater creative control.

Rise of Contemporary Street Lit

The contemporary street lit movement began with two sets of occurrences: two street-themed novels published by mainstream publishing giant Simon & Schuster received large-scale attention, and several independent authors who could not find a reception with mainstream publishers achieved widespread underground success.

Mainstream Novels Sell Big

The first of two popular mainstream street-themed novels in the 1990s was *Flyy Girl* by Omar Tyree. Originally self-published in 1993, *Flyy Girl* was not widely distributed until 1996, when Simon & Schuster reissued the novel (Morris et al. 2006). The novel tells the story of Tracy Ellison, a spoiled girl from Philadelphia's Germantown neighborhood growing up in the 1980s. Sex, materialism, and street crime all play into Tracy's coming-of-age and the coming-of-age of those around her.

In 1999 Sister Souljah's *Coldest Winter Ever* became a sales phenomenon; in 2008 Simon & Schuster reported that one million copies were in print (Minzescheimer 2008). The novel describes the journey of sixteen year-old Winter Santiaga, from her pampered lifestyle as a Brooklyn drug dealer's daughter, to her fight for survival on the streets, to her eventual incarceration. Souljah, already a known hip-hop artist and activist, inserts herself as a character and moral center in an otherwise amoral universe.

Independent Authors Gain Followings

Some authors of gritty African American fiction found success outside mainstream publishing. Teri Woods, author of *True to the Game*, began her lucrative writing and publishing career selling hand-bound copies of the novel out of the trunk of her car in 1998 (Patrick 2003). Vickie Stringer, who began her writing career while serving a prison term, reports selling over 100,000 copies of her 2001 autobiographical novel *Let That Be the Reason*, which she also self-published (Smith 2004).

Zane, now widely known as a powerhouse of African American erotica, first sold erotic short stories from her Web site, then self-published her *Sex Chronicles*, a compilation of short stories that sold 50,000 copies in its first year. She had received some amount of interest from mainstream publishers but was unwilling to "clean up" her juicy, sexual prose (Patrick 2002).

Street Lit Authors Create Publishing Houses

Rather than use their success to seek the attention of mainstream houses, many of the pioneering street lit authors turned their efforts to creating publishing enterprises of their own. In 2001, the same year that she published *Let That Be the Reason*, Vickie Stringer began publishing and distributing street lit titles by other authors through her newly founded press, Triple Crown Publications (Murray 2004). K'wan's *Gangsta*, in 2002, and Nikki Turner's *A Hustler's Wife*, in 2003, were two of Stringer's smash hit titles.

Teri Woods also used her business smarts to distribute other authors' works. She signed Shannon Holmes to her label, alternately known as Teri Woods Publishing and Meow Meow Productions, and distributed his wildly successful *B-More Careful*, the story of three women's friendship in Baltimore and one drug dealer's revenge. Numerous other street lit authors became publishers in the early 2000s, including Crystal Lacey Winslow, with Melodrama Publications; Carl Weber, with Urban Books; and Mark Anthony, with the now-defunct Q-Boro Books.

Mainstream Publishers Embrace Street Lit

Recognizing the popularity and large sales figures of urban fiction titles, mainstream publishing houses turned their attention to street lit and began courting big name authors aggressively.

Mainstream Houses Publish Street Lit Authors

After his success with *B-More Careful,* Shannon Holmes got a two-book contract with Atria for a reported six figures (Patrick 2003). K'wan's *Street Dreams,* published in 2004, was St. Martin's Press's first foray into the genre. Nikki Turner, author of two successful novels with Triple Crown, published *The Glamorous Life* with Random House's Ballantine/One World imprint in 2005. Although often more rigorously copyedited than their independently published predecessors, street novels published with mainstream houses largely retained the flavor of the authors' earlier work, though features like the glossary in Shannon Holmes's *Dirty Game* would not likely have appeared in a Triple Crown volume.

Street Lit Authors Recruited as Editors

Not only were street authors wooed into publishing books with mainstream houses, but many were also offered positions of creative control. At Random House, Nikki Turner was invited to edit short story collections and acquire novels of her own, which were packaged under the label "Nikki Turner Presents . . ." . At Simon & Schuster, Zane signed a distribution deal for titles from her company Strebor Books International (Johnson 2004). Strebor Books appear in the catalog of Simon & Schuster's Atria imprint, but Zane retains editorial authority.

The Landscape Today

Mainstream publishers' foray into street lit has not dampened the success of independent urban publishing. Independent presses such as Triple Crown and Urban Books continue to thrive. At the same time, even more authors have begun publishing their own work or creating publishing companies of their own.

Deja King, author of the highly popular Bitch series, stopped selling and marketing her books through Triple Crown after *The Bitch Is Back* (2008). For the fourth and fifth books of the series, King used her own company, A King Production. T. Styles, who published *Black and Ugly* and *A Hustler's Son* with Triple Crown, created The Cartel Publications in 2008 and has successfully distributed thirteen books in two years, including Reign's *Shyt List* and Eyone Williams's *Hell Razor Honeys.* Wahida Clark, whose Thugs and Payback series are still published by Kensington, a large independent publisher known for a variety of genres, entered the publishing game herself in 2008 with a press called Wahida Clark Publishing.

As the number of books published in the street lit genre continues to grow, the boundaries of the genre itself continue to expand. Walk past street book vendors in any major metropolitan area and you will see a diverse array of titles from a variety of sources: mainstream publishers, large independent presses, and one-author self-publishing operations.

Though some critics dismiss street lit as a fad, writing and publishing in the genre show no sign of slowing. As long as fans hunger for stories that reflect the flavor of the streets, street lit will only get bigger, broader, and more diverse in range.

About This Book

Purpose

The purpose of this book is twofold: to educate librarians and booksellers about street lit and to provide access to works of street lit categorized by theme, subgenre, and appeal.

The introductory essays and lists identify and contextualize street lit as a leisure reading genre, explaining the characteristics of the genre, its unique publication history, the criticisms and controversies surrounding the genre, special issues for teen readers of street lit, and ways to identify new street lit titles for library collections. "Resources and Further Reading" in the back of this book lists articles and resources for understanding street lit as well as sources for learning about new and upcoming street lit titles. A list of significant street lit publishers appears in appendix D.

The eleven chapters are annotated bibliographies. Organized by subgenre, these bibliographies describe individual works of street fiction so that readers' advisors will better understand the books in the street lit genre and will recommend books that readers of the genre will enjoy.

Appendixes A, B, and C provide collection development resources, suggesting core collections for adults in public libraries, young adults in public libraries, and students in high school libraries. Three indexes provide access to street lit titles by author, title, and keyword (subject).

Scope

Covering a new genre on which relatively little has been written is tricky. Titles for this bibliography were selected using a variety of sources. Professional sources for librarians, including Vanessa Morris's "Urban/Street Lit Fiction Reading List Suitable for PUBLIC Library Collections" (2008), Daniel Marcou's Streetfiction.org, and *Library Journal*'s "Word on Street Lit" column provided some titles and authors.

Catalogs of independent publishers were also consulted. For independent publishers who only publish street fiction, such as Vickie Stringer's Triple Crown Publications, all titles still in print were considered for inclusion. Some publishers, such as Carl Weber's Urban Books, produce both street fiction and mainstream fiction. In the cases of those publishers, only imprints with a focus on street fiction were considered.

Books selected for the annotated bibliography were true to most if not all elements of street fiction, including an independent publication history; African American author, characters, and intended audience; an urban setting; and a focus on street life. Some books that fall slightly outside this range were also included: a few representative classics from genre godfathers Iceberg Slim and Donald Goines, seminal memoirs of street life, and books that add diversity to the list—poetry, novels featuring GLBT characters, erotica, and Christian titles.

Intended Audience

This book is primarily intended for librarians working with adults and teens, particularly in urban areas where there is highest demand for street fiction. Street lit fans, you already have your tools—we librarians are just catching up—but should this book prove useful to you, either in finding your next great read or in making sure your local library has that next hot title ready for you, this author would be honored.

Arrangement

Street lit titles are listed in eleven chapters, arranged by subgenre and subdivided by theme: novels in the "Friendship" subgenre, for example, are divided into the two themes "Friends 'Til the End" and "Frenemies." Within each theme, titles are listed alphabetically by author. Books in series are grouped together and listed in series order.

Entry Anatomy

Each bibliographic entry contains the elements listed below.

Author Name

The name of the author or editor is listed, starting with last name. Anthologies with no editor named are listed simply by title. Entries are listed alphabetically.

Series Heading

Many street lit books are published in series. If the annotated work is a series of books rather than a single title, the name of the series appears underscored. If the author and publisher do not provide a unique name for the series, the name of the first book in the series is used. For instance, Vickie Stringer's *Let That Be the Reason*, *Imagine This*, and *The Reason Why* have been listed under the heading <u>Let That Be the Reason Series</u>. If an author has both stand-alone books and series books, the stand-alone titles are listed before the series.

Bibliographic Information

Title, publisher name and location, year of publication, number of pages, and ISBN are listed here. For reprints, the original year of publication is included in parentheses.

Symbols

The gun symbol (☞) and the pepper symbol (❨) indicate the levels of violence and sexuality present in a book. Each book is assigned a rating of 1 to 3 ☞ and 1 to 3 𝟙. Books rated ☞ contain the mildest level of violence, but in books rated ☞☞☞, expect graphic brutality. Books rated 𝟙 contain mild or no sexual content, whereas books rated 𝟙𝟙𝟙 contain explicit and abundant sex.

Annotation

A short paragraph introduces the plot of the book and evokes its appeal.

Keywords

These words or short phrases indicate appeal factors or other important attributes, such as the city in which the story is set and whether the book includes a particular theme or type of character, such as teenagers, stickup artists, or GLBTQ.

Similar Reads

This paragraph sums up the appeal of the title and makes further reading recommendations. Suggested titles have elements in common with the original title, such as theme, appeal, type of character, or subject matter.

Core Collection and Classic

Titles that appear in the suggested core collections in Appendixes A, B, and C are labeled "Core Collection: Adult," "Core Collection: Young Adult," and "Core Collection: School Libraries" respectively. Classic titles are labeled "Classic."

Street Lit in the Library

Your library patrons deserve street lit! However, including street lit in library collections presents a unique set of challenges. Some of the major challenges are discussed below, including responding to common complaints, serving teen readers, and developing street lit collections.

Preparing for Controversy

Love it or hate it, street lit belongs in your library. Because the genre brings up issues of race, class, gender, and sexuality and portrays a world that is harsh, unsanitized, and full of imperfect choices, it is no surprise that street lit becomes a lightning rod for cultural anxieties about these topics.

Some of your library patrons may hate or feel threatened by the presence of street lit in your collection. Be prepared to respond to complaints with compassion and understanding, and be aware that you will probably not change their feelings about the genre. At the same time, know that street lit is a popular genre that likely holds meaning for many readers in your community and belongs in your library for that reason.

Following are some of the common complaints about street lit.

Literary Quality

Some critics of street lit complain that street lit is "bad literature." In their eyes, the genre is unworthy of attention because it focuses on plot rather than character development, contains spelling and grammar errors, or depicts unrealistic situations. These critics seem to believe that readers who find street lit meaningful are simply being duped and would stop reading street lit if only they were exposed to works with greater literary merit.

If you are used to defending other genre fiction, these accusations may sound familiar. Charges that a particular genre is "bad literature" or of less inherent value than explicitly literary fiction are levied against many kinds of books, particularly those that appeal to marginalized groups—romance novels, which appeal largely to women, and comic books, which appeal to teenagers, come to mind.

Kindly remind patrons who make this complaint that not all types of books will appeal to all readers, but that many readers do find this genre meaningful, and your job as a librarian and readers' advisor is to serve all of your readers' interests and tastes.

Portrayal of the African American Community

One of the most scathing and high-profile attacks on street lit appeared in a *New York Times* editorial by Nick Chiles, an African American writer and intellectual. After a visit to his local Borders in Lithonia, Georgia, in late 2005, Chiles described in horror what he had seen there. The African American literature section of the bookstore had expanded, Chiles reported, but it was filled with works of street lit. Chiles went on to describe the books and his own reactions to them in particularly loaded terms: he was "embarrassed," "disgusted," "mortified," and "ashamed" to see these books on the same shelves as his own work (Chiles 2006).

One of the many pernicious effects of American racism is that the actions and portrayals of one African American person or group of people are presumed to reflect on all African American people. For this reason, upwardly mobile African American readers may be concerned that the characters, situations, and language of street lit reflect on them personally. Hidden in this fear is anxiety about social class. Elements that appear in street lit, such as brash attitudes, nonstandard grammar, crime, non-nuclear family structures, and street slang, reflect a stigmatized underclass from which critics of the genre may be eager to distance themselves.

The ill effects of racism and classism are and should be a concern of public libraries, but failing to provide street lit is not a fair or effective way to address these concerns. Your job as a librarian is to maintain a collection that reflects the reading tastes of all community members, and your collection should include street lit as well as other kinds of literature featuring African American characters and concerns.

Misogyny, Homophobia, and Transphobia

Some opponents of street lit criticize the genre's treatment of gender and sexuality, or of gay, lesbian, bisexual, or transgender people. Concerns about misogyny focus on the rigidity of gender roles in many works of street fiction, double standards around infidelity, unproblematized violence against women, and the photographic covers of many street novels, which often feature women in sexualized positions. Concerns about homophobia focus on the portrayal of same-gender sexuality as aberrant or disgusting, as in a memorable scene in Wahida Clark's *Payback Is a Mutha*, in which a woman catches her male lover *in flagrante* with another man and promptly vomits. Concerns about transphobia focus on books in which transsexual women's existence is portrayed as a shocking plot twist or used to elicit shame and disgust.

Though these elements are present in many works of street lit, the treatment of women and GLBT people varies widely within the genre. For example, authors such as Reginald Hall and Laurinda D. Brown tell affirming stories about gay men and lesbians, respectively, and a number of authors, including Black Artemis and Sapphire, portray positive, empowered women characters. If you have patrons who are concerned about issues of misogyny, homophobia, and transphobia, perhaps you can use library programming to help address these issues in your community. What you can't do, however, is solve the problem by eliminating street lit.

Conflation with African American Literary Fiction

Another frequent criticism focuses on where street lit is shelved. Many libraries and bookstores feature sections for African American fiction and name those sections in a way that suggests the books therein represent the lives of all African American people—"Black Experience" is a common example. Critics argue that shelving street lit in a "Black Experience" section sends the message that all African American people's lives mirror those depicted in street lit.

When you shelve your street lit, why not shelve it as its own genre? It is insulting to street lit readers and literary fiction readers alike, not to mention ineffective readers' advisory, to put a literary opus by Toni Morrison under the same heading as a thriller by Relentless Aaron. Shelving street lit by itself allows readers looking for street lit to find it more easily and avoids sending the message that your library believes there is only one universal "Black Experience."

Effect on Teenagers

Another set of criticisms about street lit come from people who are concerned about the effect of street lit on teenagers. Critics are concerned that street lit contains "inappropriate" language or sexual content or "glorifies" sex, drugs, and criminal behavior, and that teen readers of street lit will be exposed to dangerous ideas or influenced to emulate the language and actions of characters in the books. Most of these complaints miss the point: teens are reading these books, and failing to collect street lit at the public library will not change that fact. The best way to address concerns about making street lit available to teens is not by censoring the material, but by providing a balanced library collection and offering relevant programming.

The significance of street lit to teenagers and best practices for serving teens who read street lit are discussed in detail below.

Serving Teen Street Lit Readers

Like it or not, adults are not the only street lit readers. Teens read street lit too, and the teens in your library deserve to see their needs and interests represented in your library collection. The sections below discuss why the genre of street lit speaks to teenagers and how best to supplement these sometimes controversial titles.

Significance of Street Lit to Teenagers

Street lit is written by adults with an adult audience in mind. Though the appeal to adult fans is obvious, librarians are often surprised at, bewildered by, and suspicious of the genre's appeal to teenagers. In fact, understanding teens' interest in the genre is simple. Teens choose reading material that is meaningful to them. When teens read street lit, it is because works in the genre are meeting their emotional, social, or developmental needs. Some of the needs street lit may meet for teens are discussed below.

Reflection of Lived Experiences

Teens who read street lit are often drawn to the genre because it reflects landscapes, settings, and characters that remind them of those in their own lives. Many teens who read street lit report feeling that the books are "like real life" (Morris et al. 2006). It is worth pointing out that when teen readers feel that these books reflect the lives they already lead, attempting to protect them from the books' content is a farce: street lit is meaningful to these readers *because* of its difficult content.

Identity Affirmation

Teen readers of street lit often identify with characters in the books. Teens are constantly questioning and exploring their identities, and finding a character whose speech, appearance, concerns, and circumstances mirror one's own is particularly affirming and validating for a teen reader.

Engagement at a Safe Distance

Teens who find street lit compelling may be grappling with some of its darker themes in their own lives, including abuse, drug use, violence, extreme poverty, or the loss of a friend or family member. Some novels written for young adults explore these themes, but most often the stories are character-driven and evoke painful emotions. Street lit, which focuses more often on plot than on characters' emotions, allows readers to engage with these topics without experiencing their full emotional weight.

Entertainment

Adults read for entertainment, and so do teens. Street lit provides its readers with the pleasures of a cinematically fast-paced and plot-driven story. Readers can also experience the pleasure of wish fulfillment, watching characters rise to the top of a drug empire and make opulent displays of wealth. Some readers also enjoy the voyeuristic aspect of street lit, watching characters lie, cheat, steal, fight, betray each other, and get revenge.

Risk-Free Thrill

Though some adults are afraid that giving teens access to sexually explicit material will expose them to dangerous ideas, it is much more likely that the reverse is true. Sexually graphic material gives readers the opportunity to explore their sexuality in private, without the risk of pregnancy, disease, or pressure from a partner.

Perspective

Reading about other people's choices and lives allows teen readers to gain perspective on their own. A group of Philadelphia librarians who worked with teen patrons to start a street lit book club found that their discussions changed the ways that readers saw the world around them. Having read about a particular relationship between a man and woman, participants in the group initially stated that the man treated his partner well because he gave her expensive gifts. But after further discussion, the group saw that the relationship was also violent (Morris et al. 2006). Could this insight have helped the book club members identify violence in their own communities and make more informed choices about relationships? It seems likely, and is a powerful argument for the importance of both reading and discussing these books.

Collections and Programming for Teen Street Lit Readers

Street lit brings up difficult issues, including verbal and physical abuse, street and relationship violence, racism, poverty, homophobia, prison, transphobia, drug addiction, incest, misogyny, and the lure of material wealth. This content has a place in libraries serving teens, but successful libraries do more than provide access to these materials: they also supplement works of street lit with more diverse materials and responsive programming.

Collecting Street Lit

It bears repeating: When the teens in your community are interested in street lit, your library must collect works of street lit for them. Small public libraries may shelve street lit titles for adult and teen use in a single section. Public libraries with teen spaces, however, should maintain a distinct street lit collection for teens in the teen space. Teen spaces are intended to reflect the needs and interests of teens in the library and should include all materials of interest to teens. A suggested core street lit collection for teens in public libraries appears in appendix B.

Collecting street lit in school libraries, where materials are often more susceptible to challenges, can be trickier. However, some school librarians recognize the importance of street lit to their students and collect titles in the genre. If you are collecting street lit for a school library, be prepared to defend the importance of these titles to concerned parents, teachers, and administrators. Resources discussing the significance of street lit to teenagers can be found in the section "Resources and Further Reading," and a core street lit collection for school libraries, emphasizing titles with a positive message, can be found in appendix C.

Balancing the Teen Collection

In addition to street lit, collect works of fiction and nonfiction that take similar tones or address similar themes:

- *Fiction.* For many teen readers, street lit books are a gateway into reading. After having read street lit, readers may wish to try new fiction genres. Carry a wide array, including horror fiction, which is also plot driven and sensational, and Chick Lit, which also explores relationships and interpersonal drama. Your collection should already include works by African American authors in genres other than street lit. Like all readers, African American teenagers deserve to see themselves in a wide variety of fiction.

- *Nonfiction.* To supplement street lit's treatment of sexuality, be sure to carry matter of fact, user-friendly guides to sexuality and sexual health. To support teens who may encounter police and the criminal justice system in their own lives, carry teen-friendly guides to young people's rights and the legal system. Nonfiction books focusing on other aspects of hip-hop culture, including music, celebrities, graffiti art, and spoken word poetry, may also be of interest.

Programming

You can also address many of the issues raised in street lit through library programs. Talk to the teens in your library to see what kind of programs might be of interest to them. Relevant programs may include a street lit book club or book discussion group, a workshop on navigating the legal system, a writing workshop, a facilitated discussion on sexuality, or a visit by an urban fiction author.

Collecting Street Lit for Adults

The bibliographies in this book provide a foundation for a street lit collection, but street lit is a growing genre, with new books coming out all the time. Librarians maintaining a street lit collection must keep on top of new releases and developments in the genre.

If you're used to relying on library professional journals to select new materials, you'll need some new tools for street lit. Though street lit is slowly making its way to the consciousness of the mainstream review media, much of it is still sold directly to the consumer without concern for the library or chain bookstore market. Because of this, many review journals do not review street lit, review very little street lit, or only review works of street lit produced by mainstream publishers.

If you're selecting for teens, your job is even harder. No mainstream publications and no fan sites currently review adult street lit from a teen services perspective. Unless you have the luxury of examining each book yourself before it goes into the collection, you must simply make your best guess at what materials fit your collection needs—a dicey proposition when considering edgy fiction for collections aimed at young people.

Despite these challenges, your readers deserve access to materials that meet their needs. You cannot ignore the need for street lit, so try some nontraditional collection development sources.

Talk to Readers

Fans of street lit are often experts on the genre and can tell you what's hot and what's coming up. Talk to your patrons about the books they're reading and find out who is in the know. If you have teenagers at your library who read street lit, ask them what books speak to them and where they find out about new titles. Talking to teens will inform you about what street books you should put in your young adult collection and will show them that their opinions matter.

Visit Street Vendors

In some urban areas, street lit is literally sold on the street. Book vendors who sell street lit can tell you what's selling and what their customers are asking about. As a collection development librarian, I have frequently been grateful for the book vendor on the corner of my library's block. Passing by his table on the way to work has alerted me to numerous new releases, including Mike Sanders's *Thirsty* and Anna J's *Snow White*.

Keep up with Publishers' Web Sites and Mailing Lists

Most publishers of street lit have Web sites and mailing lists and are eager to alert potential customers about new products. A list of contact information for important street lit publishers appears in appendix D.

Check Fan Web Sites

The Internet is chock-full of street lit fans and book discussions. Black Book Releases (http://www.blackbookreleases.com) maintains a substantial, continuously updated list of upcoming African American titles, many of which are adult street lit. Amazon.com is a great source of user-generated lists. Look for lists of upcoming titles, hot titles, or an individual user's favorites. Fan reviews on Amazon.com can also inform your selection decisions.

A list of additional Web sources appears in "Resources and Further Reading."

Conclusion

Developing, maintaining, and defending a street lit collection in your library can be a challenge. Nevertheless, know that you are doing a meaningful and deserved service for your patrons by taking on this challenge. By learning more about street lit and respecting its importance to your patrons, you ensure that your library stays relevant, responsive to its community, and in touch with the things that matter to readers.

References

Chiles, Nick. 2006. "Their Eyes Were Reading Smut." (Editorial Desk). *The New York Times*, January 3, A15(L).

Horton-Stallings, LaMonda H. 2003. " 'I'm Goin Pimp Whores!': The Goines Factor and the Theory of a Hip-Hop Neo-Slave Narrative." *CR: The New Centennial Review 3*, no. 3, 175–203.

Johnson, Kalyn. 2004. "Zane, Inc." *Black Issues Book Review 6*, no. 5 (September–October): 17–20.

Minzescheimer, Bob. 2008. "Sister Souljah Rejects Any Labels on Her Literary Output." *USA TODAY*, November 20. http://www.usatoday.com/life/books/news/2008-11-19-souljah-midnight_n.htm.

Morris, Vanessa. 2008. "Urban/Street Lit Fiction Reading List Suitable for PUBLIC Library Collections." http://www.jahreinaresearch.info/VJMWebsite/urbanfiction/UrbanFictionReadingList.htm.

Morris, Vanessa, Sandra Hughes-Hassell, Denise E. Agosto, and Darren T. Cottman. 2006. "Street lit: Flying Off Teen Fiction Bookshelves in Philadelphia Public Libraries." (Cover Story). *Young Adult Library Services 5*, no. 1(Fall): 16–23.

Murray, Victoria C. 2004. "Triple Crown Winner: In the Hot Category of Urban Fiction, Ex-Offender Victoria Stringer Self-Published Her Story and Launched Her Successful Independent Press." *Black Issues Book Review 6*, no. 3 (May/June): 28.

Patrick, Diane. 2002. "Sex Sells." *Publishers Weekly* 249, no. 28 (July 15): 20.

Patrick, Diane. 2003. "Urban Fiction." *Publishers Weekly* 250, no, 20 (May 19): 31.

Smith, Dinitia. 2004. "Unorthodox Publisher Animates Hip-Hop Lit." *The New York Times*, September 8, E6.

Chapter 1

Players and Hustlers

Plot-driven and sometimes violent, novels in the players and hustlers subgenre focus on gangsters, hustlers, stickup artists, street crews, and the mechanics of drug dealing or other illegal enterprise. Common themes in these novels include turf wars, hustlers coming up or rising to power, defending one's business, avoiding law enforcement, and planning and carrying out heists or robberies.

Characters in novels in the players and hustlers subgenre are often recognizable types, including wild, unpredictable gangsters; ruthless, effective drug kingpins; cold, street-savvy women hustlers; and "ride or die chicks," who are down for their men whatever the cost.

The novels in this chapter are similar to those in chapter 6, because both concern crime and hustling, and feature a lot of action. In this chapter, however, the action focuses on the day-to-day business of the hustle, whereas in thrillers, the tension is heightened, often because law enforcement is involved.

The pleasures of these novels are many: watching a character rise to the top of the drug game; savoring the material goods that successful drug dealers can afford; and wondering who will be left standing and who will pay for their misdeeds. Classic novels in this subgenre include K'wan's *Gangsta* and Teri Woods's *Dutch*.

Drug Dealers and Kingpins

Novels in this section focus on the actions of players and hustlers in the drug business. Some, like Teri Woods's <u>Dutch</u>, chart the steps in a powerful gangster's rise to power. Others, like 50 Cent and K'wan's *Blow*, follow the misadventures of low-level, ineffective drug dealers.

50 Cent and K'wan.

Blow. New York: Pocket Books, 2007. 226pp. ISBN 9781416540601, 1416540601. 𝄞𝄞 ((

Unlike your typical street lit heroes, Danny, E, Felix Guzman, and the rest of *Blow*'s cast of characters are drug dealers without much strength, heart, or daring. They take other people's orders, get high on their own product, and clown around. When one of their number gets his own connect, the men have a chance to make it big. But can these small-timers rise to the occasion?

Keywords: Light Reads; New York; Street Code

Similar Reads: *Blow* is a comic take on hustling. For other light comedies featuring male characters, try *Cut Throat* by K. Roland Williams or David Givens's *Betrayed*. For other stories of incompetent drug dealers, robbers, and hustlers, try 50 Cent and K. Elliott's *Ski Mask Way*, Joy's *Dollar Bill*, or Victor Martin's *For the Strength of You*.

50 Cent and Nikki Turner.

Death Before Dishonor. New York: Pocket Books, 2007. 194pp. ISBN 9781416531005, 1416531009. 𝄞 (

Sunni runs a hair salon in Richmond, Virginia, but before that she spent three years in prison, thanks to a man who sold her out. Now she's a strict businesswoman who believes in money before men. Trill, an up-and-coming drug dealer who has also spent time in prison, is pulled over by a racist cop while carrying a large amount of cocaine. Trill flees and ends up outside Sunni's house, and Sunni invites him in. The tension and chemistry between the two strong characters is intense! Nikki Turner herself makes a brief appearance in this first book in 50 Cent's G Unit line.

Keywords: Richmond, VA; Women Hustlers

Similar Reads: *Death Before Dishonor* is crisp and short and features a strong, assertive female character and dramatic romantic tension. For other stories about strong women, try Vickie Stringer's <u>Let That Be the Reason</u> series or Keisha Ervin's *Hold U Down*. For another odd couple thrown together by circumstance, try *Life* by Leo Sullivan or Keisha Ervin's *Gunz and Roses*.

Ace.

Teri Woods Presents Predators. New York: Teri Woods Publishing, 2007. 249pp. ISBN 0977323404, 9780977323401. 𝄞𝄞𝄞 ((

Woods's name looms large on the cover of this gritty thriller, but the story is by an author named Ace. One murder leads to another in a war for revenge and territory between crack dealers in 1988 Detroit. BJ and Thad are young players responsible for a large percentage of Detroit's murder rate. A new dealer named Busta tries to sell crack on BJ's turf, and BJ fights back. The violence between the men is gritty, but the violence between the women is even more intense. Chi Chi, who hangs out with BJ'.s crew, torments crack addict Lisa by forcing her to debase herself in exchange for drugs. In between these horrific acts, side characters—a Christian preacher and a Black Nationalist—speak inspiringly against black-on-black violence.

Keywords: Abuse; Detroit; Drug Addiction; Prison; Revenge; Social Commentary

Similar Reads: Bleak, gritty, and action-oriented, *Predators* focuses on a turf war between drug dealers and violent encounters between drug dealers and drug users. K'wan's *Gangsta* and Erick S. Gray's *Ghetto Heaven* both feature turf wars and high murder rates. *Crack Head* by Lisa Lennox, Treasure E. Blue's *Street Girl Named Desire*, and Endy's *Deal with Death* all feature brutal physical, emotional, and sexual abuse of drug users. The book's political center, which focuses on Christianity and Black Nationalism, can also be found in the works of Leo Sullivan and Jihad.

Ashley and JaQuavis.

Supreme Clientele. West Babylon, NY: Urban Books, 2009 (2007). 342pp. ISBN 1601621507, 9781601621504. ⌐ ((

Jules, Zya's boyfriend, is a major drug dealer in Harlem. But when Jules gets caught and sent to prison, Zya takes over moving the many kilos of cocaine for which Jules used to be responsible. Leaving Jules behind, Zya climbs to the top. The challenge: staying on top. The obstacles: her best friend's devious man and a marijuana-loving cop who's made it his personal mission to take New York's biggest drug lords down.

Keywords: New York; Prison; Women Hustlers

Similar Reads: *Supreme Clientele* is a typical Ashley and JaQuavis tale, full of fast-paced action, juicy drama, and relatively conventional gender roles—Zya may be hustling while Jules is behind bars, but she still looks to men more than to her own strength. For more of Ashley and JaQuavis's trademark drama, try other titles the pair have cowritten, particularly *The Trophy Wife* and *Dirty Money*. For a classic story of a woman fending for herself while her man is locked up, try Nikki Turner's <u>Hustler's Wife</u> series.

Core Collection: Adult

Dixon, Gregory.

The Cake Man. West Babylon, NY: Urban Books, 2009. 257pp. ISBN 9781933967844, 1933967846. ⌐⌐ ((

Big George King, a high-level drug dealer in Houston, Texas, showed his son Chris the basics of the drug game but never let him get too involved. Then Big George got caught by the feds and sentenced to ten years. Now Chris is coming up fast. A rival gang member shoots at him, so Chris retaliates violently. He gets his father's drug connect and builds himself a crew. All the while, he is falling in love with Jasmine, the woman who is part of his crew. This fast-paced and sometimes brutal story teaches the rules of the game.

Keywords: Houston; Mentors; Prison; Street Code

Similar Reads: The appeal of *The Cake Man* is learning the rules of the drug game along with Chris. For more stories about young hustlers learning how to win success in the drug game, try 50 Cent's memoir *From Pieces to Weight*, Dana Dane's *Numbers*, or Vickie Stringer's Let That Be the Reason.

Core Collection: Young Adult

Fleming, Eric.

Lust, Love, and Lies. **Wilmington, DE: Street Knowledge Publishing, 2008. 277pp. ISBN 9780979955679, 097995567X.** 🖙🖙🖙 ℭ

This tale of wealth, relationships, and brutal violence stars two men and two women. Brandon, known as Tank in his younger days, has just come back to Dallas, Texas, after going to college to play football. DJ, Brandon's closest friend growing up, now runs parts of the town, including a car wash that doubles as a soliciting ground for prostitution and a lucrative drug business. Tabitha, a lonely, attractive accountant, and Shon, Tabitha's friend, become close to Brandon and DJ without knowing the full extent of their depravity. While Tabitha is becoming involved with Brandon, Brandon is becoming a cold-blooded killer. Scenes of lurid and extreme violence illustrate Brandon's rise to professional hit man status.

Keywords: Assassins; Dallas; Multiple Perspectives

Similar Reads: *Lust, Love, and Lies* is told from multiple perspectives and features two high school buddies whose lives have diverged: one directionless college graduate and one opulently wealthy drug lord. For another story of high school friends reconnecting later in life, try Anya Nicole's *Corporate Corner Boyz*, in which two former friends go into the music business together. For another celebration of wealth, try Leondrei Prince's Bloody Money series, which begins with a hustler returning from prison and receiving lavish gifts from his friends.

Givens, David.

Betrayed. **Columbus, OH: Triple Crown Publications, 2008. 280pp. ISBN 9780979951770, 0979951771.** 🖙🖙 ℭℭ

Darrell is the head of Waterloo, Iowa's GMC, or Get Money Crew. But the city is filled with rivalries. The L-Block Boys are moving in on GMC territory, the cops are on Darrell's trail, and one of the guys who works for Darrell is coming up short of cash. Not only that, but there's drama—and plenty of sex—with the women in Darrell's life.

Keywords: Light Reads; Street Code; Waterloo, IA

Similar Reads: *Betrayed* is a breezy, funny, outrageous drama focused on male characters. For more drama centered on men, try Dwayne S. Joseph's *Womanizers* or the collection *Gigolos Get Lonely Too*. For light stories about hustlers, try K'wan's *Blow*, Michael Covington's *Chances*, or K. Roland Williams's *Cut Throat*.

Gray, Erick S.

Crave All, Lose All Series. ⌐⌐ ((

In two companion volumes, Gray explores themes of family, opportunity, and the dangers of greed.

Keywords: Queens, NY; Social Commentary; Street Code

Similar Reads: This series is notable for its round characters and its critique of crime and street life. Gray's *Money Power Respect* features similar character depth and also investigates the dangers and pitfalls of crime. For more novels that critique hustling, try Shannon Holmes's *Never Go Home Again* or Lena Scott's *O. G.*

Crave All, Lose All. New York: Augustus Publishing, 2008. 255pp. ISBN 9780979281617, 097928161X.

> There are two kinds of hustlers, Gray writes in his preface, the kind who need the money to support themselves and their families and the kind who love the fancy cars, clothes, jewelry, and women that money can buy. Initially Vince is the first kind of hustler. Loyal to the memory of the father who wanted him to work hard and legally, Vince used to let his drug-dealing friends do their thing while he did his. But after September 11, Vince gets laid off from the airline he's been working for, and he is tired of being broke when his mother and his child both need his support. The problem is that the fast life is easier to get into than to leave.

Love & a Gangsta. New York: Augustus Publishing, 2009. 261pp. ISBN 9780979281648, 0979281644.

> More a companion to *Crave All, Lose All* than a sequel, this volume focuses on characters Soul and America and the question of whether a hustler who has spent four years in prison should get back into the game.

King, Joy.

Stackin' Paper Series. ⌐⌐ ((

This action-packed series is a multi-city drama with an unusually strong female character. Joy King, the author, is better known as Deja King, author of the <u>Bitch</u> series. The first volume also lists a coauthor, Joe Joe.

Keywords: Atlanta; Philadelphia; Revenge; Women Hustlers

Similar Reads: *Stackin' Paper* is an action-heavy story of players coming up in the drug game, featuring a partnership between a ruthless man and a street-savvy woman. For more stories of midlevel players finding street success, try Gregory Dixon's *Cake Man.* For more women characters who can hold their own in the drug game, try 50 Cent and Nikki Turner's *Death Before Dishonor*, Vickie Stringer's <u>Let That Be the Reason</u>, or 50 Cent and Mark Anthony's *Harlem Heat*.

Core Collection: Adult

Stackin' Paper. Wilmington, DE: Street Knowledge Publishing, 2008. 212pp. ISBN 9780975581117, 0975581112.

> Genesis spent his adolescence in a juvenile facility after killing his abusive father in self-defense. As a free man, he's a midlevel player in the drug game. But he gets a break when he robs a stickup crew and finds far more drugs and cash than he imagined. Genesis and his friend and business partner Deuce fly to Atlanta to meet a drug connect, and the connect turns out to be a very attractive, very powerful pair of sisters, CoCo and Chanel. Genesis also meets a compelling woman, Tanisha, who just happens to be the girlfriend of a major Atlanta drug dealer.

Stackin' Paper II: Genesis' Payback. Collierville, TN: A King Production. 217pp. ISBN 9780975581162, 0975581163.

> Genesis, the up-and-coming drug dealer from *Stackin' Paper*, returns to seek revenge on those who got in his way.

K'wan.

Gangsta Series. 𝒓𝒓 ((

This classic shoot-'em-up stars two wild members of Los Angeles's Crips gang, fighting for turf in New York City.

Keywords: Gangs; New York

Similar Reads: *Gangsta* is a classic street story of gang warfare featuring a wild gangster and his legendary exploits. For a grimmer take on gangs, try James Hendricks *A Good Day to Die* or Reymundo Sanchez's memoir *My Bloody Life: The Making of a Latin King.* For another outrageously ambitious and violent gangster character, try Teri Woods's <u>Dutch</u> series or Cash's *Trust No Man.*

Classic

Core Collection: Adult, Young Adult

Gangsta: An Urban Tragedy. Columbus, OH: Triple Crown Publications, 2003 (2002). 198pp. ISBN 0970247214, 9780970247216.

> One of urban publishing giant Triple Crown's original titles, *Gangsta* tells the story of Lou-Loc, a founding member of the Harlem Crips. After helping to murder a racist cop in Los Angeles, Lou-Loc and his fellow Crip Gutter move across the country to New York and fight the Blood gang for territory in Harlem. The *Loc* in Lou-Loc's name comes from *loco,* and the book includes plenty of flashbacks to his wildest stunts. K'wan also tells a love story: enrolling at community college in hopes of becoming a writer, Lou-Loc meets beautiful but hard-to-get Satin Angelino and falls for her instantly, despite having another woman at home and a baby on the way.

Gutter. New York: St. Martin's Griffin, 2008. 406pp. ISBN 9780312360092, 0312360096.

> In this sequel to *Gangsta*, wild but sensitive Lou-Loc's fellow Crip Gutter takes center stage. In Harlem and bent on getting revenge on the Bloods, Gutter is ready for all-out war.

Malone, Mikal.

Pitbulls in a Skirt Series. 🐾🐾 (

> In this series set in a vividly rendered housing project called Emerald City, four street-savvy women work together to control Emerald City's drug economy.
>
> **Keywords:** Multiple Perspectives; Street Code; Washington, DC; Women Hustlers
>
> **Similar Reads:** The <u>Pitbulls in a Skirt</u> series features a crew of women with warm friendships as well as a business relationship and has a strong sense of place. For more women hustling together, try Allysha Hamber's *Northside Clit*, J. M. Benjamin's *Down in the Dirty*, or Nisa Santiago's *Cartier Cartel*. For more warm friendships between women, try Deja King's *Trife Life to Lavish*, Jacki Simmons's *Stripped*, or Nikki Turner's *Glamorous Life*. Other novels with a sense of place include Erick S. Gray's *Ghetto Heaven*, which is set in Brooklyn's Coney Island, and Tracy Brown's *Criminal Minded*, which evokes the desolation and isolation of Staten Island by calling the island Shaolin.

Pitbulls in a Skirt. Owings Mills, MD: The Cartel Publications, 2008. 203pp. ISBN 9780979493126, 0979493129.

> Mercedes, Yvette, Carissa, and Kenyatta live in D.C.'s Emerald City, a housing project nicknamed for the buildings' green awnings. The four women are part of the set that runs Emerald City's drug trade, but everyone knows the top players are Stacia and Dex. Then a group of thugs viciously murder Stacia and Dex, and a struggle for power begins. Can the four women climb to the top? Each chapter is told from a different character's perspective, and the warm relationships between the women are as compelling as the fast action.

Pitbulls in a Skirt 2: The Finale. Owings Mills, MD: The Cartel Publications, 2009. 215pp. ISBN 9780979493195, 0979493196.

> In Emerald City, a notorious D.C. housing project named for its green awnings, the four "pitbulls" who rose to the top of the drug game in *Pitbulls in a Skirt* return for more drama, turf wars, and looking out for each other.

Martin, Blaine.

Hustle Hard: For All Debts, Public and Private. **New York: Augustus Publishing, 2007. 237pp. ISBN 9780979281631, 0979281636.** 🐾🐾 ((

> A senior in high school, Jaden is one of his school's star football players. Colleges are offering scholarships, and he needs the money to take care of

his sick mother. Jaden thinks drug dealing is selfish, but his best friend Devlin is drawn to the thug life. Devlin sabotages Jaden's football career, and in an instant Jaden loses everything he's got. He figures the only way to make money is to hustle for it. But can he become a hustler and hold on to his ideals and his girl?

Keywords: New York; Street Code

Similar Reads: *Hustle Hard* is a slice-of-life story about a young man who leaves college and becomes a reluctant hustler. Anthony Whyte's <u>Ghetto Girls</u> series and Victor L. Martin's *For the Strength of You* also have a slice-of-life feel. Other characters who feel ambivalent about hustling appear in Erick S. Gray's <u>Crave All, Lose All</u> and Shannon Holmes's *Never Go Home Again*.

Martin, Victor L.

A Hood Legend Series. ✍ ✍ ❨❨

This series stars Menage Unique Legend, an outrageously powerful and successful hustler in Miami.

Keywords: Law Enforcement; Miami

Similar Reads: The joy of reading about Menage and his exploits is his outrageous power and status. For more opulently rich, high-status, sexually successful men, try Quentin Carter's *Hoodwinked*, 50 Cent and Relentless Aaron's *Derelict*, Relentless Aaron's *Platinum Dolls*, or White Chocolate's *Sex in the Hood*.

A Hood Legend. Columbus, OH: Triple Crown Publications, 2004. 221pp. ISBN 0974789569, 9780974789569.

> In this raw fantasy of male power in Miami, Menage Unique Legend is the flyest guy in the hood. He's got a wifey at home and countless strippers and attractive young women begging for his attention. Life is good, . . . except for two things: one, police are closing in on his criminal operations, and two, someone is making threats against his life.

Menage's Way. Columbus, OH: Triple Crown Publications, 2004. 180pp. ISBN 0970247222, 9780970247223.

> Menage Unique Legend was once thought to be the flyest guy in his corner of Miami. Now he claims to be keeping things together even while his life falls apart.

Rhodes, Evie.

Street Vengeance. **New York: Dafina, 2008. 302pp. ISBN 9780758216687, 075-8216688.** ✍ ✍ ❨

This story of a girl gangster starts with a rap about "The Lost Generation," meaning the young men and women who die in the streets. Brandi Hutchinson experiences her own loss at age eighteen when her best friend Q is beaten by the cops and ends up paralyzed. She fights with her father about politics and music: he insists that rap music is just noise, and she insists there's no point in getting a job because the money never goes very far. After a heated argument, Brandi's father puts her out of the house, and from there Brandi assembles a ruthless girl posse determined to make money and take down oppressors. Her mother thinks Brandi has made a deal with the devil. Can anything stop Brandi's rage?

Keywords: Los Angeles; Revenge; Women Hustlers

Similar Reads: *Street Vengeance* explores themes of revenge, rap music, police violence, and the generational divide, with a fierce female character leading the way. For another story of a character avenging wrongs done to his loved ones, try Relentless Aaron's *Push*. For more about girl gangs, try Nisa Santiago's *Cartier Cartel*, Mikal Malone's *Pitbulls in a Skirt*, or Eyone Williams's *Hell Razor Honeys*. K'wan's *Eve* also features a young woman who leads a crew and is bent on revenge.

Core Collection: Young Adult

Stevens, Travis "Unique".

I Ain't Mad at Ya. **Amiaya Entertainment, 2005. 208pp. ISBN 0974507555, 9780974507552.** ☞ ((

Freedom, a small-time hustler in Harlem, starts seeing big money after he hooks up with Havoc, a ruthless mastermind of robberies, heists, hits, and more. After making $45,000 from a robbery, Freedom invests in new clothes and in Harlem's finest cocaine. With the help of his sexy first love Mercedes and her friend Bish, Freedom is hard at work getting paid. But can he trust his partners and avoid getting caught?

Keywords: New York; Street Code

Similar Reads: *I Ain't Mad at Ya* focuses on a man climbing higher into the drug trade and revels in women's sexuality. *Stackin' Paper* is another story of a small-time hustler getting a big break. For more examples of sexually compliant women, try Quentin Carter's *Hoodwinked* or White Chocolate's *Sex in the Hood*.

Tysha.

The Boss: The Story of a Female Hustler. **West Babylon, NY: Urban Books, 2008. 290pp. ISBN 9781601620729, 1601620721.** ☞ ((

What happens in Bossy's crib stays at Bossy's crib, according to Bossy and her friends Aisha and Terry. Bossy has been fending for herself since age thirteen, when her older brother and last surviving relative got locked up. Cynical, practical, and all business all the time, Bossy believes in having a legitimate job and a hustle. She and her two friends own a hair salon, but Bossy's claim to fame is her special technique for cooking and packaging drugs, from weed to crack. Adapted from Tysha's short story "Bossy" in *Street Chronicles: Girls in the Game*, the novel focuses on Bossy and her friends making deals and dealing with drama from the jealous girlfriend of one of Bossy's business partners.

Keywords: Women Hustlers; Youngstown, OH

Similar Reads: *The Boss* is a breezy story of friendship, drama, and a no-nonsense woman with strong business sense. For another story of friendship mixed with jealousy and payback, try K'wan's <u>Hood Rat</u> series. For another business-savvy female character with some drama in her emotional life, try Sha's *Harder*. To learn more about Bossy's origins and meet other women doing for themselves, try the short story collection *Girls in the Game*.

Woods, Teri.

Dutch Series. 🖋 🖋 (

Set in Newark, New Jersey, this series focuses on master gangster Bernard James, better known as Dutch. Though the series was initially planned as a trilogy, a dispute about authorship has kept Teri Woods from being able to publish the last volume. Although Woods's name appears on both *Dutch* and *Dutch II*, author Kwame Teague is widely credited with writing both volumes while in prison. Teague wrote a third volume, *Dutch III*, which was self-published but not widely distributed.

Keywords: Newark, NJ; Street Code; Women Hustlers

Similar Reads: *Dutch* is a courtroom drama with a classic gangster feel that focuses on a ruthless, flawless, compassionless gangster and his take-no-prisoners rise to wealth and power. For more classic stories of a gangster's rise to power, try Iceberg Slim's *Trick Baby* or Donald Goines's *Whoreson*. For more courtroom drama, try *Diary of a Street Diva* by Ashley and JaQuavis or *Stacy* by Darrell DeBrew. Fans of the character Angel may enjoy other stories that include hard-nosed lesbian gangsters, including Allysha Hamber's *Northside Clit* and Amaleka McCall's *Hush*.

Classic

Core Collection: Adult

Dutch. New York: Grand Central, 2009 (2003). 231pp. ISBN 9780967224947.

> Street lit meets classic gangster story in this tale of ambition and ruthlessness. From a young age, Bernard James, aka Dutch, has his eyes on money and power, and there's no one he won't betray, or kill, to get what he wants. The story begins in court, looking back at Dutch's latest shocking crime spree. Will Dutch get taken down? Or does the man responsible for the "month of murder" have something else up his sleeve? Unlike most street novels, *Dutch* pays little attention to interpersonal relations and focuses solely on courtroom drama and the master gangster's shocking rise to power.

Dutch II: Angel's Revenge. New York: Teri Woods Publishing, 2005. 290pp. ISBN 0967224969, 9780967224961.

> Butch, ruthless Angel was part of the gang of notorious kingpin Bernard James, aka Dutch. She was sentenced to life in prison for her role in Dutch's Month of Murder, but after three years she is released. Now Angel seeks to rebuild the empire she and Dutch shared.

Thieves and Stick-up Artists

Novels in this section focus on thieves, who rob shops and homes, and stickup artists, who rob other hustlers. Turf wars, revenge, and watching one's back are central themes here.

50 Cent and Derrick R. Pledger.

The Diamond District. **New York: Pocket Books, 2008. 163pp. ISBN 978-1416551799, 1416551794.** ⚐⚐ (

After getting a college degree at the prestigious University of Pennsylvania, D. J. comes back to Harrisburg and his boys in the League, a group known for partying and going wild. What starts as a bar fight ends with Dre stealing diamond jewelry from the men he beats. D. J. goes to sell the diamonds, and crooked jeweler Tony offers D. J. top dollar if he can bring Tony more diamonds. The League begins a crime spree, but with money in the picture, D. J.'s friends begin to show their true colors. A quick read about the dangers of loving money.

Keywords: Harrisburg, PA; Stick-Up Artists; Street Code

Similar Reads: *The Diamond District* is a short, fast-paced story of a crew of well-intentioned young men hustling together. For other novella-length books, try others in the G-Unit line, particularly 50 Cent and K'wan's *Blow* and 50 Cent and Noire's *Baby Brother*. For more stories of young, college-educated men trying their hands at hustling and getting in over their heads, try Mark Anthony's *Paper Chasers* or Randy Thompson's *Ski Mask Way*.

50 Cent and K. Elliott.

The Ski Mask Way. **New York: Pocket Books, 2007. 213pp. ISBN 978-1416531012, 1416531017.** ⚐⚐ ((

Fresh out of prison, New Yorker Seven is small time. But smoking weed one night with Butter, a local gangster from Charlotte, North Carolina, Seven decides to start getting his money the ski mask way—by robbing other players. Seven and Butter pull off robberies with the help of Seven's girl Elise. Crime gets more complicated when Elise tries to set up a major player named Reno and Reno catches on. A short, fast-paced tale of stealing, dealing, and the differences between North and South.

Keywords: Charlotte, NC; Stick-Up Artists

Similar Reads: *The Ski Mask Way* is a story of a young man just out of prison with aspirations of making it big. For other stories of men trying to establish themselves after prison, try Kevin Bullock's *In the Cut* or Michael Covington's *Chances*. Daniel Serrano's *Gunmetal Black* gives a slower, more contemplative take on reestablishing oneself after serving time. *Blow*, by 50 Cent and K'wan, features a similar set of hustlers who are not quite at the top of their game. K'wan's *Road Dawgz* features dialogue that is funny and warm, much like the interactions between Seven and his buddies.

Benjamin, J. M.

Down in the Dirty. **New York: Flowers in Bloom Publishing, 2006. 268pp. ISBN 0970819161, 9780970819161.** ☞ ☞ ☞ 𝄆

Ever since the first murder they pulled off together as teenagers, Keisha and Desiree have been tight. Now they run with a crew of four women who scheme together to get money from men, either by sleeping with high rollers or robbing them blind—or both. When a group of hustlers from the North ride into Durham, North Carolina, aka "The Dirty," in their Range Rovers, the crew spots potential victims. But in Stacks and his boys, the four of them may just have met their match.

Keywords: Durham, NC; Street Code, Women Hustlers

Similar Reads: *Down in the Dirty* features a crew of young women who target men for high stakes extortion and robberies. For other all-female hustling crews, try K'wan's *Eve* or Allysha Hamber's *Northside Clit*. Mikal Malone's *Pitbulls in a Skirt* is a warmer story of young women hustling together, and Brandon McCall's *Spot Rushers* offers a cautionary tale of women with aspirations similar to Keisha and Desiree's, who lose everything after one heist goes terribly wrong.

Carter, Quentin.

Amongst Thieves. **Columbus, OH: Triple Crown Publications, 2007. 316pp. ISBN 9780979951725, 0979951720.** ☞ ☞ ☞ 𝄆

It's all about money and staying on top in this grim, action-packed story. When the brother of Hershey, his child's mother, robs his house, Ramon beats Hershey and murders her brother. One fifteen-year sentence later, Ramon is back on the streets and back to new business ventures, new robberies, and new entanglements with women.

Keywords: Drug Addiction; Kansas City, MO; Prison

Similar Reads: *Amongst Thieves* is a bleak, violent story about a man returning from prison. For more bleak violence, try Iceberg Slim's classic *Pimp* or Michael Evans's *Son of a Snitch*. Y. Blak Moore's *Triple Take* is another brutal story of a man returning home from prison.

Contagious. **Columbus, OH: Triple Crown Publications, 2007. 248pp. ISBN 9780976789482, 0976789485.** ☞ ☞ 𝄆

Carter brings together the stories of two very different hustlers. Maurice, a car salesman, "hustle[s] cars the way a dope man hustle[s] dope." In the case of beautiful women, he'll also accept sex as partial payment. Nekole, girlfriend of stickup artist Sirron, uses her sexuality to set men up to be robbed. When Maurice and Nekole's paths cross, the results are explosive.

Keywords: Kansas City, MO; Prison; Stick-Up Artists; Women Hustlers

Similar Reads: *Contagious* focuses on a relationship between a powerful male salesman and a woman who uses sex to get what she wants. For more female characters who use sex to lure in male victims, try J. M. Benjamin's *Down in the Dirty* or Brandon McCalla's

Spot Rushers. Nekole's sexuality is also portrayed for the enjoyment of the male reader. For other women whose sexuality fulfills male fantasies, try Carter's other novels, especially the <u>Hoodwinked</u> series, as well as Victor Martin's <u>Hood Legend</u> series.

Cash.

Trust No Man Series.

Published by street lit great Wahida Clark, this pull-no-punches series follows determined Youngblood, a thorough stickup artist from the age of sixteen; his business partners; and the many women in his orbit. Author Cash writes from prison.

Keywords: Atlanta; Drug Addiction; Prison; Street Code

Similar Reads: The <u>Trust No Man</u> series gives a brutal, violent account of Youngblood's rise to power and his conduct at the top. For more stories of unforgiving stickup artists and drug dealers, try Shannon Holmes's *B-More Careful*, K'wan's *Gangsta*, or DeJon's *Ice Cream for Freaks*. Theo Gangi's *Bang Bang* offers a more thoughtful take on stickup artists and their work.

Core Collection: Adult

Trust No Man. East Orange, NJ: Wahida Clark Presents Publishing, 2008. 345pp. ISBN 9780981854564, 0981854567.

> In this volume, Youngblood deals with disloyal partners, his girl Shan and her crack-addicted mama, and the ups and downs of the fast life. Gritty, fast-paced, sexy, and sometimes shocking, *Trust No Man* begins with one of Youngblood's mentors putting a stickup victim's baby in a microwave.

Trust No Man 2: Disloyalty Is Unforgiveable. East Orange, NJ: Wahida Clark Presents Publishing, 2009. 211pp. ISBN 9780981854526, 0981854524.

> Still hustling in this second series volume, Youngblood finds himself betrayed by one woman and choosing between two others.

DeJon.

Ice Cream for Freaks. **Jamaica, NY: Q-Boro Books, 2008 (2005). 303pp. ISBN 9781933967448, 1933967447.**

Set in Queens, *Ice Cream for Freaks* follows two hustlers: Ice, a bold and violent stickup artist, and Preme—short for Supreme—a high-ranking drug dealer. Ice holds up Preme for his platinum chain and it's on. Ice is coming up, and Preme won't rest until he's found out who robbed him. Though the characters are tough, each has a softer side that comes out around female lovers and friends.

Keywords: Queens, NY; Stick-Up Artists; Street Code

Similar Reads: Both of the main characters of *Ice Cream for Freaks* are in-control hustlers with a softer side. For similar characters, try Cash's <u>Trust No Man</u> or Shannon Holmes's *B-More Careful*. For other stories of hustlers coming up in the game, try Gregory Dixon's *Cake Man* or rap artist 50 Cent's memoir *From Pieces to Weight*.

Ervin, Keisha.

Hold U Down. **Columbus, OH: Triple Crown Publications, 2006. 288pp. ISBN 0977880427, 9780977880423.** ☞ ☞ ❨❨

Unique has never believed in love. Hated by her schizophrenic mother, she's been relying on herself and only herself as long as she can remember. A skilled and ruthless car thief, Unique has been with the same man for five years but doesn't love him. Then she meets Bigg, an up-and-coming drug dealer, and sparks fly. What happens when Unique lets her guard down?

Keywords: St. Louis; Women Hustlers

Similar Reads: *Hold U Down* features an emotionally closed off narrator who is looking out for herself and only herself. More ruthless women can be found in T. N. Baker's *Sheisty*, Shannon Holmes's *B-More Careful*, and Chunichi's <u>Gangster's Girl</u> series. Tu-Shonda Whitaker's *Flip Side of the Game* is another story of a self-possessed woman letting her guard down and falling in love.

Gangi, Theo.

Bang Bang. **New York: Kensington, 2007. 244pp. ISBN 9780758220547, 0758220545.** ☞ ☞ ❨

Izzy's wavering sense of identity colors much of this crime novel by Columbia MFA Gangi. Thirty-eight and still ripping off drug dealers, Izzy wonders if he can still rightly be called a stickup *kid*. Still, Izzy and his partner Mal have a code when it comes to stickups: leave no witnesses. Izzy has killed before, but the memory still makes him sick, and he's never killed an innocent bystander. So when Eva, a friendly social worker Izzy met at a bar, happens to witness one of Izzy and Mal's robberies, Izzy's code—and his humanity—are put to the test. Where is the line between business and compassion? What does it mean to be a man? Who will take the fall? These questions and more are explored in this crafted but still action-oriented tale.

Keywords: Contemplative; Queens, NY; Stick-Up Artists; Street Code

Similar Reads: *Bang Bang* offers a contemplative take on crime and street violence. For more thoughtful looks at hustling and robbing, try the works of Leo Sullivan, particularly *Life*, which features a similar relationship between a male hustler and a woman with a critique of street life. For other crafted street stories, try Kenji Jasper's *Snow*.

Jasper, Kenji.

Snow. **New York: Vibe, 2007. 147pp. ISBN 9781601830012, 1601830017.** ☞ ❨

Journalist Kenji Jasper gives us this taut, evocative story of a hustler who finds himself becoming a family man. Snow, so named for the white birthmark on his cheek, has been dealing, robbing, and killing for years. Now he's got a wife with a legitimate job and a newborn child, Kayi. Snow bursts into a poker game, shoots up the room, and exits with a fat bag of money. But afterwards he's haunted by the cry of a child whose mother he shot dead. Snow's starting to wonder if it's time to get out of the business. But getting out is so much harder than getting in . . . .

Keywords: Noir; Paranormal Fiction; Street Code; Washington, DC

Similar Reads: *Snow* is an evocative, crafted story of a hustler haunted by his deeds. For another character haunted by a dead person—his stillborn baby sister—try C-Murder's *Death Around the Corner*. For more crafted approaches to street storytelling, try D's <u>Got</u> series or Solomon Jones's *C.R.E.A.M.*

Relentless Aaron.

Rappers 'R in Danger: An Urban Drama. **New York: St. Martin's Press, 2009 (2000). 463pp. ISBN 9780312949709, 0312949707.** ☞ ☞ ☞ ℭℭ

Cooksie, Ringo, and Brice are no older than eighteen when they plan the stickup that changes their lives. Brice is the mastermind, and though he assures the others that no one in the Just Right Check Exchange will be harmed, he is far more ruthless than he lets on. After several bloody casualties, the police arrive, and Ringo escapes with $58,000 cash. He leaves his native Queens and takes the Metro North train to its last stop in Bridgeport, Connecticut. Reinventing himself, Ringo uses his money to venture into the rap industry. But with his past haunting him, he may never be truly free. A thick, high-stakes tale of a man reinventing himself—and using women to get what he wants.

Keywords: Bridgeport, CT; Music Industry; Queens, NY; Street Code

Similar Reads: Like many of Relentless Aaron's novels, *Rappers R in Danger* is a fast-paced, pulpy, long, and action-packed read. Reginald Hall's *In Love with a Thug* features another character blindsided by his partner in crime's cruel behavior. A number of street novels also take place within the rap industry, including Mark Anthony's *Take Down* and Rahsaan Ali's *Selfish Intentions*.

Sanders, Mike.

Thirsty. **East Orange, NJ: Wahida Clark Presents Publishing, 2008. 250pp. ISBN 9780981854540, 0981854540.** ☞ ☞ ℭℭ

This entry in the Wahida Clark Presents . . . publishing line centers around street savvy Justice and her younger brother Monk. Originally from Chicago, the siblings took their street smarts with them when they moved to Charlotte, North Carolina. Now Monk's got a hustle doing stickups, and Justice gets paid to put him onto people to rob. This story of hustling and drama is told from a variety of viewpoints: those of Justice, Monk, Justice's ex Carlos, and Justice's best friend Sapphire.

Keywords: Charlotte, NC; Multiple Perspectives

Similar Reads: *Thirsty* features multiple perspectives and involves both high-action hustling and juicy drama. Eric Fleming's *Lust, Love, and Lies* also explores hustling and relationships from multiple perspectives. Chunichi's <u>California Connection</u> series similarly flips between street action and interpersonal affairs. For another abundance of perspectives, try Sonny F. Black's *Gangsta Bitch*.

Santiago, Nisa.

Cartier Cartel. **Bellport, NY: Melodrama Publishing, 2009. 249pp. ISBN 978-1934157183, 193415718X.** ☞ ☞ ⊂⊂

Tired of her irresponsible mother leaving her hungry, fifteen year-old Cartier gets together a crew of girls to start making real money. They start by boosting designer clothes, but soon move into drugs. The story follows Cartier and her girls through a variety of moneymaking ventures, arrests, and romances. Cartier is a street-smart, business-savvy girl who knows she's just as strong as the boys, and readers looking for a strong, female character will appreciate that almost every chapter comes from Cartier's point of view.

Keywords: Brooklyn, NY; Prison; Street Code; Women Hustlers

Similar Reads: *Cartier Cartel* features a strong female protagonist and a girl gang. For other stories of girl gangs, try K'wan's *Eve*, Allysha Hamber's *Northside Clit*, or Eyone Williams's *Hell Razor Honeys*. Tonya Ridley's *Takeover* is another story of a street-savvy teenage girl who supports herself by any means necessary when her mother can't.

Core Collection: Adult; Young Adult

Slim, Iceberg.

Trick Baby: The Story of a White Negro. **Los Angeles: Holloway House, 1997. 312pp. ISBN 0870679775, 9780870679773.** ☞ ☞ ⊂

At the start of this gritty classic, notorious pimp Iceberg Slim finds himself in a prison cell with a light-skinned black man. The man recognizes Slim, and with a bit of coaching, Slim remembers him too: a con man known by his friends as "White Folks" and by his enemies as "Trick Baby." As the men come to trust each other, White Folks tells his story: how he learned the tricks of the trade and how a top-notch con man like himself ended up in jail.

Keywords: Chicago; Street Code

Similar Reads: *Trick Baby* is a classic story about a con artist and his rise to wealth and power. For other classic, gritty street tales, try Slim's *Pimp* or any of Donald Goines's titles. For other stories about gangsters coming to power, try Erica Hilton's coming-of-age tale *10 Crack Commandments*, Cash's gritty and violent *Trust No Man*, or Teri Woods's <u>Dutch</u> series.

Classic

Woods, Teri.

Angel. **New York: Teri Woods Publishing, 2006. 256pp. ISBN 0977323420, 9780977323425.** 🖛 🖛 🖛 ((

Not to be confused with the character of the same name in the <u>Dutch</u> series, this Angel is Kareemah El-Amin, raised a devout Muslim, turned a ruthless killer. As a teenager, Angel kills the father who is abusing her and her sister. In college, she kills a popular athlete as revenge for his seducing her and then blowing her off. Years later, she ties her cocaine dealer boyfriend to their bed, claiming sexual intentions, and then shoots him, telling a sob story to the cops and making off with over $1 million. Then her sister is killed, and Angel is out for revenge. She's making money and she's making enemies. It's only a matter of time before her deeds catch up with her.

Keywords: Abuse; Assassins; Prison; Revenge; Street Code; Washington, DC

Similar Reads: *Angel* is the brutal tale of an unrepentant, materialistic killer out for revenge. For other characters who murder with no remorse, try Dakota Knight's *Sola*, the story of a female assassin, or Cairo's erotic novel *The Kat Trap*. For more stories of seemingly unstable characters who seek revenge, try K'wan's *Eve*, in which a teenage girl wants to "pay back" all of the parties responsible for putting her in jail, or Reign's *Shyt List*, in which a wronged woman goes to outrageous lengths to hurt, kill, or humiliate those who have brought her misery.

Strippers, Pimps, and Prostitutes

Novels in this section focus on those hustlers who choose to work in the sex industry. Novels such as Iceberg Slim's *Pimp* and Treasure Hernandez's *Pimp's Life* follow male pimps who manage—often violently—a workforce of female prostitutes. Deborah Mayer's *Love & Loyalty* and Vickie Stringer's <u>Let That Be the Reason</u> feature driven women in the sex trade, a stripper and an escort service boss respectively. For stories of women working in the sex industry against their will, see chapter 7.

Goines, Donald.

Whoreson: The Story of a Ghetto Pimp. **Los Angeles: Holloway House, 2007 (1972). 319pp. ISBN 0870679716, 9780870679711.** 🖛 🖛 ((

Originally published in 1972, this classic pulp novel tells the story of Whoreson Jones, a man whose mother named him so that he would never forget where he came from. Growing up in 1940s Detroit, Whoreson grows up in the company of his mother and other prostitutes and is encouraged at a young age to become a pimp. His transformation into a violent, effective pimp is the subject of this simple, fast-paced novel.

Keywords: Detroit; Sex Industry

Similar Reads: Goines is known for his conversational prose, and *Whoreson*'s appeal lies in its matter of fact language and coming-of-age narrative. Other Goines novels have a similar classic, conversational feel, particularly *Black Girl Lost*, which also tells a story of a young person growing up in harsh conditions. For more contemporary coming-of-age stories about growing up on the streets, try Dana Dane's *Numbers* and Leondrei Prince's Tommy Good series. Crystal Lacey Winslow evokes her own childhood among "prostitutes and pimps" in *Up Close & Personal*, her book of poetry.

Classic

Core Collection: Adult

Hernandez, Treasure.

A Pimp's Life. West Babylon, NY: Urban Books, 2009. 280pp. ISBN 9781601621511, 1601621515. ☞ ☞ ℂℂ

Mack is a pimp who works for a man named Cocaine. Anton is Mack's buddy, who has a warrant out for having shot a cop. Sade is Mack's girl, and she's beginning to suspect she's not the only one. Life gets more complicated for all three when Sade goes home to Virginia and kills the mother who stood by while her stepfather abused her. Meanwhile, Mack tries to bring an attractive woman named Joi into his business, but little does he know that Joi herself has a history. The life of a pimp is full of drama and near misses.

Keywords: Abuse; Queens, NY; Sex Industry

Similar Reads: *A Pimp's Life* provides readers with the gritty details of the work of a pimp and also addresses child abuse. For other stories about the day-to-day details of being a pimp, try the classics: Iceberg Slim's *Pimp* and Donald Goines's *Whoreson*. For grimmer stories of prostitution from the other side, try *Lady's Night* by Mark Anthony or *Brooklyn Brothel* by C. Stecko. K'wan's *Street Dreams* and Jihad's *Baby Girl* also deal with child sexual abuse.

Lindsay, Tony.

Street Possession. West Babylon, NY: Urban Books, 2007 (2004). 256pp. ISBN 9781601620118, 160162011X. ☞ ☞ ℂℂ

One rainy night on the South Side of Chicago, the lives of two prostitutes, a crack addict, and a rogue cop intersect. This whirlwind street adventure jumps from character to character as the night and the days that follow unfold. Johnny, the cop, hires Pam for sex and keeps sticking around for more. Mary Beth Olsen, a biracial former foster child, is loath to tell Pretty Tony, the man she's working for, that her purse full of blank credit cards has been stolen. Mike Brown, the notoriously thieving crack addict, is the one who stole the purse, and Johnny steps in to help. A raucous tale of sex, drugs, grit, and vice.

Keywords: Abuse; Chicago; Drug Addiction; Sex Industry

Similar Reads: *Street Possession* is a raucous story of Chicago's gritty underworld and characters involved in crime who are barely getting by. For more on hustlers who are not top of the line, try 50 Cent and K'wan's *Blow* or Victor L. Martin's *For the Strength of You*.

Mayer, Deborah.

Love & Loyalty. **Columbus, OH: Triple Crown Publications, 2006. 258pp. ISBN 0976789426, 9780976789420.** ☞☞ ℭℭ

There's a code of honor to the game. Peaches, a stripper, knows it's about using her body to get what she deserves. Derrick, a hardcore hustler, knows it's about love and loyalty. Javon, Derrick's partner, wants to leave the drug world and get into the cutthroat music industry, where battles are fought on stage and in boardrooms. But the code of honor—and Derrick's need for support—keeps Javon in the streets. This thick book combines tales of a no-nonsense strong woman, a rising star, and two ruthless gangsters who are bound to bring down the whole operation when their misdeeds catch up to them.

Keywords: Brooklyn, NY; Contemplative; Music Industry; Sex Industry; Street Code

Similar Reads: *Love & Loyalty* is a slower-paced novel that reflects on the rules of drug dealing, stripping, and the music industry. For other reflective takes on how street crime is done, try Iceberg Slim's classic *Pimp*, about a young man's rise to becoming a violent and universally feared pimp, or 50 Cent's memoir *From Pieces to Weight*. For more stories about the music industry, try Anya Nicole's *Corporate Corner Boyz*, Thomas Long's gritty *Cash Rules*, or Nikki Turner's *Ghetto Superstar*. Short stories about the music industry by a variety of street authors can be found in the collection *Backstage*.

Simmons, Jacki.

The Madam. **Bellport, NY: Melodrama Publishing, 2007. 219pp. ISBN 9781934157053.** ☞ ℭℭ

Jade Wilcox has a six-figure job representing celebrities, from rapper Shotta to wholesome teen pop stars. But when her business partner runs out of money, he forces her at gunpoint to set up a lucrative but highly illegal scheme. Without wanting to, Jade becomes a madam of an elite prostitution ring. With her keen business sense, Jade turns her new venture into a successful operation. But tensions—and stakes—are high.

Keywords: Music Industry; New York; Sex Industry; Street Code

Similar Reads: *The Madam* is about prostitution and business sense, but the joy is in seeing the lives of the rich and influential and watching how they wield their power within the professional world. For a story of a powerful lawyer who gets her way by hook or by crook, try Kiki Swinson's <u>Playing Dirty</u> series. For more stories of the entertainment industry and its demanding personalities, try K. Roland Williams's *Cut Throat*, Rahsaan Ali's *Backstabbers*, and the short story collection *Backstage*. To read more about prostitution and its mechanics, try Vickie Stringer's <u>Let That Be the Reason</u>.

Slim, Iceberg.

Pimp. **Los Angeles: Holloway House, 2007 (1967). 317pp. ISBN 9780870679353, 087067935X.** *☞ ☞ ☞* **((**

Subtitled *The Story of My Life*, this fictional autobiographical narrative details the career of Robert Beck, better known as Iceberg Slim. Molested at a young age, Slim transformed himself into a brutal pimp, controlling a large number of women with unyielding cruelty. Reflective, gritty, and bitter in tone, *Pimp* shows a changed man looking back at his wicked but financially successful ways. A classic work of street literature.

Keywords: 1940s; Chicago; Street Code

Similar Reads: *Pimp* is a classic, violent narrative of male power and cruelty. For another classic story of a pimp, try Donald Goines's *Whoreson*. Treasure Hernandez's *Pimp's Life* tells a contemporary story about being a pimp. To read about prostitution from the point of view of women who work as prostitutes, try Erica Hilton's *Dirty Little Angel* or Treasure Hernandez's <u>Flint</u> series.

Classic

Core Collection: Adult

Stringer, Vickie.

Let That Be the Reason Series. *☞* **(**

Stringer, who later founded Triple Crown Publications, wrote *Let That Be the Reason* while in prison, and the story is based on her personal experience supporting herself and surviving her sentence.

Keywords: Columbus, OH; Prison; Sex Industry; Street Code; Women Hustlers

Similar Reads: The <u>Let That Be the Reason</u> series explores Pamela's transformation into a savvy, pragmatic businesswoman, as well as her tender feelings for her young son. For other stories of women who run their own operations, try Ashley and JaQuavis's *Supreme Clientele* or Nikki Turner and 50 Cent's *Death Before Dishonor*. The short story collection *Girls in the Game* also focuses on women hustlers. *Let That Be the Reason* is one of contemporary street lit's original titles. For other early street novels, try Teri Woods's *True to the Game*, K'wan's *Gangsta*, or Nikki Turner's *Hustler's Wife*.

Classic

Core Collection: Adult

Let That Be the Reason. **Columbus, OH: Triple Crown Publications, 2001. 247pp. ISBN 9780970247209.**

Pamela may be meek, but to provide for her young son, she pulls out her alter ego Carmen, a self-made businesswoman. In warm, casual tones, Carmen guides the reader through Columbus, Ohio's, street slang and through the gritty details of her work: running an escort service, fencing stolen goods, and eventually selling drugs.

Imagine This. New York: Simon & Schuster, 2004. 256pp. ISBN 978-0743493475.

> Pamela, the likable heroine of *Let That Be the Reason*, returns, behind bars and with a lot on her mind. The feds offer her the chance to cooperate for a shorter sentence. Pamela wants nothing more than to see her son again, but her street-minded alter ego Carmen can't stand the thought of becoming a snitch. Much more character-driven than most street fiction, *Imagine This* focuses on the protagonist's internal struggle to make the right choice.

The Reason Why. New York: Atria, 2009. 291pp. ISBN 9781439166093, 1439166099.

> This prequel introduces Pamela and her first love Chino, before ruthless alter ego Carmen ever existed. Fans of *Let That Be the Reason* can finally find out what Chino was like before he betrayed the naïve girl who loved him.

Sullivan, Leo L.

Dangerous. **Columbus, OH: Triple Crown Publications, 2007. 313pp. ISBN 9780977880447, 0977880443.** ☞ ☞ ((

This brutal, politically conscious saga follows the intersecting lives of two men and two women. Jack is freshly out of prison and ready to get his street life back up and running and get revenge on the cops and snitches who got him locked up. Gina learned the streets from Jack, and since he's been gone, she's grown up and her game has gotten deadly. Monique, the only black stripper at an exclusive gentleman's club, is learning how to make even bigger money with the help of a white stripper who calls herself Game. Rasheed, the man who left Monique when he learned she was stripping for a living, is also Jack's best friend and can't help but get involved. Throughout the fast-paced and often brutal action, Sullivan comments on police violence and the state of the African American community.

Keywords: Music Industry; New York; Revenge; Sex Industry; Social Commentary; Street Code

Similar Reads: *Dangerous* is a longer read that explores themes of racism, police violence, and revenge. Sullivan's *Life* explores similar themes. Evie Rhodes's *Street Vengeance* also stars a character whose life has been adversely affected by police violence: cops beat her best friend and he ended up paralyzed.

Short Stories and Anthologies

These books contain short stories and novellas in the players and hustlers subgenre. These are great suggestions for those looking for a quick read or to try a new author.

Concrete Jungle. **New York: Jackson Press, 2005. 217pp. ISBN 0976911205, 9780976911203.**

Shannon Holmes, A. J. Rivers, and Anthony Whyte headline in this broad-reaching collection of urban short stories. At an average of ten pages apiece, these stories are bite-sized pieces of urban drama. Many of the writers are new authors making their first forays into the genre.

Keywords: Multiple Authors; Prison; Short Stories; Street Code

Similar Reads: *Concrete Jungle* features short-form short stories about street life. *The Game*, published by Triple Crown, features short stories of similar length and focus. Readers who enjoy these authors' offerings may also wish to try Holmes's *B-More Careful* or *Bad Girlz*, A. J. Rivers's *Cash Money*, or Anthony Whyte's <u>Ghetto Girls</u> series.

Holmes, Shannon, ed.

The Game: Short Stories About the Life. **Columbus, OH: Triple Crown Publications, 2003. 225pp. ISBN 0970247230, 9780970247230.**

One of the first offerings from Triple Crown, this compilation of twenty short stories about street life reads like street lit's version of "Before They Were Stars." An early snippet of Tracy Brown's *Black* appears as the story "Black Butterfly." Shannon Holmes tells a story that will later become part of *Dirty Game*. Although readers well-versed in the genre may recognize the stories from their later versions, the book is a perfect starting point for readers new to the genre. The stories, at around five to ten pages apiece, will introduce street lit readers to their new favorite authors, most of whom now have short stories in other compilations as well as full-length novels.

Keywords: Multiple Authors; Prison; Short Stories

Similar Reads: *The Game* is a perfect introduction to some of street lit's biggest names. Readers who find an author they enjoy will surely want to pick up the author's full-length offerings. For another collection of short-form short stories, try *Concrete Jungle*, edited by Jackson Press.

Classic

Menace. **Bellport, NY: Melodrama Publishing, 2009. 336pp. ISBN 1934157163, 978-1934157169.**

Street lit author Shannon Holmes introduces this collection of street stories by Erick S. Gray, Al-Saadiq Banks, Crystal Lacey Winslow, Mark Anthony, and J. M. Benjamin. Turf wars, steamy sex, betrayals, and more keep this collection hot and fresh.

Keywords: Multiple Authors; Short Stories; Street Code

Similar Reads: *Menace* is full of street action, interpersonal drama, and steamy sex. For more varied collections, try *Flirt*, *Tales from Da Hood*, or Jackson Press's *Concrete Jungle*.

Teague, Kwame.

The Adventures of Ghetto Sam and The Glory of My Demise. **New York: Teri Woods Publishing, 2003. 231pp. ISBN 0967224926, 9780967224923.** ☞ ☾

Kwame Teague, who many credit as the original author of the <u>Dutch</u> series, puts two novellas back to back in this witty, stream-of-consciousness journey through international affairs and the 'hood. In *The Adventures of Ghetto Sam*, a regular guy from Newark, New Jersey, sweet talks his way into a beautiful woman's car in New York's Times Square and finds out later he's riding with a body in the trunk and an African princess at the wheel. In *The Glory of My Demise*, the narrator takes an imaginary white observer on a tour of the ghetto, debunking myths and laughing at the expense of white "liberals" everywhere. Like good rap lyrics, the snappy, fast-paced narration plays with words and a variety of cultural elements, from *Star Wars* to the West African "Door of No Return." Two wholly unusual takes on street drama.

Keywords: Newark, NJ; Street Code

Similar Reads: *The Adventures of Ghetto Sam and The Glory of My Demise* feature a stream-of-consciousness narrative and wordplay. For more stream-of-consciousness narratives, try Charles D. Ellison's *Tantrum* or D's *Got*. For more wordplay, try Hickson's free verse piece *Ghettoheat*.

Turner, Nikki, ed.

Nikki Turner Presents . . . Street Chronicles: Girls in the Game. **New York: Ballantine/One World, 2007. 286pp. ISBN 9780345484024.** ☞ ☞ ☾☾

This collection of five novelette-length short stories is an ode to women in street life. Chunichi opens with an unapologetically scheming heroine in "Crowning Miss Baby Mama," and LaKesa Cox, Meisha C. Holmes, Joy, and Tysha follow with stories of women both self-possessed and insecure. Guest essays from famous names in street lit Free, Wahida Clark, and series compiler Nikki Turner add a personal touch, and the streetwise definitions of terms such as "baby mama," "beeyatch," and "game face" tie the collection together.

Keywords: Multiple Authors; Short Stories; Women Hustlers

Similar Reads: *Girls in the Game* highlights some of street lit's all-stars and focuses on women who hustle and scheme. For more about women who scheme, try Vickie Stringer's *Dirty Red* or Chunichi's *California Connection*. Tysha revisits her character Bossy in the full-length novel *The Boss*.

Nikki Turner Presents . . . Street Chronicles: Tales from Da Hood. **New York: One World/Ballantine Books, 2006. 282pp. ISBN 0345484010, 9780345484017.** ☞ ☞ ☾☾

The first entry in Nikki Turner's <u>Street Chronicles</u> series features stories by known and obscure street authors, including Y. Blak Moore and Nikki

Turner herself. Sex work, thug love, and violent drug-dealing operations are all well-represented here.

Keywords: Multiple Authors; Sex Industry; Short Stories; Street Code

Similar Reads: *Tales from da Hood* is the first entry in One World/Ballantine's Nikki Turner Presents . . . line of books edited by the successful author of *A Hustler's Wife*. For more of Turner's editorial work, try short story collections *Christmas in the Hood*, *Girls in the Game*, or *Backstage*, or full-length novels *Gorilla Black*, by Seven, and *Against the Grain*, by Freeze. For a similar collection featuring street crime and drama, try the <u>Girls from da Hood</u> series.

Chapter 2

Coming-of-Age

Many street novels are coming-of-age stories, exploring the struggles and satisfactions of growing up in a street setting. Some of the most emotional and character-driven works of urban fiction can be found here, and many have strong appeal to teenage readers. Protagonists in coming-of-age novels are often teenagers, though sometimes they are younger children. Some of these stories continue into the character's adulthood, while others focus only on the character as a young person.

Coming-of-age novels often explore painful topics, including sexual abuse, poverty, parental drug addiction, having family in prison, or having to take on adult responsibilities while still a child. Many stories also describe a young person's acculturation into a moneymaking "game" or "hustle," including drug dealing, robberies, or the sex industry. Childhood friendships and relationships with mentors or older family members are often central to coming-of-age narratives.

Classic coming-of-age stories include Omar Tyree's *Flyy Girl*, Sister Souljah's *Coldest Winter Ever*, and Donald Goines's seminal *Black Girl Lost*.

Britt, A. C

London Reign. **New York: Ghettoheat, 2007. 221pp. ISBN 97809742982-3-8.** ⚓ 〔〔
Hot-headed seventeen-year-old London usually presents as male, but self-identifies alternately as "chick" and "nigga." Angry that London is not a conventional daughter, London's alcoholic father kicks London out of the house. Leaving Boston for Detroit, London finds an apartment, a job at an auto repair shop, and drama in the form of flirtatious Mercedes, who initially thinks London is uncomplicatedly male, and Saul, a drug dealer who helps London, but at a price. London's relationships with family members and sometime-girlfriend Lexi form the center of the novel, along with London's experience of passing as a man. Shifting perspectives and jumpy pacing may be off-putting to some readers, but London has a strong, sympathetic voice and an unusual, authentic story.

Keywords: Boston; Detroit; GLBTQ; Teenagers

Similar Reads: *London Reign* is a story of supporting oneself as a teenager, first loves, and family relationships, with strong themes of gender and sexuality. For another story of a masculine teenager navigating an abusive past, fraught parental relationships, and first loves, try *Strapped* by Laurinda D. Brown or Felicia "Snoop" Pearson's memoir *Grace After Midnight*. Karen Williams's *Harlem on Lock* features another sympathetic teenage character fending for herself.

Core Collection: Young Adult; School Libraries

Brown, Tracy.

Criminal Minded. **New York, St. Martin's Griffin, 2005. 292pp. ISBN 0312336462, 9780312336462.** ☞ (

Set in Brown's native Staten Island, which she also calls Shaolin, this family drama focuses on a young man named Lamin and those closest to him in the early 1990s. Frustrated with a racist teacher, Lamin leaves school a few months before he would have graduated, and his unemployed mother kicks him out of the house. Lamin turns to drug dealing to make a living and becomes involved with Lucky, a privileged senior at a Catholic school whose father can't stand her daughter's choice of boyfriend. Meanwhile, Lamin's cousin Curtis brings a gun to school to fight off a bully and ends up in a ten-year prison term upstate, and Lamin's younger sister Olivia becomes more and more a part of Lamin's life and the life of his fellow drug dealer, Zion. Unusually character-driven, the novel focuses on relationships and personal beliefs more than on action.

Keywords: Character-Driven; Prison; Staten Island, NY; Teenagers

Similar Reads: *Criminal Minded* is a character-driven coming-of-age story with a strong sense of place. For more character-driven coming-of-age stories, try *Gorilla Black* by Seven or *Crossroads* by Rochan Morgan. For more novels with a strong sense of place, try Erick S. Gray's *Ghetto Heaven* or Mikal Malone's *Pitbulls in a Skirt*. C-Murder's *Death Around the Corner* is another coming-of-age story in which a teenage boy and his cousin become involved in criminal activities.

Core Collection: Adult; Young Adult; School Libraries

C-Murder.

Death Around the Corner. **New York: Vibe Street Lit/Kensington Publishing, 2007. 276pp. ISBN 1601830009, 9781601830005.** ☞ ☞ (

At five years old, Daquan Watson sees his father come home early from work and shoot the lover of his drug-addicted wife. His father goes to prison, and Daquan is sent to live with his Grandma Mama in CP3, New Orleans's notorious Calliope Projects. Grandma Mama tries to raise him straight, but Daquan's cousin Jerome entices him into street culture and street life. At age twelve, police catch Daquan and his cousin Nut stealing a car stereo system, and the two are sent to a juvenile prison where violence is brutal from guards and inmates alike. Behind bars, Daquan discovers his passion for hip-hop music, and he comes home with dreams of becoming a rapper. Can he make it, with the odds stacked against him and the allure of the streets still strong? Dream sequences involving Daquan's stillborn sister intensify the internal drama behind the action-packed story.

Keywords: Music Industry; New Orleans; Prison; Teenagers

Similar Reads: *Death Around the Corner* is the story of a teenage boy with a painful family history learning the rules of the drug game from his peers. *10 Crack Commandments* by Erica Hilton features a similar learning process. Tracy Brown's *Criminal Minded*, in which protagonist Lamin's drug-dealing cousin takes him under his wing when Lamin is kicked out of his house, has similar family relationships. Readers who like the dream sequences' role in the novel can try Kenji Jasper's *Snow*, in which the protagonist is haunted by a child whose mother he killed.

Core Collection: Young Adult; School Libraries

Dane, Dana.

Numbers. **New York: One World/Ballantine Books, 2009. 240pp. ISBN 9780345506054, 0345506057.** ☞ (

1980s rapper Dana Dane turns author in this third "Nikki Turner Presents . . ." novel. Dupree is the given name of a young man from the Fort Greene projects in Brooklyn, but he soon earns the nickname Numbers for his way with math and gambling. Crispy Carl, an old pimp who now runs a numbers game, takes a liking to Numbers, and the young man comes of age under Crispy Carl's wing. At first he makes his money gambling, despite the regular intrusions of vicious, racist cops. Then one of his twin sisters is diagnosed with breast cancer, and Numbers has to step up his earnings. To do it, he gets into drug dealing. He's riding high, but the one thing he doesn't have is an exit strategy. How does a hustler get out of the game?

Keywords: Brooklyn, NY; Mentors; Street Code; Teenagers

Similar Reads: *Numbers* features a boy learning the rules of the drug game under the watchful eye of an experienced mentor. For more stories of mentoring, try Gregory Dixon's *Cake Man* or Darrell King's <u>Dirty South</u> series. Shannon Holmes's *Never Go Home Again* is another story of a teenage boy still learning that he needs an exit strategy. To hear Dana Dane's take on the music industry, check out the short story collection *Backstage*.

Core Collection: Young Adult

Desiree, Dawn.

Sunshine & Rain. **Columbus, OH: Triple Crown Publications, 2007. 260pp. ISBN 9780977880485, 0977880486.** ☞ ((

Sunshine is the teenage daughter of an HIV-positive mother. Rain's father is addicted to crack. Both lose their parents and are sent to live with Cathy

Stone, a white foster mother who is emotionally giving and lavishes her children with gifts. Can the two girls with painful pasts learn to love themselves and their new family? Where does Cathy get all her money, anyway? What happens when men come into the picture? Part wish-fulfillment, part story of friendship and sisterhood, this is an uplifting, satisfying tale.

Keywords: Overcoming Adversity; Teenagers; Washington, DC

Similar Reads: *Sunshine & Rain* is an uplifting story of family closeness and overcoming abuse. Sherrie Walker's *Mistress of the Game* also features foster children who grow close to each other after losing their birth families, and Mallori McNeal's <u>Down Chick</u> series tells another story of a girl with a difficult childhood coming into a family that loves her. For more uplifting stories, try Nikki Turner's *Ghetto Superstar* or Treasure E. Blue's *Harlem Girl Lost* or *Street Girl Named Desire*.

Core Collection: Young Adult; School Libraries

DeVaughn, LaShonda.

A Hood Chick's Story. **Streetdreamz Publications, 2007. 300pp. ISBN 9780615168678, 0615168671.** *☞ ☞* ((

When Tina and her brother Trè were young, their mother took them away from their abusive father and moved the family to Boston. After bouncing from relative to relative and staying in shelters, Tiara and Trè learn to live in the streets. As a teenager, Trè considers himself the man of the house and supports the family with money from drugs and robberies. Tiara starts running with a crew of girls who are down for each other no matter what. Can this hood chick ever rise above the streets?

Keywords: Boston; Teenagers

Similar Reads: In *A Hood Chick's Story*, two teenagers fend for themselves to support their family. For more about teenagers supporting a family on their own, try Tonya Ridley's *Takeover* or Tanika Lynch's bleak *Whore*. *My Time to Shine*, by Ed McNair, also features a family of teenage siblings hustling together to stay afloat.

Core Collection: Young Adult

Ervin, Keisha.

Chyna Black. **Columbus, OH: Triple Crown Publications, 2004. 259pp. ISBN 0976234912, 9780976234913.** *☞ ☞* ((

When she meets sexy Tyreik, seventeen-year-old Chyna changes. She stops going to school and getting good grades. She gets kicked out of her mom's house. She grows distant from her two best girlfriends. Tyreik buys her clothes, and she lets him tell her how to dress like a woman. How far is Chyna willing to go? Can she please her man and still stay true to herself? A scene in which Tyreik convinces Chyna to transport drugs on an airplane against her better judgment provides an emotional center to the story of sacrificing one's values for the affections of a loved one.

Keywords: St. Louis; Teenagers

Similar Reads: *Chyna Black*'s narrator looks back at her teenage years and is wiser than the young girl caught up in the action. Nikki Turner's *Riding Dirty on I-95* stars a narrator with similar regrets. Many young women in street lit jeopardize their freedom and safety for the men in their lives, including Loretta in KaShamba Williams's *Driven* and Isabel in Meisha Camm's *You Got to Pay to Play*.

Core Collection: Adult; Young Adult; School Libraries

G, Divine.

Baby Doll. **Jamaica, NY: Q-Boro Books, 2008. 435pp. ISBN 9781933967455, 1933967455.**

Pretty Brooklyn teenager Baby Doll Winbush is fighting off a gang of five jealous classmates when reformed gangster Big Daddy Blue drives by. Big Daddy, who spent thirty years in prison and now works with youth to prevent gang activity, feels concern for Baby Doll's safety and stops the car. Thus begins a father-daughter-like relationship between the two. Big Daddy, an entrepreneur who runs several clubs and clothing stores, offers Baby Doll a job as long as she stays in school, and she takes him up on it. There Baby Doll learns a new measure of success, and that if she stays out of trouble, she may be able to make her lifelong dream of becoming rich a reality.

Keywords: Abuse; Brooklyn, NY; Mentors; Teenagers

Similar Reads: *Baby Doll* is a thick book featuring a feel-good story and a caring relationship between a young woman and a father figure. For another uplifting story of a young woman's achievement, try Nikki Turner's *Riding Dirty on I-95*. For more on father–daughter relationships, try Shannon Holmes's *Dirty Game* or Mallori McNeal's <u>Down Chick</u> series.

Core Collection: Young Adult

G, Mike.

Young Assassin. **Brandywine, MD: Life Changing Books, 2007. 224pp. ISBN 1934230987, 9781934230985.**

His older brother is a rich hustler, and the boys in his crew do robberies and small-time drug dealing, but Maurice has always stayed away from crime. His life changes when a vicious drug dealer and his accomplices kidnap him to collect money from his older brother. Though Maurice escapes, his urges toward violence grow. When his girl Tia comes home injured from visiting her baby's father Craig, Maurice decides to take matters into his own hands. Killing Craig is just the first of many violent acts Maurice perpetrates in this action-oriented page-turner set in Washington, D.C.

Keywords: Drug Addiction; Prison; Teenagers; Washington, DC

Similar Reads: *Young Assassin* begins with brutal, frightening violence and tells the story of a teen boy's transformation from law-abiding citizen to violent hustler. For more brutal violence, try Michael Evans's <u>Son of a Snitch</u> series. For another teenage boy's transformation into a killer, try T. Styles's <u>Hustler's Son</u> series.

Core Collection: Young Adult

Goines, Donald.

Black Girl Lost. **Los Angeles: Holloway House, 2007 (1973). 207pp. ISBN 0870679856, 9780870679858.** ☞ ☞ ⟨⟨

In Los Angeles, a skinny, hungry eight-year-old girl waits for her drunk mother to come home and feed her. Five years later, she's learned how to feed herself. Sandra steals clothes, hitches rides, and uses her street-smarts to take care of herself. Then she sees a drug dealer's car pursued by the cops. In desperation, the driver throws a bag out the window—a package of heroin. Sandra takes the package and partners with Chink, a dope dealer at her high school. Their partnership becomes both business and emotional connection, till death do them part.

Keywords: Drug Addiction; Los Angeles; Prison; Street Code; Teenagers

Similar Reads: *Black Girl Lost* is a classic, grim story of a teenage girl providing for herself, with a warm, mutually respectful relationship between the heroine and her business partner. For more grim stories of young girls coping with parents who cannot provide for them, try Anna J's *Snow White* or Tanika Lynch's *Whore*. For more relationships that mix business and emotion, try J. M. Benjamin's *Ride or Die Chick* or Treasure E. Blue's *Keyshia and Clyde*.

Classic

Core Collection: Adult; Young Adult

Hilton, Erica.

10 Crack Commandments. **Bellport, NY: Melodrama Publishing, 2009. 244pp. ISBN 9781934157213, 193415721X.** ☞ ☞ ⟨⟨

Little Nut is fifteen years old and five feet, two inches tall when he first asks local drug dealer Blue Bug to give him work. It's 1984, and conventional wisdom has it that everyone is either selling crack or smoking it. Over the next year, Little Nut becomes ruthless and rich. He almost loses everything, though, when a group of stickup artists surprise him at his apartment. This well-plotted story shows Little Nut organizing revenge on the men who robbed him, dealing with his now crack-addicted father, and becoming a man. Each chapter begins with a line from the Notorious B.I.G.'s song of the same name.

Keywords: 1980s; Brooklyn, NY; Drug Addiction; Street Code; Teenagers

Similar Reads: *10 Crack Commandments* lyrically explores the rules of drug dealing and incorporates themes of revenge, proving oneself, and becoming a man. Dana Dane's *Numbers* shows another teenage boy coming up in the drug game while still making mistakes. T. Styles's <u>Hustler's Son</u> series deals with a teenage boy becoming the man of the house and how his actions affect his relationship with his girlfriend and his mother.

Core Collection: Young Adult; School Libraries

J, Anna.

Snow White. **West Babylon, NY: Urban Books, 2009. 215pp. ISBN 9781601621641, 1601621647.** *ⅇⅇⅇ* **((**

Journey Clayton is nine years old and already knows too much. For years, she's been cooking up crack and helping her mother inject it. And for years, her heartless uncle has been forcing her into sexual acts in exchange for her mother's drugs. Joey Street is a father trying to make enough money to support his son, but he keeps getting involved with violent business partners. Vince Clayton, Journey's uncle, is running schemes, hoping to use Journey and her mother to his benefit. And Khalid Street, Joey's son, is a young man growing ever closer to Journey. Each character narrates several chapters in this harsh story of addiction and abuse.

Keywords: Abuse; Drug Addiction; Multiple Perspectives; Philadelphia; Teenagers

Similar Reads: The character Journey is the emotional heart of *Snow White*. Readers who wish to read more about abused children can try Antoine "Inch" Thomas's *Flower's Bed*, Jihad's *Baby Girl*, Mark Anthony's *Lady's Night*, or Noire's *Hittin' the Bricks*. Treasure E. Blue's *Street Girl Named Desire* depicts a similarly abused and neglected character who ultimately finds success and happiness.

Core Collection: Adult; Young Adult

Johnson, S. M.

It Can Happen in a Minute. **New York: Augustus Publishing, 2006. 237pp. ISBN 0975945378, 9780975945377.** *ⅇⅇ* **((**

In this coming-of-age drama, Samone, the older of two sisters, is known as the fast one in her family. In middle school, Samone gets in trouble with her strict Mamacita for flirting with boys, and family members are always telling her to behave more like her sister Shellie. Samone also faces abuse: men molest her, rape her, and beat her over the course of the novel, and she must decide whether and how to stand up for herself. The bonds between family are strong, but family arguments and family secrets may be stronger.

Keywords: Abuse; Miami; Teenagers; Washington, DC

Similar Reads: *It Can Happen in a Minute* is a family drama with a strict mother figure and themes of abuse. For another story of a teenage girl whose mother plays favorites among her siblings, try Karen Williams's *People vs. Cashmere*, in which Cashmere's mother expects her—but not her older sister—to support their family. For other stories of abuse, try Antoine "Inch" Thomas's *Flower's Bed* or Jihad's *Baby Girl*.

Core Collection: Young Adult

King, Darrell.

Dirty South Series. ⚞⚞ ⟨⟨

Set in the small town of Peola, Georgia, King's <u>Dirty South</u> books tell two different stories with a few overlapping characters.

Keywords: Law Enforcement; Mentors; Savannah, GA; Teenagers

Similar Reads: The <u>Dirty South</u> series includes a coming-of-age story about a young boy growing up with a hustler uncle and a hit man at odds with a high-ranking police officer. Leondrei Prince's <u>Tommy Good</u> series also involves a young boy ushered into the drug game by his uncle. For more about hit men, try Eric Fleming's *Lust, Love and Lies*.

Core Collection: Young Adult

Dirty South. Columbus, OH: Triple Crown Publications, 2005. 211pp. ISBN 0976234955, 9780976234951.

> Rae Kwon Lake has always been a rebellious child. After his parents die in a car crash, Rae Kwon moves in with his uncle Marion "Snookey" Lake. Snookey is generous with money, and it's not long before Rae Kwon learns from his cousins that his uncle is a "baller." As Rae Kwon grows up, he becomes more involved in his uncle's business . . . and then he becomes Snookey's rival. The town of Peola, Georgia—and its law enforcement— might be too small for the two of them.

Mo Dirty: Still Stuntin'. West Babylon, NY: Urban Books, 2008. 288pp. ISBN 1601620683, 9781601620682.

> Whiskey Battle, a hit man operating in Peola, Georgia, killed his first man at age sixteen. He flies to LA to visit his old friend and business partner David Ambrosia, and Ambrosia gives him an assignment: kill a man in the Federal Witness Protection program who plans to testify against several of Ambrosia's gang. Whiskey carries out the hit but learns of a bigger threat to Georgia's drug trade: Police Chief Mickey O'Malley. O'Malley is cracking down on Dafuskie, an island where cocaine is imported, and a group of dealers and crooked cops have put a price on his head. Can Whiskey carry out a hit this big?

McNeal, Mallori.

A Down Chick Series. ⚞ ⟨⟨

Written when author McNeal was a teenager, *A Down Chick* and its sequel are emotional stories of a teenage girl, her newly found family, and the dangers of associating with family and lovers involved in crime.

Keywords: Cincinnati; Prison; Teenagers

Similar Reads: *A Down Chick* is an emotional story involving a teenage girl and her relationship with a caring father and brother. For more about relationships between young women and supportive father figures, try *Baby Doll* by Divine G or Shannon Holmes's

Dirty Game. Ana'Gia Wright's *Lil' Sister* is another emotional story of a teen girl taken in by loving brotherly figures.

Core Collection: Adult; Young Adult; School Libraries

A Down Chick. Columbus, OH: Triple Crown Publications, 2005. 209pp. ISBN 0976234947, 9780976234944.

> Seventeen-year-old Amina lives in Cincinnati with a single mother who's more interested in going out with men than taking care of her daughter. So Amina hangs out with her friends Kelly and Trina. Then she comes home to find a letter from Damen Costello—the father she's never known. She agrees to meet him and also meets her older brother Azelle. They spoil her, even when Mina reveals that she has become pregnant after a drunken night with Kelly's cousin. But when the law starts cracking down on her family, Mina is caught in the middle. Not even the love of a man named Kayne can help her now.

The Set Up: The Sequel to a Down Chick. Columbus, OH: Triple Crown Publications, 2007. 234pp. ISBN 9780979951701, 0979951704.

> In *A Down Chick*, teenage Amina first met her father and brother, drug dealers who loved and spoiled her. Then the law cracked down, and she ended up behind bars. In this sequel, Amina returns from prison, hoping to put her life back in order.

Miasha.

Sistah for Sale. **New York: Simon & Schuster, 2008. 166pp. ISBN 9781416553373, 1416553371.** ☞☞ ❨❨

After losing her parents at age five, Sienna grows up in the house of a man named Chatman. Chatman operates in the sex trade, buying and selling women and the use of their bodies. Chatman spoils Sienna when she is a child, but when she turns sixteen, she too is inducted into the trade. Although she takes her new duties in stride, Sienna also learns to "think like an owner" and plan to get out from under Chatman's thumb. A surprisingly warm story of growing up in unusual circumstances and becoming one's own person.

Keywords: Miami; Sex Industry; Teenagers

Similar Reads: *Sistah for Sale* is the story of a determined young woman growing up in an unusual alternative family situation. For another young woman coming of age around women in the sex trade, try Sidi's *Fatou: An African Girl in Harlem*, in which a twelve-year-old girl from West Africa is sold by her family to be a child bride. Tracy Ellison, the heroine of Omar Tyree's *Flyy Girl*, is a similar character to the spoiled but resourceful Sienna.

Core Collection: Young Adult; School Libraries

Moore, Shavon.

Baby Girl Series. ☞ ((

This series follows golden child Kyla Brown and the dangerous object of her affections, Rayshard Phaylon.

Keywords: St. Louis; Teenagers

Similar Reads: The <u>Baby Girl</u> series is a coming-of-age story featuring a spoiled teenage girl and a dangerous love interest. For more spoiled teenage girls like Kyla, try Sister Souljah's *Coldest Winter Ever* or Cynthia White's *Queen*.

Core Collection: Adult; Young Adult

Baby Girl. Columbus, OH: Triple Crown Publications, 2009. 266pp. ISBN 9780982099650, 0982099657.

> Kyla Brown has inherited her family's looks—everyone in St. Louis calls them the *badass Browns*—and, starting with her freshman year of high school, she's the center of attention. The one person who doesn't pay attention to her is the object of her schoolgirl crush, Rayshard Phaylon. Rayshard, better known as Shard, is a notorious drug dealer with a reputation for being cold and ruthless, but all Kyla sees are his good looks. When the two of them finally connect, Kyla finds herself in way over her head. This coming-of-age drama comes with a stark lesson about the dangers of teenage love.

Baby Girl II. Columbus, OH: Triple Crown Publications, 2009. 248pp. ISBN 9780982099674, 0982099673.

> This series follows golden child Kyla Brown and the dangerous object of her affections, Rayshard Phaylon. In this second volume, Kyla has suffered heartbreak at Shard's hands, and now she's starting a family on her own.

Morgan, Rochan.

Crossroads. Jamaica, NY: Q-Boro Books, 2006. 383pp. ISBN 1933967099, 978-1933967097. ☞☞ (

Pooney, known as Allen Richards to his teachers, is a high school student with a good work ethic and a gift for football. But when he joins the Deuce-Nine Crips, he finds himself enmeshed in a violent organization. Despite the concerns of those who care about him—his sister Sheila, his football coach, his mother, and his history teacher—Pooney becomes more and more involved in the Crips' illegal and dangerous activities. Then one of the Deuce-Nines becomes interested in Sheila. Pooney knows he needs to get out, but leaving an organization like the Crips is nearly impossible to do cleanly.

Keywords: Character-Driven; Galveston, TX; Gangs; Teenagers

Similar Reads: *Crossroads* is a story about a teenage boy who is a sympathetic, moral character and his involvement with a violent gang. For more sympathetic teenage boy characters, try Seven's *Gorilla Black*, Tracy Brown's *Criminal Minded*, or T. Styles's <u>Hustler's Son</u> series. For more stories about teen boys' gang involvement, try James Hendricks's *A*

Good Day to Die or Reymundo Sanchez's memoir *My Bloody Life: The Making of a Latin King*.

Core Collection: Young Adult; School Libraries

Prince, Leondrei.

Tommy Good Series. ⚓⚓ ❨❨

Prince's <u>Tommy Good</u> series follows a young man from his childhood with a neglectful mother into his adulthood as a successful drug dealer.

Keywords: Abuse; Drug Addiction; Mentors; Street Code; Teenagers; Wilmington, DE

Similar Reads: The <u>Tommy Good</u> series begins as a story of a sympathetic young boy growing up in difficult circumstances, then learning to be a hustler. For another story of a sympathetic young man and his painful childhood in a housing project, try Seven's *Gorilla Black*. For more on teen boys becoming successful hustlers with the help of a mentor, try Darrell King's <u>Dirty South</u> series, Gregory Dixon's *Cake Man*, or Dana Dane's *Numbers*.

Core Collection: Adult; Young Adult

The Tommy Good Story. Bear, DE: Precioustymes Entertainment, 2006. 255pp. ISBN 097765074X, 9780977650743.

> Tommy Good is eight years old, growing up with his family in Wilmington, Delaware, when his mom smokes crack for the first time with a man she's been seeing for two weeks. After that, Tommy grows up virtually alone. To guide him, he has a group of friends from the neighborhood, including a pair of twins, and his Uncle Bear, a hustler. When Tommy gets older, he becomes interested in hustling himself, and Uncle Bear becomes his mentor. But as Bear tells Tommy, hustling is a dangerous way of life, and things can change at any moment. When things change for Bear, Tommy has to step up.

The Tommy Good Story II: You Reap What You Sow. Wilmington, DE: Street Knowledge Publishing, 2008. 277pp. ISBN 0982251505, 9780982251508.

> Tommy Good, once a gentle boy from the projects, has grown up learning the hustler's code. Now, older and hardened, Tommy is out for money and revenge.

Quartay, Nane.

Come Get Some: A Novel. **Largo, MD: Strebor Books, 2008. 252pp. ISBN 9781593091767,1593091761.** ⚓⚓ ❨❨

Mugwump, Whiteboy Paul, Truitt, and Willmon Angel grew up in the ghetto together. Now they're teenagers, coming of age and coming to understand their place in the world . . . and the realm of sexuality. Truitt, at sixteen, feels like the world's oldest virgin, while Paul is secretly having sex with his English teacher, Miss Jones. Paul tells his friends about the affair with Miss Jones, and the three dare him to prove it. What happens instead tests their friendship and their manhood.

Keywords: Social Commentary; Teenagers

Similar Reads: *Come Get Some* is a story about friendship between teenage boys with plenty of social commentary about racism and generational divides. Evie Rhodes's *Street Vengeance* also addresses generational divides, contrasting hip-hop loving Brandi, who refuses to work for minimum wage, with the father who thinks rap music is just noise and employment is inherently dignified. Mark Anthony's *Paper Chasers* is another story of friendship that reflects on racism and the limited set of opportunities available to young black men.

Core Collection: Young Adult

Ridley, Tonya.

The Takeover. **Brandywine, MD: Life Changing Books, 2006. 235pp. ISBN 0974139440, 9780974139449.** ⌐ (

In Raleigh, North Carolina, a teenage girl comes of age and comes up in the drug game. Kim hates seeing her mother struggle to pay bills and hates the look of disappointment on her mother's face each time her father fails to send child support money. She asks Binky, her friend's older brother and a local heavyweight drug dealer, to put her on his payroll. Binky takes her on as a protégé, constantly shaping her approach to drug dealing and cautioning her that business comes before pleasure. But Kim knows the student will soon outdo the teacher. Watch Kim's rise and its effect on her friendships, her mother, and her community.

Keywords: Raleigh, NC; Street Code; Teenagers; Women Hustlers

Similar Reads: *The Takeover* is the story of a business-minded young woman who steps up because her mother won't. For another young woman providing for her family, try LaShonda DeVaughn's *Hood Chick's Story*. To read more about the process of a teenager learning to hustle, try Erica Hilton's *10 Crack Commandments*. T. Styles's *Hustler's Son*, which stars a teenage boy supporting himself and his mother, similarly explores the relationship between mother and child.

Core Collection: Adult; Young Adult

Seven.

Gorilla Black. **New York: One World/Ballantine Books, 2008. 361pp. ISBN 9780345500526, 0345500520.** ⌐⌐ (

In this character-driven bildungsroman, the first novel in One World's "Nikki Turner Presents . . ." line, grade school-aged Bilal moves with his mom and younger brother Keon into Richmond, Virginia's Fairfield Court Projects. Almost immediately, he meets Putt, the boy who becomes his lifelong best friend, and Starr, his first love. He also earns the nickname Gorilla Black in response to Starr's taunt. Black is sensitive, smart, and loyal to his friends. His mother, an alcoholic, is callous toward Black and Keon in favor of their vulgar, freeloading stepfather.

When Keon is killed by a stray bullet, Black's anger against his stepfather explodes, and he is sent to jail for several years. He comes home swearing to lead an honest life, but his friends are involved in the drug trade, and soon Black is, too. The action is secondary to watching Black's character, relationships, and neighborhood unfold.

Keywords: Character-Driven; Prison; Richmond, VA; Teenagers

Similar Reads: *Gorilla Black* is a slower-paced, character-driven, coming-of-age story focused on a boy and the friends he meets in the projects where he grows up. For more stories of children growing up together under difficult circumstances, try Leondrei Prince's *Tommy Good Story* or C-Murder's *Death Around the Corner*. For another character-driven story about a first love between a girl and boy who stay close, try J. M. Benjamin's *Ride or Die Chick*.

Core Collection: Young Adult; School Libraries

Sidi.

The Lesbian's Wife. **New York: Harlem Book Center, 2006. 281pp. ISBN 0976393913, 978097639391.** ☞ ☞ ☞ ⟨⟨

Nikki Kone—once named Aisha—rejected her Muslim upbringing and became an atheist the day she saw a group of Muslim men beating her mother in the name of religion. Growing up in her father's house, Nikki, who named herself after street author Nikki Turner, endures vicious physical and sexual abuse. In the waiting room at New York's Department of Youth and Family Services, Nikki meets Beyonce, the daughter of an abusive Christian. The two girls realize they are attracted to one another and soon fall in love and move into an apartment together. But when Nikki realizes her father is using her sexuality as an excuse to abuse her mother, she moves back home, against the wishes of Beyonce and Nikki's social worker Sharyn. Reunited with her father, Nikki takes a trip to the Ivory Coast that becomes a violent, terrifying nightmare.

Keywords: Abuse; GLBTQ; New York; Teenagers

Similar Reads: *The Lesbian's Wife* is a sympathetic coming-of-age story about a teenage girl struggling with abuse and embracing her sexuality. For more stories of teenage girls facing abuse, try Sidi's <u>Fatou</u> series, Shavon Moore's *Ecstasy*, or K'wan's *Street Dreams*. For more about romance between LGBT teens, try A. C. Britt's *London Reign* or Laurinda D. Brown's *Strapped*.

Core Collection: Young Adult; School Libraries

Souljah, Sister.

The Coldest Winter Ever. **New York: Simon & Schuster, 1999. 534pp. ISBN 9781416521693.** ☞ ☞ ⟨⟨

What happens when a ghetto princess loses her throne? The daughter of New York City's top drug dealer, seventeen-year-old Winter Santiaga is used to being the flashiest girl in the room. Then the FBI arrests her father and seizes his assets. All Winter's got left are her name, her style, her street-smarts, and her ruthless desire to stay on top. Souljah's intention is to steer readers away from the fast life, but her anti-heroine is compelling even as she descends into desperation. A riveting cautionary tale, this novel is often credited with revitalizing the street lit genre.

Keywords: Brooklyn, NY; Teenagers

Similar Reads: *The Coldest Winter Ever* is a classic cautionary tale featuring a spoiled, materialistic heroine struggling for survival. For more spoiled and self-centered characters, try Cynthia White's *Queen*, Deja King's <u>Bitch</u> series, or Shavon Moore's *Baby Girl*. Danielle Santiago's *Little Ghetto Girl* is another novel that emphasizes glamour and the pleasures of material goods. For other early contemporary street lit titles, try Teri Woods's *True to the Game* and Vickie Stringer's *Let That Be the Reason*. Readers can learn more about Midnight, the object of Winter's unrequited affection, in Souljah's companion novel, *Midnight: A Gangster Love Story*.

Classic

Core Collection: Adult; Young Adult; School Libraries

Midnight: A Gangster Love Story. New York: Washington Square Press, 2009 (2008). 496pp. ISBN 9781416545361, 1416545360. ⌕ ☾

Before becoming the somber, ruthless lieutenant for Winter Santiaga's father in *The Coldest Winter Ever*, Midnight had a boyhood of his own. At age seven, he immigrated to Brooklyn from Sudan with his mother and learned quickly how to hold his own against the tough teenagers in his housing project. At age fourteen, Midnight is fully versed in street survival but retains his Islamic values. One day in Chinatown, Midnight meets a Japanese girl, Akemi, who seems equally serious. Their relationship, as well as Midnight's love for his mother, colors much of this contemplative, slower-paced street story.

Keywords: Brooklyn, NY; Teenagers

Similar Reads: *Midnight* is a slower-paced love story that explores Islam, love, and the immigrant experience. For another slower-paced, character-driven love story, try Tracy Brown's *White Lines*. For a more critical take on Islam and gender roles within the religion, try Sidi's *Lesbian's Wife*. For more about where Midnight ends up, be sure to read Souljah's original classic, *The Coldest Winter Ever*.

Core Collection: Adult; Young Adult; School Libraries

Styles, T.

A Hustler's Son Series. ⌕ ⌕ ⌕ ☾☾

This series focuses on Kelsi, a young man who is becoming a hustler to provide for his mother, who has a few skeletons in her own closet.

Keywords: Bladensburg, MD; Multiple Perspectives; New York; Revenge; Teenagers

Similar Reads: The <u>Hustler's Son Series</u> is a fast-paced story with round characters and themes of manhood and family closeness. For more teen boys' coming-of-age stories with round characters, try Seven's *Gorilla Black*, Rochan Morgan's *Crossroads*, or Tracy Brown's *Criminal Minded*. For another story of a parent-child hustling team, try 50 Cent and Mark Anthony's *Harlem Heat*.

Core Collection: Adult; Young Adult

A Hustler's Son. Columbus, OH: Triple Crown Publications, 2006. 210pp. ISBN 0976789493, 9780976789499.

> He's still close with his mom, but fifteen-year-old Kelsi is becoming a man. While his mom keeps letting the cheating, begging Delonte back into her life, Kelsi is selling weed and dating Lakeisha, the hottest girl in school. But when Lakeisha's jealous ex starts threatening Kelsi and his girl, Kelsi commits the ultimate crime to defend himself. Now he's going to see just how down his mom can be, and just how many secrets of her own she's hiding. Because the story is told in the voices of both Kelsi and his mom, Janet, the reader can see where each character is playing the other.

A Hustler's Son II: Live or Die in New York. Owings Mills, MD: The Cartel Publications, 2008. 187pp. ISBN 9780979493157, 0979493153.

> Teenage Kelsi's mom looked out for him when he committed a crime of passion. But when he leaves Maryland for New York, both Kelsi and his mother are exposed to danger. When an enemy attacks Kelsi's mother, Kelsi seeks his revenge.

Thompson, Randy.

The Ski Mask Way. New York: Flowers in Bloom Publishing, 2008. 281pp. ISBN 9780970819185, 0970819188.

Not everyone on Long Island is rich—just ask Isaiah "Ski" Thompson, a high school basketball star who never had the right clothes until his friends got him started boosting and selling weed. The youngest of his crew, Isaiah resents being treated like a child. But as the game gets deeper and the stakes get higher, Isaiah becomes a man and a witness to murder, brutality, and the loss of his friends' humanity.

Keywords: Revenge; Street Code; Teenagers

Similar Reads: *The Ski Mask Way* tells a story of young men who become involved in crime together and get in over their heads. Mark Anthony's *Paper Chasers* and 50 Cent and Derrick R. Pledger's *Diamond District* both feature similar groups of young male friends who surprise themselves with the violence and destruction that accompany illegal enterprise.

Tyree, Omar.

Flyy Girl Series. 🐎🐎 ⟨⟨

Flyy Girl, the story of a spoiled, materialistic teenage girl growing up in Philadelphia's Germantown neighborhood in the 1980s, is considered one of contemporary street lit's original hot titles—even though Tyree himself does not wish to have his work considered street fiction. In *Flyy Girl*'s sequels, Tyree tones down the street drama and gives protagonist Tracy Ellison a white collar career.

Keywords: 1980s; Middle Class Setting; Philadelphia; Teenagers

Similar Reads: *Flyy Girl* is the story of a self-centered, materialistic teenager growing up in the 1980s. For similar characters, try Miasha's *Sistah for Sale* or Deja King's Bitch series. Readers nostalgic for the 1980s or early 1990s can try Alex Tyson's *Compton Chick* or Keisha Seignious's *Boogie Down Story*. Readers who like the upscale tone of *For the Love of Money* and *Boss Lady* might enjoy Tyree's *Last Street Novel* or the short story collection *The Womanizers*.

Classic

Core Collection: Adult; Young Adult; School Libraries

Flyy Girl. New York: Scribner Paperback Fiction, 2001 (1996). 480pp. ISBN 0743218574, 9780743218573.

> This street classic details the coming-of-age of spoiled, materialistic Tracy Ellison, a young African American girl growing up in the Germantown neighborhood of Philadelphia in the 1980s. Tracy starts as a grade-school-age princess on her birthday. Later, as a teenager, she discovers boys, fashion, and popularity, while her peers discover sex and the drug trade.

For the Love of Money. New York: Simon & Schuster, 2003 (2000). 408pp. ISBN 0684872927, 9780684872926.

> Tracy Ellison, the spoiled heroine of *Flyy Girl*, has mellowed out and developed a career in this sequel. Now twenty-eight and a successful writer, Tracy returns to her childhood neighborhood to inspire other young girls to follow in her footsteps.

Boss Lady. New York: Simon & Schuster, 2006 (2005). 336pp. ISBN 0743228723, 9780743228725.

> Tracy Ellison, the driven heroine of *Flyy Girl* and *For the Love of Money*, is now a famous screenwriter. In this installment, Tracy takes her twenty-year-old cousin Vanessa under her wing.

Walker, Sherrie.

Mistress of the Game. Columbus, OH: Triple Crown Publications, 2008. 345pp. ISBN 9780977880454, 0977880451. 🐎🐎 ⟨⟨

In this novel's fast-paced opening sequence, three sets of children lose their parents. Que helps his younger sister LaKiesha hide from the drug dealers who murder their mom and dad. Elise accidentally kills her stepfather, who is abusing her younger sister. Aparis, whose parents were the first African Americans to move into their wealthy neighborhood, loses her family to a fire set by white supremacists. The children grow up together—LaKiesha and Elise in a crooked orphanage and Aparis nearby with her aunt—and become lifelong friends, who stick together and promise to take their shared secrets to the grave.

Keywords: Cleveland, OH; Women Hustlers

Similar Reads: *Mistress of the Game* is about street-smart foster children who grow up together under difficult circumstances. For more about foster children, try Allison Hobbs's *Double Dippin'*, a disturbing tale of two brothers in the foster care system, or Dawn Desiree's *Sunshine & Rain*, an uplifting story of foster children who become sisters. For more about caring for a sibling who is being abused, try Seven's *Gorilla Black* or Shavon Moore's *Ecstasy*.

Core Collection: Young Adult

White, Cynthia.

Queen Series. 🐎🐎 ((

The Queen series focuses on a teenage girl named Queen and is full of street action, relationship drama, and steamy bisexual encounters.

Keywords: GLBTQ; Prison; St. Louis; Teenagers

Similar Reads: The Queen series focuses on the well-to-do daughter of a high-powered hustler and involves both romantic drama and street action. For another story of a kingpin's daughter struggling when her father goes to jail, try Sister Souljah's classic *Coldest Winter Ever*. For more stories that mix street action and romance, try Chunichi's Gangster's Girl series or Deja King's Bitch.

Core Collection: Adult; Young Adult

Queen. Columbus, OH: Triple Crown Publications, 2007. 308pp. ISBN 9780977880409, 0977880400.

> Daughter of the Don of the Black Mafia, Queen has grown up in a life of luxury. Her father loves and spoils her. At sixteen, Queen shoots her mother in anger, and her father goes to jail for her crime. Now Queen must fend for herself. Supported by the wisdom of her imprisoned father and the paternal love of his closest business associate, Uncle Moe, Queen learns to navigate the worlds of crime, love, and sex. A steamy, well-realized page-turner.

Always a Queen. Columbus, OH: Triple Crown Publications, 2008. 282pp. ISBN 9780982099605, 0982099606.

> After murdering her mother and losing her father, Queen, the daughter of the Don of St. Louis's Black Mafia, is in Hawaii, pregnant with her first child. Then a member of the Black Mafia appears in her life and lures her back to St. Louis.

Williams, Karen.

The People vs. Cashmere. **West Babylon, NY: Urban Books, 2009. 271pp. ISBN 9781933967790, 193396779X.** ⟋⟋ ⟋⟋ ⟋⟋

According to Cashmere's mother Pearla, some people are born with the right stuff, and others just can't do any good. Both Pearla and Desiree, Cashmere's big sister, can't do any good, so it falls to fourteen-year-old Cashmere to take care of her beloved father after a car accident leaves him paralyzed. Pearla leaves the family, and Cashmere and Desiree are left with their mean-spirited Aunt Ruby. To pay for their room at Ruby's and for their father's hospital care, the two begin stripping and cooking up drugs. Their involvement with a ruthless pimp leads the sisters down a dark road. Kindhearted Cashmere's story will have particular appeal for teenagers.

Keywords: Abuse; Character-Driven; Compton, CA; Drug Addiction; Prison; Sex Industry; Teenagers

Similar Reads: *The People vs. Cashmere* is a Cinderella story in which a teenage girl's family burdens her with the work of supporting all family members. For more stories of love between a daughter and her father, try Cynthia White's <u>Queen</u> series or Nikki Turner's *Riding Dirty on I-95*. For more about teenage girls forced to support themselves through stripping, try Marlon McCaulsky's *Pink Palace* or Shavon Moore's *Ecstasy*.

Core Collection: Adult; Young Adult; School Libraries

Chapter 3

Drama

In street lit, "drama" doesn't mean plays. Drama is the juicy, voyeuristic "oh no she didn't" factor. Like the best of daytime talk shows or the worst of the tabloids and reality TV, novels in the drama category titillate readers with characters' outrageous behavior: lying, cheating, stealing, betrayal, and outlandish revenge.

Novels in the drama subgenre are more likely to star female characters, though some, such as Quentin Carter's *Stained Cotton* or Dwayne S. Joseph's *Womanizers*, focus on men. To say that emotions run high may be an understatement. Characters are more likely to be adults than children or teenagers, and the tone is more likely to be light or funny than in other genres. Many of street lit's longest running series are in the drama subgenre, including Wahida Clark's popular Thugs series, Chunichi's Gangster's Girl, Kiki Swinson's Wifey, and Deja King's Bitch.

Common themes in the drama subgenre include women fighting over men, backstabbing friendships, romantic or sexual partners fighting with each other, and wronged parties seeking revenge. Characters are often recognizable types, including "gold-digging" women out to scam money from the men in their lives, womanizing men looking to cheat and seduce women without taking responsibility for the consequences, and characters with attitude who refuse to be disrespected and will fight anyone who tries.

Light Reads

Some drama is so over-the-top, it's funny. Novels in this section are often intended to be comedies, and rarely is anyone's life, livelihood, or freedom on the line. The pleasure in light reads is in laughing at the ridiculousness of characters' behavior—for example, the outrageous womanizing of Pastor Goodlove in P. L. Wilson's *Holy Hustler* or the bickering between Mina and Andrew in Keisha Ervin's *Mina's Joint*.

Ali, Rahsaan.

Backstabbers. West Babylon, NY: Urban Books, 2009. 300pp. ISBN 9781601621603, 1601621604. ☞ 〔

Tracy Kane is a high-maintenance model for well-known designer Christian Elijah. Known as the face of the company, Tracy thinks he can get away with anything because Christian needs him. What Tracy doesn't know is that Christian is involved with a ring of serious criminals: bootleggers, crooked cops, and two immigrants from the Congo who are plotting a revolution. When the drama heats up, it is unclear who will be left alive.

Keywords: Fashion Industry; Middle Class Setting; New York

Similar Reads: *Backstabbers* is a plot-driven story featuring a high-maintenance personality and a setting within the fashion industry. For more comically high-maintenance characters, try Crystal Lacey Winslow's <u>Life, Love & Loneliness</u> series or Allison Hobbs's *Bona Fide Gold Digger*. For more on men in fashion and other glamorous, entertainment-related industries, try Ali's *Selfish Intentions* or Omar Tyree's *Last Street Novel*.

Selfish Intentions. West Babylon, NY: Urban Books, 2008. 268pp. ISBN 9781601620606, 1601620608. ☞ 〔〔

Nate moves to New York eager to pick up new work after losing his job writing about rappers for a Baltimore music magazine. To get on his feet, Nate stays with his best friend Moe and Moe's belligerent drama queen girlfriend Kaneecha. Suddenly, Nate's life is full of Moe and Kaneecha's fights and Kaneecha's unsolicited attention. When Nate meets and brings home a new woman, Janettea, the tension gets intense. In the meantime, an old friend of Nate's is having trouble with her baby's father and sees Nate as a way out. Short chapters, nonstop drama, and a risky investigation into the rap industry make this a fast, light, funny read with a hint of danger.

Keywords: Light Reads; Music Industry; New York

Similar Reads: *Selfish Intentions* is a story of white collar professionals and the music industry, but outlandish drama is what makes this read worthwhile. For more lighthearted drama from a male perspective, try *Chances* by Michael Covington. La Jill Hunt's *Drama Queen* describes over-the-top relationship issues from a female perspective. For more on the music industry, try K. Roland Williams's *Cut Throat* or the short story collection *Backstage*.

Camm, Meisha J.

Mistress. West Babylon, NY: Urban Books, 2007 (2006). 264pp. ISBN 9781893196841, 1893196844. ☞ 〔〔

At age eight, Alexis Gibbs saw what happens when a man cheats: after catching her husband tongue-kissing another woman at a bar, Alexis's mother Vivian threw him out of the house at knifepoint . . . only to take him back a few days later. With these parents as role models and a few girlfriends giving advice, teenage Alexis begins a lifelong exploration of love, sex, and romantic drama. A light story that focuses as much on Alexis's relationships with friends and family as on her interactions with men.

Keywords: Light Reads; Norfolk, VA

Similar Reads: *Mistress* is a light, comic tale about love, friendship, family, and cheating. For more light stories about relationship dramas, try La Jill Hunt's <u>Drama Queen</u> series or the short story collection *A Dollar and a Dream*, in which characters' lives and relationships change in surprising ways after someone wins the lottery.

Carter, Quentin.

Stained Cotton. Columbus, OH: Triple Crown Publications, 2008. 290pp. ISBN 9780979951718, 0979951712. 🖝🖝 ❨❨❨

Brothers Qu'bon and O'bon sleep with most of the women in Kansas City, Missouri in this fast-paced and humorous story of creeping, cheating, using, and abusing from a man's perspective. The cast of characters includes Lady, Qu'bon's strong-willed baby mama; Terry, the best friend who goes behind Qu'bon's back; and Katrina and Nancy, two naïve white girls who want to have a "black experience." Add STDs, arrests, and drug smuggling for maximum drama.

Keywords: Kansas City, MO; Light Reads

Similar Reads: *Stained Cotton* is a raunchy comedy about cheating and using women. For more comedic relationship drama from male perspectives, try Brandie's *Don't Hate the Player . . . Hate the Game,* Dwayne S. Joseph's *Womanizers,* or Dwayne S. Joseph, Roy Glenn, and Jihad's *Gigolos Get Lonely Too.* Carter's other novels, including *Hoodwinked* and *Contagious,* also feature raunchy treatment of female characters.

Ervin, Keisha.

Mina's Joint. Columbus, OH: Triple Crown Publications, 2005. 265pp. ISBN 0976789450, 9780976789451. 🖝 ❨

Mina, a plus-sized girl from the hood, runs a beauty salon called Mina's Joint, where she works with funny, outrageously gossipy stylists. She got the money to start the salon from her fiancé, Andrew Wellington Jr., and money is the only reason she keeps Andrew around. Andrew is the son of St. Louis's mayor, and his well-heeled family can't stand Mina. Lately, Mina can barely stand Andrew; he criticizes her clothes and even slapped her once. Then, at a club, Mina runs into Victor Gonzalez, her sweetheart from the school playground days. Victor wants Mina and won't take no for an answer. Will Mina follow her head or her heart?

Keywords: Middle Class Setting; St. Louis

Similar Reads: *Mina's Joint* is a story of an ill-matched romantic couple and a clash between social classes. Erick S. Gray's *Ghetto Heaven* is a love story between a stripper from the projects and the son of Long Island socialites. Allison Hobbs's

Bona Fide Gold Digger also explores the class divide from the point of view of an upwardly mobile woman who can't stand her "ghetto" family.

Hunt, La Jill.

Drama Queen Series. ☞ ((

This lighter series leaves street action aside and focuses on relationships, cheating, and a high-strung drama queen.

Keywords: Light Reads; Middle Class Setting

Similar Reads: *Drama Queen* is a light comedy focused on cheating and its aftermath. For another comedic take on relationships and infidelities, try Dwayne S. Joseph's *Womanizers*. For more high-drama takes on cheating, try Kiki Swinson's Wifey series or P. L. Wilson's *Holy Hustler*.

Drama Queen. West Babylon, NY: Urban Books, 2006 (2003). 228pp. ISBN 097436360X, 9780974363608.

> The drama begins when Kayla comes home to find her man Geno in bed with her sister. Kayla's friends tell her to move on, which is how she meets Craig, a smooth player with a mink comforter and a hot tub. But one pregnancy and a few infidelities later, it's clear that Kayla is still a drama queen.

No More Drama. West Babylon, NY: Urban Books, 2008 (2004). 316pp. ISBN 9781601620699, 1601620691.

> The original *Drama Queen* starred Kayla, a woman with a record for dating players and playing the men she dated. Now Kayla is just one of the characters starring in La Jill Hunt's follow-up, and the drama has only gotten more intense.

Joseph, Dwayne S.

The Womanizers. **West Babylon, NY: Urban Books, 2007 (2004). 399pp. ISBN 9781601620149, 1601620144.** ☞ ((

This over-the-top comedy stars three male friends: Mike, who can't quite seem to stay faithful to his woman; Ahmad, whose wife Shay has stopped having sex since she gave birth to their daughter four months ago, and Max, who is carrying on an affair with his bourgeois wife's "ghetto" mother. The three men spend the book telling each other wild stories, covering for each other, and watching each other's dramas unfold. Chapters are short, and even the ladies get a chance to tell their side.

Keywords: Light Reads; Middle Class Setting; Multiple Perspectives

Similar Reads: *The Womanizers* is a light comedy about cheating and men's relationships with women. For other relationship-focused comedies from men's perspectives, try Quentin Carter's *Stained Cotton* or the compilation *Gigolos Get Lonely Too*. To read about women commiserating about cheating men, try Rechella's *Players Got Played* or the collection *Diamond Playgirls*.

Rechella.

Players Got Played. **West Babylon, NY: Urban Books, 2007. 282pp. ISBN 9781601620200, 1601620209.** ☞ ☞ ⁅⁅⁅

Tired of their husbands cheating on them, five female professionals from the small town of Coldwater, Alabama, decide to cheat right back. Every year, Parrish, Myilana, Dhelione, Emberly, and Renalia meet in a house just outside town to discuss their secret conquests. Each story is steamier than the last, and each man is wilder in bed than the man before. But wilder still is what happens when two of the women realize they have cheated with the same man.

Keywords: Coldwater, AL; Middle Class Setting

Similar Reads: *Players Got Played* is an outrageous story of cheating and sexual exploits. For another story in which cheating hits close to home, try Miasha's *Diary of a Mistress*. For more over-the-top sexual exploits, try Storm's *Eva, First Lady of Sin* or Zane's *Sex Chronicles*. Risqué's *Red Light Special* also mixes a sexual plotline with an upscale setting.

Williams, Wendy.

The Ritz Harper Chronicles. ☞ ⁅

Radio personality Wendy Williams lends her name to these stories of a radio personality whose propensity for gossip makes her a star . . . then takes her down. The first two volumes were coauthored by Karen Hunter and the third by Zondra Hughes.

Keywords: Film Industry; Middle Class Setting; New York; Revenge

Similar Reads: The Ritz Harper Chronicles focus on a high-maintenance personality in the entertainment industry. For more high-drama celebrities, try Omar Tyree's *Last Street Novel* or Rahsaan Ali's *Backstabbers*.

Drama Is Her Middle Name. New York: Harlem Moon/Broadway Books, 2006. 212pp. ISBN 076792486X, 9780767924863.

Ritz Harper has an evening show on WHOT, and one night she gets to reminiscing about the adolescent misdeeds of one Delilah Summers, now a respected reporter on world affairs. Next thing she knows, Ritz is all over the morning talk shows. She's famous, glamorous, and dodging paparazzi. But can she also dodge bullets?

Is the Bitch Dead, or What? New York: Harlem Moon/Broadway Books, 2007. 249pp. ISBN 9780767924870, 0767924878.

In the first volume, Ritz made a name for herself trashing a TV news reporter. Now, after a drive-by shooting, Ritz struggles to get back into the spotlight.

Ritz Harper Goes to Hollywood. New York: Pocket Books, 2009. ISBN 1416592881.

Ritz Harper made a name for herself as a gossip radio personality. In this volume, the queen of drama takes her show business to the next level: Hollywood!

Wilson, P. L.

Holy Hustler. **West Babylon, NY: Urban Books, 2009 (2007). 231pp. ISBN 1933967706, 9781933967707.** ☞ ⟨⟨

Houston's Pastor Goodlove sleeps with both women and men, and his three sons cheat on their spouses and even on their mistresses! Each chapter shows another Goodlove in another sexual situation, or the congregation gossiping about the Goodloves. The drama is over-the-top and played for comic effect. Sex scenes are explicit but sometimes more funny than sexy. Unlike grittier street lit, *Holy Hustler* involves no street level crime. A lighthearted, sometimes sexy comedy.

Keywords: GLBTQ; Houston; Light Reads; Middle Class Setting

Similar Reads: *Holy Hustler* is a comedy about hypocrisy in the church and a family of unstoppably outrageous players. For more light, comic reads about sex, try Erick S. Gray's *Booty Call *69* and Omar Tyree's short story collection *Dirty Old Men*. For another man who sleeps promiscuously with both women and men, check out Chris in Anya Nicole's *Corporate Corner Boyz.*

High Drama

The action gets juicy, deadly, and dark in high-drama novels. Here we see gruesome revenge in Wahida Clark's *Payback Is a Mutha*, brutal hate violence in Miasha's *Secret Society*, and vicious payback schemes in Reign's *Shyt List*. These are books for readers with a high tolerance for—or delight in—cruelty, violence, and heartbreak.

50 Cent and Méta Smith.

Heaven's Fury. **New York: Pocket Books, 2007. 208pp. ISBN 1416562087, 978-1416562085.** ☞ ⟨

Heaven Diaz is a devout Catholic. When she marries Rico, she is as naïve about sex as about where he gets his seemingly endless supply of cash. But even though she's been taught to obey her husband, Heaven is starting to have her suspicions. Is Rico cheating? Why does he have drug paraphernalia in his car? And what will happen when Heaven finds out the truth?

Keywords: Chicago

Similar Reads: *Heaven's Fury* is a short novel about a naïve woman and her dangerous husband. For more stories of naïve women surprised and dismayed by the truth about the men in their lives, try Mark Anthony's disturbing abuse novel *Reasonable Doubt* or C. Stecko's *Brooklyn Brothel*, in which a devoted girlfriend finds that her beloved has sold her into prostitution. For more stories about cheating, try Keisha Ervin's *Torn* or Ashley and JaQuavis's *Dirty Money*.

Anthony, Mark.

Queen Bee: A Novel. **Jamaica, NY: Q-Boro Books, 2008. 230pp. ISBN 9781933967899, 1933967897.** ⚭⚭ ((

In this high-stakes tale, everyone's got a hustle and everyone's out for revenge. Essence owns Promiscuous Girl, a strip club in Queens that makes its real money running a prostitution ring. Destiny and Brazil, friends who work for Essence, are skimming off her money. So Essence puts into play a revenge scheme that will blow all three women's lives apart. From the action-packed first scene, in which Essence and her man King Tut threaten to kill Brazil in front of her child, *Queen Bee* is a page-turner filled with steamy sex, twisted revenge plots, and dire consequences.

Keywords: GLBTQ; Prison; Queens, NY; Revenge; Sex Industry

Similar Reads: *Queen Bee* is a story of powerful women trying to outmaneuver each other. For more of this sort of competition, try T. N. Baker's *Sheisty* or Shannon Holmes's *B-More Careful*. Wahida Clark's <u>Payback Is a Mutha</u> series also explores revenge. For another war between women in a strip club, try *The Cat House* by Anna J, Brittani Williams, and Laurinda D. Brown.

Baker, T. N.

Dice. **New York: St. Martin's Griffin, 2007. 242pp. ISBN 9780312355746, 0312355742.** ⚭⚭ ((

Indecent Proposal meets the hood. Wasuan has two loves: his girl Enychi and shooting dice. He gets into a game with a high roller, Tone, and loses big. Tone tells him there is only one way to pay off the debt: allow Tone to spend a night with Enychi. Baker writes from both Wasuan and Enychi's points of view as both members of the couple deal with the ways their relationship changes.

Keywords: Multiple Perspectives; Norfolk, VA; Revenge

Similar Reads: Besides its irresistible premise, *Dice* is a he-said, she-said story from the perspective of both partners in a relationship. For more novels that feature both partners' perspectives, try Erick S. Gray's erotic *Booty Call *69* or K'wan's love story *Street Dreams*.

Barnes, Erica K.

I Ain't Saying She's a Gold Digger. **Jamaica, NY: Q-Boro Books, 2008. 256pp. ISBN 9781933967424, 1933967420.** ⚭ (

Written when the author was a senior in high school, this is the story of an unapologetically materialistic eighteen-year-old. After graduating from LA's Crenshaw High School, Kentia is ready to make money. She can't sell weed anymore now that she's no longer dating the boy who sold it to her. At her friend Shanti's suggestion, she starts selling her handmade jewelry and soon meets Dante, the first of many rich members of LA's Crips gang whom she uses for their cash. But the game Kentia is playing has consequences. Can she learn from her mistakes?

Keywords: Los Angeles; Teenagers

Similar Reads: Kentia is a teenage girl determined to make money, either by her own wits or from the men she attracts. For more stories of enterprising teenage girls, try Tonya Ridley's *Takeover* or Sister Souljah's *Coldest Winter Ever*. For more about women looking for rich men, try Ericka Williams's *All That Glitters* or Chunichi's *California Connection*.

Brown, Tracy.

Dime Piece Series. *🐎🐎* ((

Unlike Brown's more contemplative stand-alones, the <u>Dime Piece</u> series is full of fiery drama and high-stakes street action.

Keywords: Atlanta; Prison; Staten Island, NY

Similar Reads: *Dime Piece* is both action-packed and funny, with themes of cheating and standing by someone in prison. For more on cheating, try Kiki Swinson's <u>Wifey</u> series or La Jill Hunt's *Drama Queen*. Wahida Clark and Kiki Swinson's *Sleeping with the Enemy* contains two novellas that deal with cheating and having a romantic partner in prison.

Core Collection: Adult

Dime Piece. Columbus, OH: Triple Crown Publications, 2004. 187 pp. ISBN 0974789577 9780974789576.

Celeste is Staten Island drug dealer Rah-Lo's woman on the side, the Lil Kim to his B.I.G. But Rah-Lo is being hunted, and the hunters come first to Celeste. A masked man invades the hair salon Celeste owns, orders Celeste to open the salon's safe, and forcibly undresses her. At the last minute, Rah-Lo's partner Ishmael arrives and shoots the would-be rapist, but this only escalates the war. Then someone brings in the police and Rah-Lo is sent to jail. How will Celeste stay safe? Will she continue to stand by a man who isn't even hers? In a comic and dramatic subplot, hairstylists Nina and Charly compete for territory at the salon and for Ishmael's affection.

Twisted. New York: St. Martin's Griffin, 2008. 338pp. ISBN 9780312336509, 0312336500

In her old life, Celeste ran a hair salon on Staten Island and got caught up in the drama when her lover Rah-Lo and his partner Ishmael made enemies in their drug-dealing business. After the destruction of her salon, Celeste moves to Atlanta. But she can't escape Rah-Lo, Ishmael, or the drama that continues to surround them.

Carter, Quentin.

Hoodwinked Series. ⋖⋖ ((

The <u>Hoodwinked</u> series focuses on two players in Kansas City, Missouri: womanizing KB and street-smart Tukey, whose Jamaican accent is written in off-puttingly stereotypical dialect.

Keywords: Kansas City, MO; Law Enforcement; Multiple Perspectives; Sex Industry; Women Hustlers

Similar Reads: <u>Hoodwinked</u> has themes of cheating, the sex industry, and female sexuality as seen through the eyes of men. For more women's sexuality as seen by the men who desire them, try Carter's *Contagious* or *Stained Cotton*. For more about cheating from the perspective of a man using women, try Sharron Doyle's *If It Ain't One Thing, It's Another*.

Core Collection: Adult

Hoodwinked. Columbus, OH: Triple Crown Publications, 2005 (2004). 277pp. ISBN 0976234963, 9780976234968.

> KB is a major player in the drug game with a major weakness for attractive women. When a hot-bodied Puerto Rican woman drives up behind him and gives him her number one evening, KB doesn't think twice about spending the night in her hotel room. But KB's affair with Selina might be the downfall of his longtime relationship with his Jamaican American girlfriend Tukey, not to mention the end of his drug career. Alternating chapters give both KB's and Tukey's perspectives.

In Cahootz: The Sequel to Hoodwinked. Columbus, OH: Triple Crown Publications, 2006. 243pp. ISBN 9780977880430, 0977880435.

> In *Hoodwinked*, Jamaican American Tukey endured the insults and betrayals of her man KB. Now Tukey is in charge of her own life and some other lives besides. She's got a sex club and a group of crooked cops under her command. But can she stay successful, or will her enemies bring her down?

Chunichi.

California Connection Series. ⋖⋖ ((

In this sexy series featuring multiple characters, self-proclaimed gold digger Jewel stops scamming money from men and starts hustling in her own right.

Keywords: GLBTQ; Multiple Perspectives; Sex Industry; Virginia Beach

Similar Reads: *California Connection* features a self-proclaimed gold digger and is told from a variety of perspectives. For more women hoping to make money from their relationships with men, try A. J. Rivers's *Cash Money* or Ericka Monique

Williams's *All That Glitters*. For more books told from multiple perspectives, try Brittani Williams's *Daddy's Little Girl* or T. N. Baker's *Sheisty*. Chunichi's <u>Gangster's Girl</u> series features a similarly strong-minded female character and also includes sexuality between women.

California Connection. West Babylon, NY: Urban Books, 2009. 203pp. ISBN 9781601620750, 1601620756.

> Her name is California Jewel, but most people just call her Jewel. She's a diva in Virginia Beach with a ghostwriting gig and lives by something she calls *The Golddigger's Guide to Financial Security*. In this story, Jewel shares the stage with Sasha, a stripper readers may recognize from her relationship with Ceazia in Chunichi's <u>Gangster's Girl</u> series; Touch, Jewel's best friend, who has a bit of a drinking problem; and Calico, a sexy hustler whose name is short for California Connection. Short chapters from multiple perspectives give readers a 360-degree view of the drama that unfolds among the friends, lovers, and hustlers.

California Connection 2. West Babylon, NY: Urban Books, 2009. ISBN 9781601621658, 1601621655.

> Jewel, a self-proclaimed gold digger, has been playing second fiddle to the hustlers and strippers in her life. Tired of playing a supporting role, Jewel decides to get on top of the game herself.

A Gangster's Girl Series. ✐ ✐ ⟨⟨

> This sexy, high-drama saga stars Ceazia, her man Vegas, and Ceazia's friends and lovers. The first volume was originally published in three installments: *A Gangster's Girl*, *The Naked Truth*, and *Married to the Game*.

Keywords: GLBTQ; Multiple Perspectives; Prison; Virginia Beach

Similar Reads: The <u>Gangster's Girl</u> series is a high-drama story focusing on friendship and including themes of cheating and steamy affairs. For more about friendships full of tension, try T. N. Baker's *Sheisty* or Mark Anthony's *Queen Bee*. For more about cheating, try Kiki Swinson's <u>Wifey</u> series or Miasha's *Diary of a Mistress*. Chunichi's *California Connection* and Cynthia White's *Queen* also include steamy bisexual affairs.

Core Collection: Adult

A Gangster's Girl Saga. West Babylon, NY: Urban Books, 2007. 440pp. ISBN 9781601620248, 1601620241.

> Ceazia begins working as an escort. She likes the money but hates that the job makes her feel cheap. Her first week as an escort, she meets Vegas, a seductive, good-lucking, rich gangster, and the two of them are together from then on. Drama follows Ceazia and her friends: Mickie, who continues working as an escort despite Ceazia's wishes; Tionna, who loses her sister to a stalker and faces an HIV scare; and sexy Arizelli, who pulls Ceazia and Vegas into a wild threesome. Ceazia's world is full of sexual experiments, affairs, and STDs, but when she catches her man cheating, she's prepared

to commit the ultimate crime of passion. Ceazia narrates most of the early chapters, but the story continues from the perspectives of a wide variety of characters.

The Return of a Gangster's Girl. West Babylon, NY: Urban Books, 2007. 198pp. ISBN 9781601620279, 1601620276

Ceazia rode high in the original *Gangster's Girl Saga*, consorting with gangsters and enjoying wild sexual escapades. Now Ceazia is heartbroken and no longer the center of attention. She decides to get back to basics and scheme her way back to the top . . . at the expense of her friends.

Clark, Wahida.

Payback Is a Mutha Series. *☞ ☞ ☞ ⟨⟨*

This series about cheating, stealing, and violent revenge in Memphis stars a variety of characters.

Keywords: Detroit; Memphis; Multiple Perspectives; Prison; Revenge; Women Hustlers

Similar Reads: *Payback Is a Mutha* is a gritty story about dramatic revenge and friends who are very different from each other. For more on high-drama revenge, try Reign's *Shyt List* or K'wan's *Eve*. For more friends who are different from each other, try Tonya Ridley's *Talk of the Town* or Geavonnie Frazier's *After Hours Girls*.

Core Collection: Adult

Payback Is a Mutha. New York: Kensington, 2006. 227pp. ISBN 9780758212535.

Steamy sex, brand names, and backstabbing fill the pages of this dramatic story of friendship and revenge in Memphis. Shan and Brianna have been best friends since childhood but couldn't be more different. Shan works at a prison for a living and dresses casually, while Brianna has expensive tastes and makes her money by playing men against each other . . . and straight into her pocket. But what happens when naïve Shan gets caught up in an inmate's game? And when Brianna crosses someone she never should have crossed? Be warned: the outlandish revenge schemes are not for the faint of heart!

Payback with Ya Life. New York: Grand Central, 2008. 323pp. ISBN 9780446178082, 044617808X.

The original *Payback Is a Mutha* followed Shan and Brianna through hookups, heartbreaks, hustles, and a take-no-prisoners revenge scheme. In this installment, Shan moves to Detroit, and her brother Peanut is caught in his own quest for revenge.

Thugs Series. ☞ ☞ ☞ ⟨⟨

The violent and nonstop drama in the <u>Thugs</u> series focuses on Angel, Kyra, Jaz, and Roz, four women involved with dangerous men.

Keywords: Drug Addiction; Los Angeles; Multiple Perspectives; New York; Revenge

Similar Reads: <u>Thugs</u> is a violent, high-drama series told from multiple perspectives, featuring themes of revenge. For more stories about revenge from multiple perspectives, try Mark Anthony's *Queen Bee* or Shannon Holmes's *B-More Careful*. Clark's <u>Payback Is a Classic Mutha</u> series is similarly gritty and also explores revenge.

Classic

Core Collection: Adult

Thugs and the Women Who Love Them. New York: Kensington Publishing, 2005 (2002). 232pp. ISBN 0758212860, 9780758212863.

> Meet four women and several dangerous men. Angel, whose hustle is writing bad checks, lives with a pimp named Snake, who regularly beats the women who work for him. The two have violent fights until Snake's actions go too far and someone decides to exact revenge. Kyra is fourteen when Marvin introduces her to sex . . . and heroin. Jaz cooks up meth for money but has a run-in with the law and with her sister Micki. Steamy sex scenes and extreme, graphic violence follow these heroines and the men in their lives.

Every Thug Needs a Lady. New York: Kensington Publishing, 2006. 312pp. ISBN 0758212887, 9780758212887.

> In this installment, Roz is in love with Trae. The question is whether she can keep him in her life.

Thug Matrimony. New York: Kensington Publishing, 2007. 277pp. ISBN 9780758212559, 0758212550.

> In this third installment Angel, who used to make money writing bad checks, has become a lawyer—and a married woman. But what happens when Angel's past in the hood catches up with her?

Thug Lovin'. New York: Grand Central, 2009. 342pp. ISBN 9780446178099, 0446178098.

> This fourth installment takes place in Los Angeles. Returning characters Trae and Tasha move to LA to run a nightclub. Are they up to the job?

Ervin, Keisha.

Me and My Boyfriend. **Columbus, OH: Triple Crown Publications, 2004. 193pp. ISBN 0974789526, 9780974789521.** ☞ ⟨⟨

Meesa, a stylish fashion design student at community college in St. Louis, has her eye on drug dealer Black. But when they see each other in the VIP section of the Spotlight Club, Black won't give her the time of day. Black finally reveals that he is attracted to Meesa, but she and her friends have a reputation as "paper-chasers," after men's money only, and Black is too busy avoiding the eye of the feds to risk getting involved. But when Darryl, the boyfriend of Meesa's friend Destiny, tries to attack Meesa at the Spotlight, Black protects her and admits his love. The resulting relationship is passionate, but Black is not always faithful, and Darryl is out for revenge.

Keywords: Fashion Industry; St. Louis

Similar Reads: *Me and My Boyfriend* depicts a tension-filled romance between a self-possessed woman and an arrogant man. Tu-Shonda Whitaker's *Flip Side of the Game* features a similarly self-possessed heroine who is determined not to fall in love, until she meets a man she can't get enough of. Meesa makes appearances in some of Ervin's other novels, including *Torn*.

Folkes, Nurit.

Triangle of Sins Series.

This action-packed series follows a white collar worker and the high school student bent on revenge against her.

Keywords: Brooklyn, NY; GLBTQ; Middle Class Setting; Prison

Similar Reads: *Triangle of Sins* is a high-drama romance with a professional setting and themes of cheating and revenge. For more about characters who want revenge, try Willie Dutch's *Day After Forever* or Evie Rhodes's *Street Vengeance*. For more about cheating and love triangles, try Tracy Brown's *Dime Piece* or Azárel's *Carbon Copy*.

Triangle of Sins. New York: Teri Woods Publishing, 2004. 335pp. ISBN 0967224934, 9780967224930.

> Rich, and with a job speaking out against violence, Natalia leads a comfortable but boring life. Her fiancé Mark is gentlemanly but predictable, especially in the bedroom. As Mark gets busier and busier with his career, Natalia spends more time going out with her best friend Andre, a gay hairdresser who always knows how to cheer her up. When she speaks at a high school, a student named Shawn recognizes Natalia as the witness who helped get his friend sent to prison. Shawn sets into motion Operation Payback, a scheme that is supposed to make Natalia's life hell, but ends up kindling a romance between hunter and hunted.

Rectangle of Sins. New York: Teri Woods Publishing, 2005. 335pp. ISBN 0967224993, 9780967224992.

> In *Triangle of Sins*, a high school student, Shawn, began an operation intended to wreak vengeance on Natalia, an antiviolence worker whose testimony in court helped send his friend to prison. Instead, Shawn and Natalia became romantically interested in each other. *Rectangle* picks up where *Triangle* left off, following Natalia and her star-crossed love life.

Frazier, Geavonnie.

After Hours Girls: A Choose Your Own Adventure Story. **Jamaica, NY: Q-Boro Books, 2007. 242pp. ISBN 9781933967165, 1933967161.** ☞☞ ⟨⟨

As teenagers, "milk chocolate" wild child Lisa learned to get money and gifts from older men, and half-white, half-Dominican naïf Tosha became involved with Antwan, a dangerous abuser with a long criminal record. Now in their early twenties, Lisa and Tosha are hanging out in clubs, getting what they can from men. Then Pretty Tony, who once convinced the two of them to join him in a threesome, invites Lisa and Tosha to a party for his friend Lamar, who has just been signed to the NFL. Lamar is interested in both women equally—and suddenly the reader is invited to choose the outcome of the story. As in a *Choose Your Own Adventure* children's book, the text contains multiple endings, and the reader decides which story line to follow by turning to the appropriate page. This unusual format is more than just a gimmick: with tight, high-drama prose and well-built characters, readers will be invested in the outcome. Poetry written from the points of view of various characters adds depth and rhythm to the already tense and well-realized story. A list of domestic violence resources appears at the end of the text.

Keywords: Abuse; Detroit; Poetry

Similar Reads: Aside from its innovative format, *After Hours Girls* is a gossipy, drama-filled story involving a close friendship between women and themes of abuse. For more close friendships, particularly between an experienced woman and a naïve one, try Deja King's *Trife Life to Lavish* or Tonya Ridley's *Talk of the Town*. For more on abusive relationships, try Azárel's Bruised series or Mark Anthony's *Reasonable Doubt*.

King, Deja.

Bitch Series. ☞☞ ⟨⟨

As a child, Precious Cummings sees her mother having sex for money, then watches her abuse drugs until her body gives out. Precious decides never to lower herself like her mother, to use her good looks to get as much money as possible, and to put her own interests first no matter what. Combine these goals with a hot body and an attitude, and you've got one dangerous woman.

Keywords: Brooklyn, NY; Drug Addiction; Women Hustlers

Similar Reads: The Bitch series has multiple installments featuring a woman with high standards who is willing to fight to get what she wants. For more characters like Precious, try Vickie Stringer's *Dirty Red* or Tiphani's *Expensive Taste*. For another multi-installment series featuring a determined woman, try Chunichi's Gangster's Girl.

Core Collection: Adult

Bitch. Columbus, OH: Triple Crown Publications, 2004. 196pp. ISBN 097623498X, 9780976234982.

Precious seduces a young "ghetto nerd" to practice having sex, then graduates to older men and drug dealers. But don't think for a minute that she's not willing to sell her men out or play high rollers against each other.

Bitch Reloaded. Columbus, OH: Triple Crown Publications, 2007. 201pp. ISBN 9780977880478, 0977880478.

> Hot, determined, and ruthless Precious Cummings returns in King's second <u>Bitch</u> novel. Reeling from a betrayal, Precious is out for revenge.

The Bitch Is Back. Columbus, OH: Triple Crown Publications, 2008. 239pp. ISBN 9780979951763, 0979951763.

> Precious Cummings, the heroine of King's first two <u>Bitch</u> novels, returns for a third helping of drama. Having escaped her old life and moved to Beverly Hills, Precious feels safe and blessed, until an old enemy escapes from prison to wreak havoc on her family.

Queen Bitch. Collierville, TN: A King Production, 2008. 208pp. ISBN 0975581155, 9780975581155.

> Still hot and still determined, Precious Cummings starts this fourth installment of the <u>Bitch</u> series at her lowest point. But having lost it all makes Precious even more determined to come out on top.

Last Bitch Standing. Collierville, TN: A King Production, 2009. 254pp. ISBN 0975581186, 9780975581186

> Precious Cummings is still standing when this fifth <u>Bitch</u> novel begins. But that's before her archenemy Maya gets to her. Now it's an all-out battle between tenacious Precious and her adversary. Which one will come out victorious?

K'wan.

Hood Rat Series. 𝄇 𝄇 𝄾𝄾

For K'wan, a hood rat is a woman with no aspirations, someone whose mission is to get money by any means available. Four such women, all friends, star in this high-drama series.

Keywords: GLBTQ; Multiple Perspectives; New York; Sex Industry

Similar Reads: The <u>Hood Rat</u> series is a story of four female friends, told from multiple perspectives. For more dramatic stories about women friends, try Wahida Clark's *Thugs and the Women Who Love Them* or T. N. Baker's *Sheisty*.

Hood Rat. New York: St. Martin's Griffin, 2006. 356pp. ISBN 9780312360085, 0312360088.

> In this breezy, scandalous, drama-filled tale, Yoshi, Billy, Reese, and Rhonda, four women in Harlem, get by, get paid, and sometimes get in over their heads.

Still Hood. New York: St. Martin's Griffin, 2007. 340pp. ISBN 031236010X, 9780312360108.

> This second installment finds Yoshi, Billy, Reese, and Rhonda still dealing with love, money, and the music business.

Section 8: A Hood Rat Novel. New York: St. Martin's Griffin, 2009. 358pp. ISBN 9780312536961, 0312536968.

> Yoshi, Billy, Reese, and Rhonda are four women hanging around Harlem. In the third installment, more action and more drama test the friendships of these "hood rats."

Miasha.

Secret Society Series. 𝒸𝒸 ((

Miasha's conversational series tells the story of a woman who uses her body to get what she wants . . . and finds that her body also gets her unwanted attention and hostility.

Keywords: GLBTQ; Music Industry; Philadelphia; Women Hustlers

Similar Reads: *Secret Society* and *Never Enough* are short, conversational stories about women who play men for money. For more about women playing men for money, try Storm's *Eva, First Lady of* Sin or Tonya Ridley's *Talk of the Town*.

Core Collection: Adult

Secret Society. New York: Simon & Schuster, 2006. 213pp. ISBN 0743281586, 9780743281584.

> Short, conversational, and to the point, Miasha's first novel tells the stories of Celess and Tina, two women who play men for money like it's a full-time job. Celess is seeing a hustler, a baller, and a businessman, while Tina's hooking the two of them up with basketball players and club superstars. But the two women are playing a dangerous game with violent men. When the men turn on them, the consequences are dire.

Never Enough. New York: Simon & Schuster, 2008. 226pp. ISBN 9781416553380, 141655338X.

> At the end of *Secret Society* Celess, the proud, confident gold digger, was attacked. After a long recovery, Celess is discovered by a modeling agency and makes her way into the entertainment business.

Mink, Meesha, and De'nesha Diamond.

Bentley Manor Series. 𝒸𝒸 ((

Don't be fooled by the name: Atlanta's Bentley Manor is a rundown apartment building full of addiction, poverty, and people desperate to get out and live anywhere else. In each installment, four characters living in Bentley Manor tell their stories in alternating chapters.

Keywords: Atlanta; Multiple Authors; Multiple Perspectives

Similar Reads: The <u>Bentley Manor</u> series is told from a variety of perspectives and has a strong sense of place. For more dramatic stories told from multiple perspectives, try K'wan's <u>Hood Rat</u> series or Wahida Clark's *Thugs and the Women Who Love Them*. For another story with a strong sense of place set in a housing project, try Mikal Malone's *Pitbulls in a Skirt*.

Core Collection: Adult

Desperate Hoodwives. New York: Simon & Schuster, 2008. 312pp. ISBN 9781416537526,141653752X.

> Aisha's man Maleek has enough drug money to get a nicer place, but he wants to wait until he's quit the drug business. Devani thought her pro footballer boyfriend would help her out, but that was before he got traded to Pittsburgh and failed to let Devani know. Lexi, who used to sleep around, is happily married but finds her husband a lot less satisfying in the bedroom. Molly is white, and her violent, racist father stopped speaking to her after she moved to Bentley Manor with her black boyfriend. The four women's lives intersect in a number of ways, particularly when it comes to men.

Shameless Hoodwives. New York: Simon & Schuster, 2008. 330pp. ISBN 9781416537540,1416537546.

> In this installment, four new women characters navigate Bentley Manor: Keisha, Takiah, Princess, and Woo Woo.

The Hood Life: A Bentley Manor Tale. New York: Simon & Schuster, 2009. 308pp. ISBN 9781416577096, 1416577092.

> This volume focuses on four men of Bentley Manor: Tavon, Demarcus, Kaseem, and Rhakmon.

Reign.

Shyt List Series. 🌶🌶 ⁇

This series follows a young woman's tireless quest for revenge against everyone who has wronged her.

Keywords: Baltimore; Revenge; Washington, DC

Similar Reads: *Shyt List* is an outrageous tale about revenge. For more over-the-top revenge stories, try Wahida Clark's <u>Payback Is a Mutha</u> series or K'wan's *Eve*.

Shyt List: Be Careful Who You Cross. Owings Mills, MD: The Cartel Publications, 2008. 201pp. ISBN 9780979493119, 0979493110.

> At eighteen, Yvonna is engaged to marry Bilal Santana. Then her father attacks Bilal, shooting him dead and injuring Yvonna's baby sister. Losing Bilal is just the beginning of the horrors that unfold for Yvonna. At the hospital, she encounters her best friend Sabrina, who is giving birth to Bilal's child—a situation of which all of Yvonna's

friends were already aware. When Yvonna gets in the car with a hustler called Crazy Dave to let off some steam, the car crashes. In that moment, the old Yvonna dies, and the new Yvonna who takes her place is out for revenge.

Shyt List II: Loose Cannon. Owings Mills, MD: The Cartel Publications, 2009. 203pp. ISBN 9780979493188, 0979493188.

In the first *Shyt List*, Yvonna took brutal, vicious revenge on all those who wronged her. Now she's back to wreak even more vengeance, but some of her enemies want revenge on *her*.

Sha.

Harder. **New York: Ghettoheat, 2006. 240pp. ISBN 0974298247, 9780974298245.** *☞ ☞* (

Kai Toussaint, a young woman from Queens, is in it for the money. She doesn't get with men who are broke, and she isn't sorry when men with wives and girlfriends hook up with her. Through her involvements with ballers in the neighborhood, Kai gets introduced firsthand to New York City's drug game, and she wants a piece of it. Her ruthlessness and tenacity take her on a journey through the drug empire. But somewhere in there, Kai's got feelings for a few men, too. The plot is episodic and the sheer number of men and women involved in Kai's drama makes the story occasionally difficult to follow, but readers looking for a self-assured, take-no-prisoners, high-drama female character will not be disappointed.

Keywords: Queens, NY; Street Code; Women Hustlers

Similar Reads: *Harder's* Kai is a self-possessed, self-centered hustler. Similar characters with "diva" tendencies can be found in KaShamba Williams's *Mind Games* and Keisha Ervin's *Hold U Down*. Tu-Shonda L. Whitaker's *Flip Side of the Game* features a self-possessed protagonist who, like Kai, finds herself surprised and nearly undone by her emotional attachments.

Simmons, Jacki.

Stripped. **Bellport, NY: Melodrama Publishing, 2006. 205pp. ISBN 9781934157008, 1934157007.** *☞ ☞* ((

Life is good for Caiza. She's got a decent job as a legal secretary in a law firm, and her boyfriend of five years, Jacey, has just proposed to her. Then suddenly everything unravels. A jealous woman with an eye on Jacey snaps a cell phone picture that seems to show Caiza cheating on him, and before she knows it, the engagement is off. Then she gets fired from her job. Heartbroken, low on cash, and paying rent for the first time in years, Caiza knows she's got to find a way to support herself. The only question is, how far is she willing to go? The warm relationship between Caiza and her best friend Myeisha gives a note of hope to this story of a woman pushed over the edge.

Keywords: Middle Class Setting; New York; Sex Industry

Similar Reads: This story of a woman who reluctantly turns to stripping to support herself explores themes of friendship and heartbreak. For another professional woman who finds herself unwillingly involved in the sex trade, try Simmons's *Madam*. For more stories of warm friendships between women, try Deja King's *Trife Life to Lavish* or Nikki Turner's *Glamorous Life*.

Stringer, Vickie M.

Dirty Red Series. 🖝🖝 ⟨⟨

This series stars Red, an outrageous, manipulative woman who gets what she wants by any means necessary.

Keywords: Detroit

Similar Reads: *Dirty Red* is the story of a woman willing to go to outlandish ends to get her way. For more about characters going over the top, try Azárel's *Carbon Copy* or Crystal Lacey Winslow's *Life, Love & Loneliness*.

Core Collection: Adult

Dirty Red: A Novel. New York: Atria Books, 2007 (2006). 238pp. ISBN 9780743493635, 074349363X.

> Men, women, friends, enemies—Red knows how to get what she wants from all of them. She gets her friend Kera to give her a cup of urine so Red can fake a pregnancy, then turns around and begs Kera and her friend Sasha to move into her house and pay top dollar for the privilege. She's ditching her man in prison, soaking her supposed baby daddy for gifts and child support, and scheming with a real estate agent to sell a house that wasn't even hers to begin with. What happens when someone catches on to Red's dirty ways?

Still Dirty: A Novel. New York: Atria Books, 2009 (2008). 226pp. ISBN 1416563598, 9781416563594.

> Red, better known as Dirty Red, is a master manipulator of everyone around her. This volume follows Red and her boyfriend as they flee the country and the unwanted attentions of her ex.

Swinson, Kiki.

A Sticky Situation. **Bellport, NY: Melodrama Publishing, 2008. 272pp. ISBN 1934157090, 9781934157091.** 🖝 ⟨⟨

In this love triangle with a twist, federal parole officer Maxine is carrying on a relationship with one of her parolees! Seth is a gentleman in bed, but when he goes back to the streets, trouble begins. Seth is violating the terms of his parole, and Maxine knows there's nothing she can do about it. What she does not know is that Seth is also violating the terms of their relationship with women from the street side of his life. Kira and Nikki from the <u>Wifey</u> books make a cameo appearance, but this one is a bit slower paced.

Keywords: Norfolk, VA; Prison

Similar Reads: *A Sticky Situation* is a steamy novel about the relationship between a parole officer and a cheating former prisoner. For more stories of law enforcement officials getting involved with prisoners, try Wahida Clark's *Payback Is a Mutha* or 50 Cent and Relentless Aaron's *Derelict*. For more cheating men and steamy sex scenes, try Wahida Clark and Kiki Swinson's *Sleeping with the Enemy* or Erick S. Gray's *Booty Call *69*.

Wifey Series. ⌐⌐ ((

This series stars Kira, a hair salon owner and wifey of a drug kingpin in Virginia Beach.

Keywords: Prison; Virginia Beach

Similar Reads: The warmly narrated <u>Wifey</u> is a series about cheating and prison. For more about cheating, try Michele Fletcher's *Charge It to the Game* or Brandie's *Don't Hate the Player . . . Hate the Game*. Swinson and Wahida Clark's *Sleeping with the Enemy* also explores cheating while one's partner is behind bars.

Core Collection: Adult

Wifey. New York: Dafina, 2008 (2004). 294pp. ISBN 9780758229014, 0758229011.

Kira is a hair salon owner in Virginia Beach and the wifey of Ricky, a drug kingpin. But being wifey doesn't mean an end to the drama. Instead, Kira has to deal with Ricky constantly being out of the house, either on business or with other women. Luckily Kira's got a sense of humor about it, not to mention a few bad habits of her own, like stealing Ricky's money out of the shoe box he hides behind the refrigerator. Then someone steals an entire drug shipment from Ricky's organization, and Ricky's looking to find out who's responsible before someone gets hurt.

I'm Still Wifey. New York: Dafina, 2009 (2007). 239pp. ISBN 9780758229021, 075822902X.

Kira is Ricky's wifey. But with Ricky behind bars, Kira is spending time with other men, while Ricky attempts to run his drug operation from prison.

Life After Wifey. New York: Dafina, 2009. 279pp. ISBN 9780758229038, 0758229038.

This volume stars Kira's cousin Nikki and Nikki's boyfriend Syncere. Is Syncere on the up and up? Or is there something he's not telling Nikki?

Still Wifey Material. Bellport, NY: Melodrama Publishing. 232pp. ISBN 9781934157107, 1934157104.

This fourth installment stars both high-drama Kira and her cousin Nikki. The two cousins are close, but drama erupts when both women have their eyes on the same man.

Tiphani.

Expensive Taste. Brandywine, MD: Life Changing Books, 2008. 224pp. ISBN 9781934230831, 1934230839. ☞ ℂℂ

Meet Mirror Carter. She grew up on the streets, begging for money with her mom, but you wouldn't know it from the way she looks and dresses now. Mirror has a taste for the finer things in life: designer fashion, cosmetic surgery, high class dining, and men who can fund her habits. She's also got an attitude: step out of line in the boutique where she sells stolen clothing, and she'll kick you out of the store. Mirror's tendencies can get her into trouble, like when the wife of the doctor who performed plastic surgery finds out that Mirror and the doctor have a sexual arrangement. Find out what happens when Mirror finally goes too far.

Keywords: Houston; Middle Class Setting

Similar Reads: *Expensive Taste* is a story of materialism and a character who is an unapologetic, over-the-top diva. For characters with similar diva behavior and high opinions of themselves, try KaShamba Williams's *Mind Games*, Leo Sullivan's *Innocent*, or Azárel's *Carbon Copy*. For other high-maintenance women in search of men to pay their way, try Ericka Williams's *I Ain't Saying She's a Gold Digger*, Miasha's *Secret Society*, or Chunichi's *California Connection*.

Williams, Brittani.

Black Diamond. Jamaica, NY: Q-Boro Books, 2009. 204pp. ISBN 9781933967677, 1933967676. ☞☞ ℂℂ

Diamond and Mica were friends coming up, but when Diamond got Mica's brother thrown in jail for killing his father, the friendship broke apart. These days Diamond confides in her girl Kiki and spends too much time with a man who's playing her. Mica's got a man who brings out the freak in her and a mom who's giving her advice she doesn't want to hear. When the two former friends reunite, each one has something up her sleeve. The question in this action-packed, steamy drama isn't who will betray whom, but who will get caught first.

Keywords: Philadelphia

Similar Reads: *Black Diamond* is a steamy story about friendships, sex, and betrayal. Chunichi's <u>Gangster's Girl</u> series has similar themes of friendship and betrayal as well as plenty of juicy sex. Keisha Ervin's *Me and My Boyfriend* also explores cheating, as does Erick S. Gray's sexually charged *Booty Call *69*. For sexual content with a similar tone, try Williams's *Sugar Walls*.

Daddy's Little Girl. Jamaica, NY: Q-Boro Books, 2009 (2007). 310pp. ISBN 9781933967691, 1933967692. ☞☞ ℂℂ

Young, hot Giselle is awaiting trial on a $500,000 bail with blood on her hands. *Daddy's Little Girl* is the story of how she got there. Three story lines make up the novel: Giselle, who loses her loving mother to her father's enemies; James, who is determined to make it to the top of the drug game; and Mimi, a fast girl who gets in over her head.

Keywords: Multiple Perspectives; Philadelphia; Prison; Teenagers

Similar Reads: *Daddy's Little Girl* is told from multiple perspectives, starting just after a violent incident. For more high-drama stories told from multiple perspectives, try Wahida Clark's <u>Thugs</u> series or Mika Miller's *And God Created Woman*. Méta Smith's *Whip Appeal* uses a similar plotting device: the novel begins with protagonist Ebony Knight disoriented next to two dead bodies, and the rest of the book follows how Ebony got to that moment.

Core Collection: Adult

Williams, Ericka Monique.

All That Glitters. **Brandywine, MD: Life Changing Books, 2007 (2003). 262pp. ISBN 9781934230947, 1934230944.** ☞ ☞ (

Twenty-four year-old Mika is in love with two men and trying her luck with others. Danny, the father of her child, gives her money, but the two fight constantly, though they still have feelings for each other. Mark is less wealthy, and though Mika enjoys spending time with him and sleeping with him, she can't settle for his UPS salary. Not only is Mika torn between two men; she's also torn between the women in her life. Her mother and sister want her to settle down and further her education, while her wild best friend Asia wants to introduce her to dangerous men with large sums of disposable income. Fights, insults, threats, and more.

Keywords: Drug Addiction; New York

Similar Reads: *All That Glitters* is a story of family tension and a woman looking for men's money. For more tension between families living together, try Sasha Raye's *From Hood to Hollywood* or Allison Hobbs's *Bona Fide Gold Digger*. For more women looking for rich men to line their pockets, try Nikki Turner's *Glamorous Life* or Erica Barnes's *I Ain't Saying She's a Gold Digger*.

Williams, KaShamba.

Mind Games. **Bear, DE: Precioustymes Entertainment, 2006. 265pp. ISBN 0977650723, 9780977650729.** ☞ ((

Serenity knows what kind of woman she is. She's no hustler's wife—those girls are weak. Serenity's a hustle bunny: slick, sly, and a little bit shady. Her husband Kyron gets locked up, and there is no way she's staying faithful. Especially when sexy Toniere's giving her plenty of attention. Too bad he's also the reason Kyron is in prison.

Keywords: Abuse; Prison

Similar Reads: *Mind Games* is all about the voice of Serenity, the slick, devious, self-proclaimed "hustle bunny." Tu-Shonda L. Whitaker's *Flip Side of the Game* features a similarly self-assured narrator relishing her own audacity. *Sleeping with the Enemy*, by Wahida Clark and Kiki Swinson, also centers on women who cheat on men who are in prison.

Winslow, Crystal Lacey.

Life, Love & Loneliness Series. ☞ ((

These two companion volumes follow New York City's most ambitious and most desperate.

Keywords: Middle Class Setting; Multiple Perspectives; Music Industry; New York

Similar Reads: *Life, Love & Loneliness* has a professional setting and involves a manipulative woman and the entertainment industry. For more manipulative characters who get what they want by any means necessary, try Vickie Stringer's *Dirty Red* or Allison Hobbs's *Double Dippin'*. For more about the movie industry, try Sasha Raye's *From Hood to Hollywood* or Nikki Turner's *Riding Dirty on I-95*.

Life, Love & Loneliness. Bellport, NY: Melodrama Publishing, 2001. 416pp. ISBN 0971702101, 9780971702103.

> This large volume centers around successful and conniving actress Lyric Devaney. Sexually involved with both the mayor of New York City and a big-time movie producer, Lyric knows how to get her way using charisma and lies. Caught in Lyric's orbit are other friends and lovers: Madison Michaels, a humble law student, and Joshua Tune, a lawyer who can't resist Lyric's charms. The characters take turns narrating this high-drama, high-society tale.

The Criss Cross. Bellport, NY: Melodrama Publishing, 2004. 356pp. ISBN 0971702128, 9780971702127.

> Lyric, Joshua, Madison, and the others from *Life, Love & Loneliness* return, but most of the second volume centers around Nikki Ling, a street-savvy woman from a Brooklyn housing project who gets involved with something called the Criss Cross.

Short Stories and Anthologies

These books contain short stories and novellas in the drama subgenre. These are great suggestions for those looking for a quick read or to try a new author.

Around the Way Girls Series. ☞ ☞ ((

Street lit's all-stars tell these novella-length short stories about young women from "around the way"—specifically, from Brooklyn.

Keywords: Brooklyn, NY; Multiple Authors; Short Stories; Street Code

Similar Reads: The stories in the Around the Way Girls series are novella-length and cover subjects from hustling to cheating. For more short stories about street life, try the Girls from Da Hood series.

Core Collection: Adult

Around the Way Girls. West Babylon, NY: Urban Books, 2007 (2004). 350pp. ISBN 9781893196803, 1893196801.

> This original volume features stories from Angel Hunter, La Jill Hunt, and Dwayne S Joseph.

Around the Way Girls 2. West Babylon, NY: Urban Books, 2007 (2005). 400pp. ISBN 1893196852, 9781893196858.

> KaShamba Williams, Thomas Long, and La Jill Hunt contribute stories to this second installment.

Around the Way Girls 3. West Babylon, NY: Urban Books, 2009 (2006). 300pp. ISBN 9781601620538, 1601620535.

> Subtitled "Double Trouble," this third volume features stories by Pat Tucker, Alisha Yvonne, and Thomas Long.

Around the Way Girls 4. West Babylon, NY: Urban Books, 2007. 293pp. ISBN 9781601620088, 160162008X.

> Dwayne S. Joseph, La Jill Hunt, and Roy Glenn contribute to volume four.

Around the Way Girls 5. West Babylon, NY: Urban Books, 2008. 305pp. ISBN 9781601620552,1601620551.

> Volume 5 includes stories by Tysha, Erick S. Gray, and Mark Anthony.

Around the Way Girls 6. West Babylon, NY: Urban Books, 2009. 313pp. ISBN 9781601621535, 1601621531.

> Mark Anthony, Meisha Camm, and Blunt contribute this volume's novellas.

Clark, Wahida, and Kiki Swinson.

Sleeping with the Enemy. **New York: Kensington, 2008. 293pp. ISBN 9780758212573, 0758212577.** ☞ ((

Dating men in prison is complicated—especially when they've got other women in their lives. Wahida Clark and Kiki Swinson's novellas reveal the danger and the drama behind relationships with men who are "the enemy." In Clark's "Enemy in My Bed," Kreesha fights with Sparkle, wifey of her lover Reign. In Swinson's "Keeping My Enemies Close," Larissa's man destroys her apartment and all of her high-price belongings. Soon, Larissa meets a new man, Supreme, but he might turn out to be even more trouble than the last. Both authors have spent time in prison themselves, and there are plenty of scenes both inside and outside prison walls.

Keywords: Multiple Authors; Prison

Similar Reads: The novellas in *Sleeping with the Enemy* focus on cheating and fights between women. Brandie's *Clique* tells the story of women who fight over a man, then get thrown in jail for fighting and decide to "clique up" to protect each other. Kiki Swinson's <u>Wifey</u> series also focuses on the drama that results from cheating, particularly the love/hate relationship between heroine Kira and her man Ricky.

Diamond Playgirls. **New York: Dafina, 2008. 298pp. ISBN 9780758223562, 0758223560.** *☞* 𝄢

In this set of intersecting stories by Daaimah S. Poole, Karen E. Quinones Miller, Deja King, and Toy Styles, four sharp, professional women move to Harlem from out of town. Dior Emerson meets a man on MySpace who won't show her his picture. Tamara, a party promoter, almost lets her boss sleep with her before realizing her job is more important. Chloe is a big spender with big ambitions, and Mona Lisa Dupree is ready to let a man into her heart again but finds there are a few complications. Each character's story is written by a different known street author, and each story ends with its heroine meeting the other women by chance at Harlem's MoBay club on Valentine's Day. A testament to female friendship in the face of romantic drama.

Keywords: Middle Class Setting; Multiple Authors; New York; Short Stories

Similar Reads: *Diamond Playgirls* is a story of professional women supporting each other through disastrous relationships with men. Rechella's *Players Got Played* also stars a group of professional women who support each other in cheating on their unfaithful husbands. Anna J's *My Woman, His Wife* and Nikki Rashan's *Double Pleasure, Double Pain* also deal with romance in an upscale setting.

A Dollar and a Dream. **New York: Kensington, 2005 (2003). 320pp. ISBN 0758207565, 9780758207562.** *☞* 𝄢𝄢

Carl Weber, La Jill Hunt, Angel Hunter, and Dwayne S. Joseph present stories about winning the lottery. One couple struggles to pay the bills, until they hit it big. A stressed out mother goes from welfare to millions. And Dwayne S. Joseph's high-energy narrator has the winning numbers but has to fight to get his hands on the ticket. Getting money can solve problems, but it also creates them.

Keywords: Light Reads; Multiple Authors; Short Stories

Similar Reads: *A Dollar and a Dream* is a collection of light short stories dealing with the theme of money. For more light stories, try Dwayne S. Joseph, Roy Glenn, and Jihad's *Gigolos Get Lonely Too.* For a different take on money and its limitations, try Sister Souljah's *Coldest Winter Ever,* in which the spoiled daughter of a drug kingpin suddenly finds herself struggling.

Even Sinners Have Souls. **Columbus, OH: End of the Rainbow Projects, 2008. 245pp. ISBN 9780970672643, 0970672640.** *☞ ☞* 𝄢𝄢

In this Christian-inflected short story collection, masters of the profane try their hand at something a little more godly: street tales in which characters experience brushes with the divine. Nikki Turner contributes the introduction to this first volume, and B.L.U.N.T., Chunichi, KaShamba Williams, Noire, and Oscar McLain contribute stories.

Keywords: Christian Fiction; Multiple Authors; Short Stories

Similar Reads: *Even Sinners Have Souls* brings overtly Christian themes to street lit. Joy, in *Mama, I'm in Love . . . with a Gangsta*, explores God's role in difficult lives. P. L. Wilson's *Holy Hustler* provides a different, profane take on Christianity in the form of a promiscuous pastor.

Girls from Da Hood Series. ☞ ☞ ℂℂ

Each volume in this series brings a new set of novellas about the outrageous, shameless, scandalous deeds of certain women from familiar neighborhoods.

Keywords: Multiple Authors; Short Stories

Similar Reads: Girls from Da Hood features novella-length stories from a variety of perspectives. For another series that compiles novella-length short stories, try Around the Way Girls, or try the collection *Tales from Da Hood*.

Girls from Da Hood. West Babylon, NY: Urban Books, 2004. 314pp. ISBN 0974702528, 9780974702520.

> This inaugural volume includes stories from Nikki Turner, Roy Glenn, and Chunichi.

Girls from Da Hood 2. West Babylon, NY: Urban Books, 2005. 283pp. ISBN 1893196283, 9781893196285.

> KaShamba Williams, Joy Turner, and Nikki Turner contribute to volume 2.

Girls from Da Hood 3. West Babylon, NY: Urban Books, 2006. 300pp. ISBN 9781893196834, 1893196836.

> This third volume features stories from KaShamba Williams, Mark Anthony, and Madame K.

Girls from Da Hood 4. West Babylon, NY: Urban Books, 2008. 294pp. ISBN 9781601620439, 1601620438.

> Ashley, JaQuavis, and Ayana Ellis contribute stories to volume 4.

Girls from Da Hood 5. West Babylon, NY: Urban Books, 2009. 294pp. ISBN 9781601621528,1601621523.

> This volume includes stories by Keisha Ervin, Brenda Hamilton, and Ed McNair.

Joseph, Dwayne S., Roy Glenn, and Jihad.

Gigolos Get Lonely Too. **West Babylon, NY: Urban Books, 2006. 296pp. ISBN 189319633X, 9781893196339.** ☞ ℂℂ

Dwayne S. Joseph, Roy Glenn, and Jihad tell three stories of men who have their hands full with love, sex, romance, and drama. A gigolo, a playa, and a cheating married man star in these lighthearted tales.

Keywords: Light Reads; Multiple Authors; Sex Industry

Similar Reads: *Gigolos Get Lonely Too* features men struggling comically with sex and relationships. For more light reads about drama from a male perspective, try Dwayne S. Joseph's *Womanizers* or David Givens's *Betrayed*.

Turner, Nikki.

Nikki Turner Presents . . . Street Chronicles: Backstage. **New York: One World/ Ballantine Books, 2009. 248pp. ISBN 9780345504296, 0345504291.** 〰 〰 ((

The music industry may seem glamorous, but these short stories are here to tell you that there's more to being a star than meets the eye. Four new street authors and superstar Nikki Turner contribute stories of talented artists, sleazy producers, and love and lust behind the music. Commentary by hip-hop artists Dana Dane and Styles P adds a dose of realism.

Keywords: Abuse; Multiple Authors; Music Industry; Short Stories; Street Code

Similar Reads: *Backstage* delves into the nitty-gritty reality behind the music business. For more stories of the music industry, try Thomas Long's *Cash Rules*, K. Roland Williams's *Cut Throat*, or, for a more uplifting take, Nikki Turner's *Ghetto Superstar*.

1

2

3

4

5

6

7

8

9

10

11

Chapter 4

Love Stories

The love stories subgenre is focused on love relationships. Street lit love stories may be warm or painful, and the characters in love may get along smoothly or have a relationship full of strife. Elements of other subgenres, including street action, prison, and drama, are often part of the story, though some street lit love stories do not focus heavily on these elements. The common thread is the relationship at the novel's center.

Some street lit love stories begin with the two partners meeting each other and follow the growth of their relationship. Others start in the middle of the action or involve characters picking up the pieces after the romance is over, as in Miasha's *Diary of a Mistress*. Others tell stories of abusive relationships. Some feature relationships between characters of the same gender, including Nikki Rashan's *Double Pleasure, Double Pain* and Reginald Hall's *In Love with a Thug*.

Classic street romances include Nikki Turner's *Hustler's Wife*, Tracy Brown's *Black*, and Teri Woods's *True to the Game*.

Crazy in Love

Novels in this section focus on partners for whom love conquers all. Warm romantic relationships either heal characters' pain or help them through hard times.

Benjamin, J. M.

Ride or Die Chick Series. 👞👞 ((

This series focuses on two street-savvy teenagers and their romantic relationship.

Keywords: Character-Driven; Prison; Teenagers; Virginia

Similar Reads: *Ride or Die Chick* is a coming-of-age story that follows a mutually respectful love relationship from a male point of view. *Gorilla Black* by Seven and *Criminal Minded* by Tracy Brown both have similar types of relationships, with a focus on thoughtful, male characters.

Core Collection: Adult; Young Adult

Ride or Die Chick: The Story of Treacherous and Teflon. New York: Flowers in Bloom Publishing, 2007. 212pp. ISBN 9780979861406, 0979861403.

> Treacherous Freeman met the love of his life, Teflon Jackson, in a juvenile detention facility. They started off fighting but quickly realized they were meant for each other. Treacherous had been raised by his gangster father, who taught him all the survival skills he would need to be a man of the streets. Teflon became his ride or die chick, the woman who stayed at his side no matter what. The book begins with a high-speed car chase and the duo's capture by the police and becomes a story of growing up, finding love, and going out with a bang.

Ride or Die Chick 2. New York: Flowers in Bloom Publishing, 2009. ISBN 9780979861413, 0979861411.

> In this second volume, Teflon takes the starring role.

Blue, Treasure E.

Keyshia and Clyde. **New York: One World/Ballantine Books, 2008. 352pp. ISBN 9780345493293, 034549329X.** ⌐ ⌐ ((

> Keyshia and Clyde meet in the women's section of an upscale department store. Clyde is trying to steal clothing, and Keyshia covers for him when security comes. Then Keyshia takes a wallet from the store detective; she realizes only later that Clyde has stolen that same wallet from her. From these beginnings comes a love that continues through a shared murder, a series of bank robberies, and a trial for Clyde that might just end explosively. Both Keyshia and Clyde have painful histories of loss, abuse, and in Keyshia's case, a habit of numbing the pain with drugs.

> **Keywords:** Abuse; Drug Addiction; New York; Teenagers

> **Similar Reads:** *Keyshia and Clyde* is an emotional novel about lovers who support each other both emotionally and as hustling partners. J. M. Benjamin's *Ride or Die Chick* has many of the same themes, including love and a man and woman who are partners in crime. For similar scenes of drug use, sex, and misery, try Noire's *Hittin the Bricks*.

> **Core Collection:** Adult

Brown, Laurinda D.

Strapped. **Jamaica, NY: Q-Boro Books, 2007. 223pp. ISBN 9781933967219, 1933967218.** ⌐ ((

> A mother comes to terms with having a lesbian daughter, and the daughter comes to terms with having survived childhood sexual abuse. The novel begins in the voice of Elise, the mother, writing a letter to her daughter Monique. Elise describes the relationship that led to Monique's conception and her current anger toward her daughter. Monique's voice recounts her childhood abuse at the hands of Mr. Luther, a lecherous candy store owner, and her hatred for herself and for the mother who never intervened. As a teenager, Monique leaves home, renames herself Mo, and begins a relationship with LaQuita, an exotic dancer who helps

Mo accept herself and her past. Mo carries a gun, but illegal activities and urban settings take a backseat to relationships and healing.

Keywords: Abuse; GLBTQ; Overcoming Adversity; Sex Industry; Teenagers

Similar Reads: *Strapped* is a character-driven, coming-of-age story about a teenage girl who loves other women. For another story of a butch teenager's loves and family struggles, try *London Reign* by A. C. Britt. For another story of love and self-discovery between two women, try Nikki Rashan's *Double Pleasure, Double Pain*. For more about healing from abuse, try Antoine "Inch" Thomas's *Flower's Bed* or the short story collection *Breaking the Cycle*. Mo first appears in Brown's short story collection *Walk Like a Man*.

Core Collection: Adult; Young Adult; School Libraries

Brown, Tracy.

Black: A Street Tale. **Columbus, OH: Triple Crown Publications, 2003. 182pp. ISBN 0970247281, 9780970247285.** ☞ (

Kaia and Aaron fall in love in high school. When Kaia becomes pregnant, Aaron heads to the streets to provide for Kaia and the baby. Then a deal goes awry. Aaron is sent to prison, and Kaia is left to support herself and her child, with or without the help of her friends. A sweet, emotional story of love and hardship.

Keywords: Prison; Staten Island, NY

Similar Reads: Readers who enjoy the character-driven love story in *Black* will find a similar tone in Brown's *Criminal Minded* and *White Lines*. *A Hustler's Wife* by Nikki Turner is another classic tale of a young woman surviving the streets while the man she loves is in prison.

Classic

Core Collection: Adult; Young Adult; School Libraries

Ervin, Keisha.

Gunz and Roses. **West Babylon, NY: Urban Books, 2009. 305pp. ISBN 9781601621566, 1601621566.** ☞ ☞ ((

When Gray Rose, editor at *Haute Couture* magazine, meets Gunz Marciano, leader of St. Louis's notorious MGM crew, the chemistry is undeniable. Gunz takes Gray home from the club where they can't stop watching each other, and the sex they have is raw, wild, and powerful. Against Gray's better judgment, she lets Gunz further and further into her life. But Gray is lonely, and Gunz trusts his nine millimeter more than he trusts any woman. Will their differences keep them apart? A steamy, captivating love story.

Keywords: Fashion Industry; Middle Class Setting; St. Louis

Similar Reads: *Gunz and Roses* is an epic, sexually charged love story about two partners with little in common. For more epic love stories, try Ervin's bittersweet *Torn* or Tracy Brown's emotional *White Lines*. For more about professional women falling in love with men involved in street life, try T. N. Baker, Tu-Shonda Whitaker, and Danielle Santiago's *Cream* or Jason Poole's *Larceny*.

Core Collection: Adult

Fournier, Tammy.

P.I.E.C.E.S.: A Booster's Story. **West Babylon, NY: Urban Books, 2008. 242pp. ISBN 9781601620354, 1601620357.** ☞ ❨❨

Tara comes from a family of hustlers. Her father is a well-known pimp, and her mother is a top-notch booster who regularly steals thousands of dollars' worth of clothing from department stores. Now Tara is following in her mother's footsteps. One night at a party, she meets Julio, a sexy Dominican drug dealer. Tara is used to using men, but with Julio—a man who respects her as a hustler—she feels an instant sexual and emotional connection. Their romance is going well until Julio unwittingly introduces her to cocaine.

Keywords: Columbus, OH; Drug Addiction; Latino Characters; Street Code

Similar Reads: *P.I.E.C.E.S.* features a materialistic woman letting her guard down and falling in love. For more brand-name conscious women like Tara, try Chantel Jolie's *In Those Jeans* or Erica K. Barnes's *I Ain't Saying She's a Gold Digger*. For more families who hustle together, try 50 Cent and Mark Anthony's *Harlem Heat* or Rahsaan Ali's *Carmello*. Kiki Swinson's *Candy Shop* and Felicia Madlock's *Back on the Block* also deal with addiction and family relations.

Gray, Erick S.

Ghetto Heaven. **Jamaica, NY: Q-Boro Books, 2006 (2004). 427pp. ISBN 097773353X, 9780977733538.** ☞ ☞ ❨❨

Coney Island in Brooklyn is known for its amusement park and boardwalk, but Toni knows it as a place full of housing projects, street violence, drug addiction, and people barely getting by. Toni is working in a seedy strip club trying to support her drug-addicted mother while her brother is in prison for killing the man who abused both Toni and her mother. When her friend Vinita takes her to a charity ball in Manhattan, Toni feels uncomfortably out of place. But there she meets Matthew, a wealthy socialite from Long Island whose fiancée, family, and country club lifestyle leave him feeling empty. As the two become closer, a turf war heats up in Coney Island. A sensitive love story with a sense of place.

Keywords: Abuse; Brooklyn, NY; Drug Addiction; Prison; Sex Industry

Similar Reads: *Ghetto Heaven* has a strong sense of place, a heroine with a heart of gold, and lovers from opposite sides of the tracks. For more novels with a sense of place, try Tracy Brown's *Criminal Minded*, set in nearby Staten Island, or Mikal Malone's *Pitbulls in a Skirt*. For another kindhearted heroine in draining circumstances, try Karen Williams's *Harlem on Lock* or Marlon McCaulsky's *Pink Palace*. Keisha Ervin's *Mina's Joint* features another pair of lovers from two different sides of the class divide.

Jones, Solomon.

Ride or Die. New York: St. Martin's Minotaur, 2005 (2004). 293pp. ISBN 0312339895, 9780312339890. ☞ ☾

Seventeen year-old Keisha Anderson is walking home along the streets of North Philadelphia when two men grab her from behind. She struggles, and then Jamal, a stranger, jumps in and fends off the attackers. The two fall instantly in love, but their families turn out to be enemies. After a shooting, the police pursue Jamal, and Keisha makes a split-second decision to flee with him, against her father's wishes. The chase makes up the rest of the novel. Although Jones begins, like many authors, by acknowledging his own familiarity with street life, the novel itself reads more like a suspense thriller than a typical street tale.

Keywords: Philadelphia; Teenagers

Similar Reads: *Ride or Die* is a love story featuring teenagers that is more crafted than most street lit. For other crafted novels with attention to language, try Jones's *C.R.E.A.M.*, the novels of Y. Blak Moore, or *Snow*, by Kenji Jasper. For another fast-paced tale of desperate young lovers fleeing, try the <u>Flint</u> series.

Core Collection: Adult; Young Adult; School Libraries

K'wan.

Street Dreams. New York: St. Martin's, 2005 (2004). 320pp. ISBN 0312333064, 9780312333065. ☞ ☞ ☾☾

Rio can't get a job because of his criminal record. Trinity endures the attentions of her abusive father. The two are in love, but when Rio turns to the streets to make a living, life gets desperate and dangerous. The street action that surrounds Rio is treated as authentically as Trinity's abuse and the couple's emotional struggles.

Keywords: Abuse; Multiple Perspectives; New York

Similar Reads: The love story and Trinity's abuse make up the core of this high-action, highly emotional novel. Treasure Hernandez's <u>Flint</u> series depicts teenagers in a similarly emotional and desperate situation. Incest is a hot topic in street lit: both *Flower's Bed* by Antoine "Inch" Thomas and *Baby Girl* by Jihad explore the effects of incest.

Core Collection: Adult; Young Adult

Majette, Danette.

Deep. Brandywine, MD: Life Changing Books, 2007. 249pp. ISBN 9781934230930, 1934230936. ☞ ☞ ☾☾

Trae is a D.C. kingpin whose troubles began at a young age: When he was seven, he watched his mother's pimp stab her to death. Now he's a coldhearted player on the streets, but women still bring out his softer side.

He meets Karina catching a bus and romances his way into her heart. Meanwhile, a skilled stripper and an accomplished hustler have made their way into Trae's operation. Little does Trae know that both are FBI agents working to bring him down. The tension builds slowly as we watch each character lead his or her double life.

Keywords: Law Enforcement; Street Code; Washington, DC

Similar Reads: *Deep* is a slower-paced love story that combines elements of thrillers, action, and tender romance. For more thrillers involving high-level drug investigations, try Relentless Aaron's *Last Kingpin* or Amaleka McCall's *Hush*. For more about men winning over women against the women's better judgment, try 50 Cent and Relentless Aaron's *Derelict* or Jason Poole's *Larceny*.

Rashan, Nikki.

Double Pleasure, Double Pain Series. ☞ (

The two volumes in this series focus on Kyla, a young woman finding herself and coming to understand her sexual identity.

Keywords: GLBTQ; Middle Class Setting

Similar Reads: The <u>Double Pleasure, Double Pain</u> series is about a female college student discovering her identity and her attraction to women. Other positive portrayals of lesbian and bisexual women include *Strapped* by Laurinda D. Brown and *And God Created Woman* by Mika Miller. Anna J's *My Woman, His Wife* provides another upscale take on same-gender-loving women.

Double Pleasure, Double Pain. West Babylon, NY: Urban Books, 2008. 232pp. ISBN 9781601620521,1601620527.

Naïve Kyla is studying social work at the local university when she meets Steph, a successful, self-confident human resources specialist to whom Kyla feels an unfamiliar attraction. Stephanie surprises Kyla by coming out as an out and proud lesbian. Kyla has a boyfriend, but as she becomes more involved with Stephanie, she begins to question her sexuality and learn more about what it means to be gay. The characters are professional and the attitudes toward homosexuality consistently positive. A warm and occasionally comic introduction to lesbian sexuality.

You Make Me Wanna. West Babylon, NY: Urban Books, 2009. 259pp. ISBN 9781601621634, 1601621639.

In *Double Pleasure, Double Pain*, college student Kyla came to accept her attractions to another woman. Now Kyla's back, and this time she knows who she is and what she wants. The question is, can she let go of her past?

Santiago, Danielle.

Little Ghetto Girl. **New York: Atria Books, 2007 (2004). 197pp. ISBN 9780743297479, 0743297474.** ⌀⌀ ((

In Santiago's first novel, Kisa is a twenty-one year-old hustler who's gotten rich running a large part of New York City's cocaine trade. The love of her life, Sincere, deals drugs too and likes that Kisa makes her own money. When the cops begin enforcing new, stronger drug laws, Kisa turns to legitimate income sources, like opening a hair salon, while Sincere and his drug enterprise come under scrutiny. Their love has endured Sincere's cheating, but the interference of the police provides a new challenge. The original, self-published edition made the *Essence* best-seller list in 2004.

Keywords: Law Enforcement; New York

Similar Reads: Santiago's *Grindin'* is a high-drama love story involving flashy material goods and the drug trade. For more protagonists with expensive taste, try Tammy Fournier's *P.I.E.C.E.S.* or Sister Souljah's *Coldest Winter Ever*. For more dramatic stories of cheating and hustling, try Ericka Monique Williams's *All That Glitters* or Kiki Swinson's <u>Wifey</u> series.

Showell, Nisaa A.

Reign of a Hustler. **Brandywine, MD: Life Changing Books, 2007. 233pp. ISBN 9781934230879, 1934230871.** ⌀⌀ ((

Quinnzel "Supreme" Sharpe is a college-educated hustler using his business degree to help his big brother run the streets. He hooks up with a girl once in a while, but no one he considers "wifey material." Imani Heaven Best is the founder of an up-and-coming media consulting agency. She lost her first true love in a car accident several years ago and has been on her own ever since. Quinnzel and Imani meet at a club, and sparks fly. Their romance is compelling, but Quinnzel's connections to the streets make him a dangerous partner.

Keywords: Middle Class Setting; Philadelphia

Similar Reads: *Reign of a Hustler* is a slower-paced love story involving college students and a professional woman attached to a street hustler. For more about professional women involved with street-oriented men, try Keisha Ervin's *Gunz and Roses* or Willie Dutch's *Day After Forever*. For more about leaving college for the streets, try Eric Fleming's *Lust, Love, and Lies* or Anya Nicole's *Corporate Corner Boyz*.

Stacy-Deanne.

Everlasting. **Largo, MD: Strebor Books, 2007. 353pp. ISBN 9781593091873, 1593091877.** ⌀⌀ (

Two teenagers with family in rival gangs fall in love in the Bronx. Nina, whose mother is being treated for cancer, moves in with her cousin Tajo, a leader of the Bronx Gangstas. Juan's brother Rico is in the rival New

York Assassins, but Juan sees no future in gang life. Nina and Juan meet in school and eventually fall in love. As violence builds around them, both teens want to rise above the gang warfare that consumes those around them. The gentle love of two young people who want no part of street violence makes for a refreshing and tender romance.

Keywords: Bronx, NY; Gangs; Social Commentary; Street Code; Teenagers

Similar Reads: *Everlasting* is a tender love story and a cautionary tale about gang violence. For more sweet stories of teenage love, try Tracy Brown's *Black: A Street Tale*, Solomon Jones's *Ride or Die*, or J. M. Benjamin's *Ride or Die Chick*. For more on the harmful effects of gang violence, try James Hendricks's *Good Day to Die*, Rochan Morgan's *Crossroads*, or Reymundo Sanchez's memoir *My Bloody Life*.

Core Collection: Young Adult; School Libraries

Turner, Nikki.

A Hustler's Wife Series. ☞ (

Turner's classic series follows the adventures of a young woman whose beloved man is in prison.

Keywords: Prison; Richmond, VA; Teenagers

Similar Reads: *A Hustler's Wife* is a warm, episodic love story. Turner's *Riding Dirty on I-95* most closely mirrors the lighthearted, episodic nature of this tale. For other episodic tales, try *Queen* by Cynthia White or Alex Tyson's *A Compton Chick*.

Classic

Core Collection: Adult; Young Adult

A Hustler's Wife. Columbus, OH: Triple Crown Publications, 2003. 259pp. ISBN 9780970247254

> Yarni is a well-behaved senior in high school when she meets lavish, seductive Des. They fall in love, and she becomes his "wifey." But when Des gets sent to prison, Yarni has to fend for herself. Can a sweet, young woman with little experience in the streets keep herself fed and stay true to the man she loves? Read past the typos for a warm story about the ups and downs of love, the streets, and getting played.

Forever a Hustler's Wife. New York: One World/Ballantine Books, 2007. 266pp. ISBN 0345493850.

> In the first volume, Yarni was a naïve teenager trying to survive on her own without her man Des. In this volume, Yarni has taken charge and become a lawyer, and she's fighting to keep Des out of prison.

Whitaker, Tu-Shonda L.

Flip Side of the Game Series. ☞ ((

Vera Wright-Turner is a self-proclaimed gold digger. Ever since her drug-addicted mother tied her in a garbage bag and dropped her out by the dumpster on the day she was born, Vera has trusted no one but herself. But what happens when a commitment-phobic gold digger falls in love? Vera's proud, humorous, engaging voice gets readers on her side, even as they see the error of her ways.

Keywords: New York; Drug Addiction

Similar Reads: *Flip Side of the Game* is a lyrical, comic story about a self-proclaimed "gold digger" falling in love. For more stories of ruthless players falling prey to their own emotions, try Keisha Ervin's *Hold U Down* or Sha's *Harder*. For more lyrical prose, try Anna J's *Snow White* or Noire's *Hittin' the Bricks*.

Core Collection: Adult

Flip Side of the Game. Columbus, OH: Triple Crown Publications, 2004. 180pp. ISBN 0974789542, 9780974789545.

> In the first volume of this series about a commitment-phobic gold digger falling in love, Vera Wright-Turner, a winning narrator with attitude, explains her origins and meets Taj, the man she comes to love.

Game Over. Columbus, OH: Triple Crown Publications, 2004. 308pp. ISBN 0976234920, 9780976234920.

> In this second installment, love has got the best of Vera, for better or for worse.

Woods, Teri.

True to the Game Series. 𝓇 𝓇 ((

Starting with one of the earliest and most popular street novels, this series stars Gena, a somewhat naïve eighteen-year-old living in Philadelphia in the late 1980s, and smooth, generous drug dealer Quadir.

Keywords: Philadelphia; Teenagers

Similar Reads: Aside from being a story of a naïve teenage girl learning to survive the streets, *True to the Game* is one of the best-recognized names in street lit. Readers looking for other classic street tales can try Sister Souljah's *Coldest Winter Ever*, Nikki Turner's *A Hustler's Wife*, Tracy Brown's *Black*, or K'wan's *Gangsta*. For more about learning to play the game, try Shannon Holmes's *Bad Girlz* or Tonya Ridley's *Takeover*.

Classic

Core Collection: Adult; Young Adult; School Libraries

True to the Game. Special Collector's Edition. New York: Grand Central Publishing, 2007 (1994). 302pp. ISBN 9780446581608.

> Gena and Quadir's fairy-tale romance begins in the first chapter. Quadir lavishes vacations, jewelry, a car, and cash on Gena, and the two fall in love, even though it's clear Quadir is keeping a few secrets.

A story of love and betrayal set against a backdrop of family drama, double-crosses, and stray bullets.

True to the Game II. 1st ed. New York: Grand Central Publishing, 2007. 232pp. ISBN 9780446581660.

In *True to the Game*, naïve teenager Gena met seductive drug dealer Quadir and, after a high-stakes climax, fled town with Quadir's drug money in her car's trunk. Now, with a trunk full of cash and a villain on her trail, Gena tries to fend for herself.

True to the Game III. New York: Grand Central Publishing, 2008. 224pp. ISBN 9780446581684.

Quadir returns for the explosive series conclusion.

Pain and Heartbreak

These are the stories in which love does not bring joy. In Reginald Hall's *In Love with a Thug* and Nikki Turner's *Black Widow*, we hear from characters who have had their hearts broken. KaShamba Williams's <u>Blinded</u> series portrays another kind of romantic relationship gone wrong: an abusive boyfriend terrorizing the woman who loves him.

Dutch, Willie.

A Day After Forever. **Wilmington, DE: Street Knowledge Publishing, 2008. 221pp. ISBN 9780979955617, 0979955610.** ☞ ❪❪

Twenty-one-year-old Miko has a respectable job working at an African American bookstore and cultural center in Houston, Texas. As a child Miko saw her father murdered for his gambling debts and promised him she'd never end up with a hustler. Then she spends a night with Seven, a powerful dealer of XTC, and she's in love for life. When she loses her second loved one to murder in the streets, Miko is devastated, and out for revenge. Her sometime relationship with her friend Jahzay helps her get through the hard times.

Keywords: Houston; Revenge

Similar Reads: *A Day After Forever* is a socially conscious love story involving warm relationships and a search for revenge. For more warm relationships between friends, try Deja King's *Trife Life to Lavish* or Keisha Seignious's *Boogie Down Story*. For another socially conscious story about revenge after a tragic incident, try Evie Rhodes's *Street Vengeance*.

Ervin, Keisha.

Finding Forever. **Florissant, MO: Prioritybooks Publications, 2008. 145pp. ISBN 9780981648347, 0981648347.** ☞ ❪❪

Koran and Whitney loved each other as teenagers, but then Whitney left St. Louis for good. Koran came up in the drug game and had a relationship with Trina, a drama queen with an eight-year-old son who now treats Koran like a father. Eight years later, Whitney shows up in St. Louis again, and she and Koran are once again drawn to each other. Ervin's tender novella follows their passionate but bittersweet reunion, as well as Koran's dramas with Trina and with his own drug crew.

Keywords: Character-Driven; St. Louis

Similar Reads: *Finding Forever* is a tender, emotional novella about lovers reuniting after years of hardship and separation. For more emotional love stories, try Ervin's *Torn* or Tracy Brown's *Black: A Street Tale* or *White Lines*. Terra Little's *Where There's Smoke* is another emotional, bittersweet story of lovers reuniting.

Torn. **Columbus, OH: Triple Crown Publications, 2007. 384pp. ISBN 978-0977880492, 0977880494.** 🖘 ((

Mo considers herself Quan's ride or die chick. They've been together nine years, but Mo knows Quan's been cheating on her for most of that time. Mo may even have cheated once or twice herself. What do you do when you love someone who treats you wrong? Crime takes a backseat in this story to romance, drama, and a love of music. Meesa, Mina, and Unique, characters from Ervin's other St. Louis–based novels, make cameo appearances in this one.

Keywords: Overcoming Adversity; St. Louis

Similar Reads: *Torn* is an emotional story about romance and making peace with a loved one's shortcomings. Ervin's *Me and My Boyfriend* also explores relationships and loving someone who is ill-suited. For another take on this theme, try *Black Widow* by Nikki Turner.

Core Collection: Adult

Hall, Reginald.

In Love with a Thug. **New York: Simon & Schuster, 2007. 240pp. ISBN 9781593091484.** 🖘🖘 ((

Gay rights advocate Reginald Hall tells a sexy cautionary tale about a gay man whose partners bring him into a life of crime. Juan is in love with Darnell and would do anything for his man. So when Darnell asks him to help rob a bank, Juan reluctantly agrees. Darnell is killed by an armed guard, but Juan escapes with bags full of cash. Heartbroken, Juan uses the money to fulfill his lifelong dream of owning a hair salon. There he meets Bryant, who seems like the man of his dreams but also seems to be hiding something. As he runs the salon and falls deeper into the drug trade, Juan realizes he's in over his head.

Keywords: GLBTQ; Philadelphia

Similar Reads: *In Love with a Thug* is a sexually charged story of love between a hustler and a man who wants to live a safe life. For more stories about reluctant partners of hustlers, try Amaleka McCall's *Myra: A Twisted Tale of Karma* or

KaShamba Williams's *Driven*. For another story of hair salons and drama, try Tracy Brown's *Dime Piece*. Other stories of men who love men include Mike Warren's <u>A Private Affair</u> series and Clarence Nero's *Three Sides to Every Story*.

Joy.

***Mama, I'm in Love . . . with a Gangsta.* West Babylon, NY: Urban Books, 2008 (2006). 288pp. ISBN 160162073X, 978-1601620736.** ☞ ☞ ℂℂ

In this book, Joy gives us two novellas about love, the streets, and redemption. In *Behind Every Bad Boy . . . Is a Bad-ass Bitch*, we meet Harlem Lee Jones, who spent her childhood wishing God would take her out of her misery. Growing up with a crack-addicted mother, she knew well the pain of being a neglected child. As an adult, Harlem hooks up with Jazzy, a gangster she thinks has moved beyond his criminal ways, but finds their love tested by both of their pasts. In the second novella, *Baby Girl McCoy*, a seventeen-year-old finds herself making the same mistakes her mother made. Emotional descriptions of both women's pain set the stage, and God's love plays a role in helping the women out of their circumstances.

Keywords: Abuse; Christian Fiction; Drug Addiction; Overcoming Adversity; Prison

Similar Reads: Joy begins this uplifting story of redemption with a prosy invocation in a style similar to Noire. *Harlem Girl Lost* by Treasure E. Blue provides another story of triumph over pain. For more stories that combine street life and Christian inspiration, try the short story collection *Even Sinners Have Souls*.

Little, Terra.

Where There's Smoke Series. ☞ ℂℂ

This romantic story focuses on an unlikely family reunited after sixteen years.

Keywords: Drug Addiction; Hartford, IL; Middle Class Setting

Similar Reads: *Where There's Smoke* is a warm, emotional romance with themes of drug addiction and father–son relationships. Tracy Brown's *White Lines* is another emotional story about a woman recovering from drug addiction and finding a supportive lover. Thomas Long's *Papa Don't Preach* is another story of a flawed father trying to keep his son from making the same mistakes he made.

***Where There's Smoke*. West Babylon, NY: Urban Books, 2009. 326pp. ISBN 9781933967783, 1933967781.**

Sixteen years ago, Alec was a teenage crack dealer who went by the name Smoke. Anne was a teenage crack addict who went by Breanne. Alec had sex with Breanne in exchange for drugs and thought nothing of it. Now a teacher who has renounced his criminal past, Alec is shocked when he gets served with papers asking for child support. He visits Anne's house in the suburbs of Chicago and meets a changed Anne and his son, a sullen teenager who seems headed down the same path as his mother. Anne needs help bringing her son in line. Can this unlikely family come together and heal?

Where There's Smoke 2: When the Smoke Clears. 288pp. West Babylon, NY: Urban Books, 2010. ISBN 9781601622624, 1601622627.

In the first *Where There's Smoke*, former drug dealer Alec, also known as Smoke, reencountered Anne, a former crack addict he had abused when the two were teenagers, and the two fell in love. Four years later, Smoke and Anne step in to protect Anne's son Isaiah from a new threat.

Miasha.

Diary of a Mistress. **New York: Simon & Schuster, 2007 (2006). 245pp. ISBN 1416547207, 9781416547204.** ☞ (

Angie has been sleeping with married men since she lost her own husband in a divorce five years ago. Her latest is Carlos, a man she loves and hopes will leave his wife for her. Monica, Carlos's wife, suspects nothing until the day a package arrives in the mail for her. It's a diary, and as she reads it, she realizes the writer is Angie and the man she describes having an affair with is her own husband. Watch the sparks fly for both women in this tight, dramatic tale.

Keywords: Middle Class Setting; Philadelphia;

Similar Reads: *Diary of a Mistress* is a dramatic story about cheating within a marriage. For more high-intensity novels about married couples cheating, try La Jill Hunt's *Drama Queen* or Dwayne S. Joseph's *Womanizers*. Anna J's *My Woman, His Wife* is the dramatic story of a couple coping with the complications of introducing a third sexual partner into their marriage. Readers who enjoy the diary conceit may also enjoy Jason Poole's *Victoria's Secret* or Ashley and JaQuavis's *Diary of a Street Diva*, both of which are told in diary formats.

Turner, Nikki.

Black Widow. **New York: One World/Ballantine Books, 2008. 285pp. ISBN 9780345493873, 0345493877.** ☞ (

Isis Tatum has had bad luck with men ever since she saw her mother murder her cheating father when Isis was thirteen. Her first love is executed by the state of Virginia, and the second cheats just like her father and then gets sent to jail. Figuring she is a black widow cursed with bad luck, Isis seeks comfort in her family: her incarcerated mother; her half-sister Phoebe, the daughter of her father's mistress; and her transgender Aunt Samantha. Then she goes to Vegas and meets Logic, a wealthy drug dealer who helps her finance her dream of starting a line of jewelry. The pace is slower than in most street lit, but the tone is hopeful.

Keywords: GLBTQ; Overcoming Adversity; Prison; Richmond, VA

Similar Reads: *Black Widow* is an uplifting story involving love and family closeness. Turner's *Ghetto Superstar* features another family that sticks together through hardship. For more uplifting reads about love and families, try Treasure E. Blue's *Harlem Girl Lost* or Meisha Camm's *You Got to Pay to Play*.

Williams, KaShamba.

Blinded Series. ⌐⌐ ((

Family, abuse, and violence all have roles to play in this series about a young woman and the drug dealer who terrorizes her.

Keywords: Abuse; Delaware; Teenagers

Similar Reads: *Blinded* is the story of a high-maintenance girl who is used to being the center of attention finding herself in an abusive relationship. For more about teen girls accustomed to being the center of attention, try Shavon Moore's <u>Baby Girl</u> series or Sister Souljah's *Coldest Winter Ever*. For more about abusive relationships, try Azárel's *Bruised*, Nikki Turner's *Project Chick*, or Mark Anthony's *Reasonable Doubt*.

Blinded. Columbus, OH: Triple Crown Publications, 2003. 193pp. ISBN 0970247273, 9780970247278.

> Mona Foster has grown up on Delaware's East Twenty-Second Street, better known as "Deuce-Deuce." Despite the negative influence of her absent, crack-addicted mother, Mona becomes the first in her family to graduate from high school. But getting the diploma was only her first challenge. Swept off her feet by a New York drug dealer named Camron, Mona finds herself caught up in a violent situation. Both Mona and Nikki, the mother of Camron's child, move into his Philadelphia apartment and are subject to his volatile temper. Mona wants to stick around because she hopes Camron will finance the shoe business she wants to start. But how much is she willing to give up?

Grimey. Columbus, OH: Triple Crown Publications, 2004. 271pp. ISBN 0974789518, 9780974789514.

> In this companion volume to *Blinded*, Mona's brother Yatta seeks revenge against the hustler who hurt his sister.

Wright, Ana'Gia.

Lil' Sister. West Babylon, NY: Urban Books, 2008. 234pp. ISBN 9781601620392, 160162039X. ⌐ ((

When Krystal was thirteen years old, her first love, Jerad, committed suicide. Krystal found his body, cold and bloody in the bathtub. Struggling to cope, Krystal ran away from home to live with the Trio, three brothers she trusted. Four years later, on the anniversary of Jerad's death, Krystal is still in pain. The Trio is there for her, particularly Yohan, with whom her relationship has become more than platonic. This warm story of family, love, and healing follows Krystal's emotional journey as she learns to cope with grief and tragedy.

Keywords: Overcoming Adversity; Teenagers

Similar Reads: *Lil' Sister* is an emotional story about grief and warm, intimate relationships. Mallori McNeal's <u>Down Chick</u> series also stars a teenage girl and the men who are kind to her, and Nikki Turner's *Black Widow* is another emotional story about healing after a tragedy. For more warm relationships between teenagers, try Treasure Hernandez's <u>Flint</u> series or Anthony Whyte's *Ghetto Girls*.

Core Collection: Young Adult

Short Stories and Anthologies

These books contain short stories and novellas in the love stories subgenre. These are great suggestions for those looking for a quick read or to try a new author.

Baker, T. N., Tu-Shonda Whitaker, and Danielle Santiago.

Cream. Columbus, OH: Triple Crown Publications, 2005 (2004). 242pp. ISBN 0976789418, 9780976789413. *☞ ☞* ((

Three women authors come together in this collection of three long (50–70pp.) short stories about street life, sex, and relationships. In Tu-Shonda Whitaker's "The Last Run," Bruh is back from prison and back to his drama-filled woman Tomkia. Danielle Santiago gives us "Fair Exchange, No Robberies," in which Lovi, a proud woman with a degree, finds herself back in the hood and falling for a hustler. T. N. Baker gives us a first peek at gambling Wasuan and his girl Enychi, who get their own full-length novel, *Dice*.

Keywords: Multiple Authors; Prison; Short Stories

Similar Reads: *Cream* is a collection of short stories with themes of love, prison, and interpersonal drama. For another high-drama compilation, try Wahida Clark and Kiki Swinson's *Sleeping with the Enemy*, which also explores the complications of love relationships, particularly with one partner in prison. Readers intrigued by Wasuan and Enychi will want to check out Baker's *Dice*.

Brown, Tracy, K'wan, and Angel Mitchell.

Flirt. New York: St. Martin's Griffin, 2009. 304pp. ISBN 9780312537012, 0312537018. *☞ ☞ ☞* ((

Love, drama, abuse, and sex are common themes in this collection of novellas. Brown, K'wan, and Mitchell all tell stories of women who get in over their heads with violent, deceptive, or simply heartbreaking men. Shannon Holmes contributes the introduction.

Keywords: Abuse; Multiple Authors; Short Stories

Similar Reads: *Flirt* is a collection that explores the painful sides of love. For more about abuse, try Azárel's *Bruised* or Mark Anthony's *Reasonable Doubt*. For more women whose hearts are broken by the men in their lives, try Keisha Ervin's *Torn* or Ashley and JaQuavis's *Dirty Money*.

Lipstick Diaries: A Provocative Look into the Female Perspective. New York: Augustus Publishing, 2007. 229pp. ISBN 9780975945391, 0975945394. *⚘⚘* **((**

In this short story collection, eight women authors tell stories from the "female perspective." Writers who have published novels with Augustus Publishing include Sharron Doyle and Vanessa Martir. Crystal Lacey Winslow contributes an introduction. Tales of love, sex, and growing up on the streets as a woman.

Keywords: Multiple Authors; Short Stories

Similar Reads: The *Lipstick Diaries* collection focuses on love and street life from a female perspective. For more short stories about women in street life, try the <u>Around the Way Girls</u> series or the collection *Girls in the Game*.

McCaulsky, Marlon, Ben Blaze, and K. Roland Williams.

Romance for the Streets. Winston-Salem, NC: Tinsley Phelps, 2009. 276pp. ISBN 9781934195697, 1934195693. *⚘⚘* **((**

This collection of novellas brings together two authors with street lit track records and one newcomer. Marlon McCaulsky, Ben Blaze, and K. Roland Williams Jr. tell stories of lovers who have to choose between street life and each other, and the friendships, families, and communities that can be torn apart when the streets win.

Keywords: Multiple Authors; Short Stories

Similar Reads: *Romance for the Streets* is a collection of novellas about the obstacles that street life creates for people in love. For more on the tension between love and hustling, try Terra Little's *Where There's Smoke*, Reginald Hall's *In Love with a Thug*, or the short story collection *Flirt*.

Street Love: A Triple Crown Anthology. Columbus, OH: Triple Crown Publications, 2007. 315pp. ISBN 9780977880461, 097788046X. *⚘⚘* **((**

Vickie Stringer introduces this collection from well-known Triple Crown authors by dedicating it to her readers. Keisha Ervin, Danielle Santiago, Quentin Carter, T. Styles, and Leo Sullivan contribute mid-length stories. Santiago's piece, from her forthcoming *Allure of the Game*, stands out: a rival gang uses Arnessa's little sister as a weapon in their turf war.

Keywords: Multiple Authors; Short Stories

Similar Reads: This high-action, high-drama collection showcases some of Triple Crown Publishing's most successful writers. For an earlier collection of street authors from Triple Crown, try *The Game: Short Stories About the Life*.

Zane, ed.

Blackgentlemen.com. **Largo, MD: Strebor Books, 2007 (2002). 410pp. ISBN 1593091672, 9781593091675.** ⌐ ⌐ ((

These five stories, two from Zane herself and one each from Shonda Cheekes, J. D. Mason, and Eileen M. Johnson, describe imaginary encounters based around a Web site where eligible women can meet the crème de la crème of African American bachelors. A married woman, a pair of twins, and a lonely widow all find what they're looking for and more on the site, and one woman finds a partner whose true self is far more chilling and violent than his Internet persona. The Web site blackgentlemen.com exists and is maintained under Zane's name. After reading these juicy stories of online love, readers can try their own luck.

Keywords: Multiple Authors; Short Stories

Similar Reads: The short stories in *Blackgentlemen.com* range from sensual to emotional to frightening and take place in upscale settings. For more on the joys and pitfalls of making matches in upscale settings, try the collection *Diamond Playgirls* and Rechella's *Players Got Played*. For more of Zane's trademark sensuality, try the <u>Sex Chronicles</u> series.

1

2

3

4

5

6

7

8

9

10

11

Chapter 5

Erotica

Shy readers beware: the erotica genre contains raw, hot, in-your-face sexuality. Some works of erotica are purely focused on sex; others have sex scenes integrated into a strong narrative. The common thread is that these books are intended to explore sexuality and to bring the reader sexual pleasure.

Authors Zane and Noire are the reigning queens of urban erotica. Noire's gritty works often portray a brutal existence—child neglect, relationship violence, or devastating drug addiction—as a frame for raw, vivid sex scenes. Zane's sensual novels and short stories often take place in upscale settings rather than in the streets and are more likely to include light drama than bleak realities.

Much urban erotica is published in themed short story collections, such as Noire's anthology *From the Streets to the Sheets*, which mixes sex with street action; Zane's anthology *Caramel Flava*, which highlights Latino characters; or Laurinda D. Brown's collection *Walk Like a Man*, which focuses on sex between women.

Erotic Novels

These full-length novels tell stories that focus heavily on the sex lives of their characters.

Cairo.

Zane Presents . . . The Kat Trap. **Largo, MD: Strebor Books, 2009. 344pp. ISBN 1593092288, 9781593092283.** 🌶🌶🌶 ❨❨❨

Katrina, better known as Kat, tells it like it is from the first chapter. She's *"that bitch,"* the envy of all the women in the room and the object of all men's desire. She's also dangerous. Kat's work is to do murders for hire. She lures men into having sex with her, and then, just before the moment of climax, she shoots them in the face—that's the Kat Trap. Proud, business-savvy, and unrepentant, Kat earns big money for her work and enjoys it, too. Her attitude and her confidence make Kat an engaging and also frightening narrator.

Keywords: Assassins; Brooklyn, NY; Street Code; Women Hustlers

Similar Reads: *The Kat Trap* is a story about a proud, confident, shameless, and highly sexual female murderer. For more cold-blooded women who use their sexuality as a murder weapon, try Dakota Knight's *Sola*, Noire's *Thong on Fire*, or Relentless Aaron's *Triple Threat*. Kat's stylized voice is similar to the prefaces that begin many of Noire's erotic novels, including *Candy Licker* and *G-Spot*.

Zane Presents . . . The Man Handler. **Largo, MD: Strebor Books, 2009. 392pp. ISBN 9781593092757, 159309275X.** ☞ ⟮⟮⟮

Thirty year-old Bianca Rivers is a confident, voluptuous woman who loves to f**k, or so she tells the reader on the first page of this no-holds-barred frenetic ride from one steamy sexual encounter to the next. Cairo graphically describes the sex Bianca has with each new man. But one man wants to stick around for longer than the time it takes to have a quickie. Will Bianca let him into her life? And will her fast lifestyle ever catch up with her?

Keywords: Middle Class Setting; New Jersey

Similar Reads: *The Man Handler* is the juicy story of a confident woman who enjoys sex with no strings attached. For more about sexually confident women, try Cairo's *Kat Trap*, Noire's *Candy Licker*, or Storm's *Eva, First Lady of Sin*. For more about letting one's guard down for a man, try Sha's *Harder* or Tu-Shonda L. Whitaker's *Flip Side of the Game*.

Dixon, Gregory D.

Sugar Daddy's Game. **Jamaica, NY: Q-Boro Books, 2008. 238pp. ISBN 9781933967417, 1933967412.** ☞ ⟮⟮⟮

Five women are attached to one powerful man in this character-driven, slower-paced story. Sugar, who runs a drug enterprise and a restaurant, enjoys being the center of attention and the focus of gossip. In his life are Nora, who is still scarred from a brutal attack when she was a teenager, from which Sugar saved her; Jessica, who is trapped in a miserable, sexually inert relationship with Bullet, a notorious gangster; and Mary, a pill-popping thrill seeker. Relations among the women in Sugar's life are harmonious, but on the streets there is a deadly struggle for power. A slice of life in Biloxi, Texas.

Keywords: Abuse; Biloxi, TX; Character-Driven

Similar Reads: *Sugar Daddy's Game* is a slice-of-life story in which several women attached to one man have warm relationships with each other. For more harmonious relationships between women who share a man, try Miasha's *Sistah for Sale*. For more warm friendships between women, try Deja King's *Trife Life to Lavish*.

Doyle, Sharron.

If It Ain't One Thing, It's Another. **New York: Augustus Publishing, 2007. 273pp. ISBN 9780975945360, 097594536X.** ☞☞ (((**1**

Petie is having sex with a vast array of women, including Share, who enjoys anal sex; Des, an oral sex expert who's developing a drug problem; and his wifey Renee, who never seems to be in the mood. In the meantime, Share is sleeping with a younger man who works at McDonald's with her, Share's friend Venus thinks about cheating on her man with a waiter, and Porscha, Venus's friend, is sleeping with a woman, Giselle. But there are two things Petie doesn't handle well: rejection and prison. When both come his way, the consequences are explosive.

Keywords: Abuse; New York; Revenge

Similar Reads: This tale involves drama, cheating, and a man who uses women solely for his sexual pleasure. Wahida Clark's <u>Thugs</u> series also features a large cast of characters cheating on each other. The sex scenes in *If It Ain't One Thing, It's Another* make up the heart of the book. For another story in which plot takes a backseat, try Stephanie Johnson's *Lakeda: A Kiss of Erotica.*

Gray, Erick S.

*Booty Call *69.* **New York: Augustus Publishing, 2006. 270pp. ISBN 0975945343, 9780975945346.** ☞ (((

This erotic tale is not a sequel to Gray's original *Booty Call* but a "remix," in which the author has added a new character and a few extra sexy scenes. Shana and her man Jakim are fighting, and each one has a new partner . . . or partners. The story goes from drama in the club to sizzle in bed.

Keywords: Multiple Perspectives; Queens, NY

Similar Reads: *Booty Call *69* mixes several enticing elements: steamy sex, cheating and relationship drama, and a variety of perspectives. For more steamy stories about cheating, try Kiki Swinson's *Sticky Situation,* in which a female parole officer carries on a relationship with an unfaithful parolee, or T. N. Baker's *Dice,* which explores a high-drama love relationship from both partners' points of view.

Hobbs, Allison.

A Bona Fide Gold Digger. **Largo, MD: Strebor Books, 2007. 255pp. ISBN 9781593091194, 1593091192.** ☞ (((

Milan grew up in the projects, but she couldn't wait to get as far as possible from her "ghetto" childhood. She got work at a spa, then set herself up at an even fancier location, a salon called Pure Paradise—so what if she had to fake a credential or two to do it? But when her employer finds out that Milan has no more than a high school diploma, Milan is fired, and her expensive purchases add up fast. Desperate to stay away from her sister's apartment, which she considers unpardonably low class, Milan accepts a live-in position with a wealthy elderly man who requires a variety of "services." Scorching hot scenes of solo sex and encounters with multiple partners keep the story juicy and fresh.

Keywords: Light Reads; Philadelphia

Similar Reads: *A Bona Fide Gold Digger* is a comic novel of family tension, wild sex, and a confident woman who is sure she deserves the best in life. For a similarly arrogant character, try Tiphani's *Expensive Taste*. For more tension between family members living together, try Sasha Raye's *From Hood to Hollywood* or Ericka Monique Williams's *All That Glitters*. Milan has sex with both men and women; for more bisexual erotica, try Storm's *Eva, First Lady of Sin* or Anna J's *My Woman, His Wife*.

J, Anna.

My Woman, His Wife Series. ☞ ₵₵₵

This marital drama set in Philadelphia explores the drama, heartbreak, and intense sexuality that ensue after a couple invite another woman into their bed.

Keywords: GLBTQ; Middle Class Setting; Philadelphia

Similar Reads: *My Woman, His Wife* is a steamy drama about infidelity that prominently features sex between women and between men and women. For another take on cheating within a professional setting, try Nurit Folkes's <u>Triangle of Sins</u> series. For more erotica featuring bisexual women, try Storm's <u>Eva, First Lady of Sin</u> or Allison Hobbs's *Bona Fide Gold Digger*.

My Woman, His Wife. Jamaica, NY: Q-Boro Books, 2004. 260pp. ISBN 0975306626, 9780975306628.

> When Jasmine's husband James suggest the two of them have a threesome with a woman named Monica, Jasmine thinks that sleeping with another woman is not for her. But afterward she finds herself drawn into Monica's drama . . . and her bed. Sizzling scenes involving both male and female sex partners make up the bulk of this steamy read.

The Aftermath. Jamaica, NY: Q-Boro Books, 2006. 207pp. ISBN 0977624749, 9780977624744.

> What happens after a married couple bring another woman into their relationship? After both have torrid affairs with the dramatic Monica, Jasmine and James try to repair their marriage. Meanwhile, Monica schemes to tear them apart.

J, Anna, Brittani Williams, and Laurinda D. Brown.

The Cat House. Jamaica, NY: Q-Boro Books, 2008. 232pp. ISBN 9781933967462, 1933967463. ☞ ₵₵₵

"Welcome to Allure," goes the tag line at a particular house of prostitution and fantasy, "we have charm and sex appeal." The ladies of Allure are considered the best of the best sex workers, and clients who can pay the price can have virtually any desire fulfilled. Behind the cool facade, however, Allure is full of drama. Lady Dee, the madam, is convinced that one of the top girls, Kimona, is stealing from the club, and will go to any lengths to expose her. Torri, one of the wildest girls, has secrets of her own. Three authors come together to write this smooth, steamy tale, each one in the voice of a different character with a different perspective on the drama.

Keywords: GLBTQ; Sex Industry; Washington, DC

Similar Reads: *The Cat House* is a high-drama, sexually charged story of a war among women working in the sex industry. Mark Anthony's *Queen Bee* features a similar war between women at a sex club. For more stories of exclusive sex clubs, try Storm's *Den of Sin*, White Chocolate's *Sex in the Hood*, or Allison Hobbs's *Bona Fide Gold Digger*.

Johnson, Stephanie, A. F.

Lakeda: A Kiss of Erotica. **West Babylon, NY: Urban Books, 2008. 212pp. ISBN 9781601620477, 1601620470.** ☞ (((

Check your inhibitions at the door! Lakeda's got a man, but what she wants is everyone. And what she wants, she gets: women, men, multiple partners, anywhere, any position, in graphic, luscious, raunchy detail. If you're looking for a story, look elsewhere—this is pure sex.

Keywords: GLBTQ

Similar Reads: *Lakeda* is a raw, raunchy, graphic tale of a woman and her constant and varied sexual exploits. For more sex with minimal plot, try Sharron Doyle's *If It Ain't One Thing, It's Another*. For more bisexual encounters, try Allison Hobbs's *Bona Fide Gold Digger* or Storm's *Den of Sin*.

Noire.

Candy Licker: An Urban Erotic Tale. **New York: One World/Ballantine Books, 2005. 291pp. ISBN 0345486471, 9780345486479.** ☞☞ (((

Candy Raye Montana grew up with love for her drug-addicted mother, dreams of hip-hop superstardom, and a penchant for touching herself in the shower. Sent into foster care, Candy hooked up with the drug-dealing Gabriano family and became a mule, transporting money and occasional drugs between airports. When she met music producer Hurricane Jackson, she thought her troubles were over. But she didn't bank on his unwanted violent behavior, both in and out of the bedroom.

Keywords: Drug Addiction; Music Industry; New York

Similar Reads: *Candy Licker* is an erotic story about growing up under harsh circumstances, navigating the music industry, and surviving an abusive relationship. Noire's *Hittin' the Bricks* is another story about a girl with dreams of music stardom and an abusive family. For more about women in abusive relationships, try Mark Anthony's *Reasonable Doubt* or Azárel's <u>Bruised</u> series.

Core Collection: Adult

G-Spot: An Urban Erotic Tale. **New York: One World/Ballantine Books, 2006 (2005). 301pp. ISBN 0345486870, 9780345486875.** ⟋⟋ ⟨⟨⟨

Juicy is nineteen years old, free from her abusive home, and the girlfriend of one of the richest and most powerful men in New York City: Granite McKay, also known as "G." The catch? Juicy craves sex, and G doesn't kiss, perform oral sex, or even tolerate female pleasure. And if he caught his girl with another man, Juicy and the man in question would both be dead. But Juicy's smart and a survivor, and she's got a plan to get out from under G's thumb—and to take her pleasure any way she can. Noire's first "urban erotic tale" expertly delivers sex and suspense.

Keywords: Abuse; New York; Sex Industry

Similar Reads: *G-Spot* is a steamy story of a young woman longing for sex while under the thumb of a dangerous, controlling man. For more stories of women's desire for sex, try Noire's *Candy Licker* or Allison Hobbs's *Bona Fide Gold Digger*. For more stories of abusive relationships, try Azárel's Bruised series or Danette Majette's *Good Girl Gone Bad*.

Hittin' the Bricks: An Urban Erotic Tale. **New York: One World/Ballantine Books, 2009. 245pp. ISBN 9780345508782, 0345508785.** ⟋⟋⟋ ⟨⟨⟨

At age fourteen, Eva was a victim of abuse: her stepfather repeatedly raped her and injected her with heroin while Eva's mother held her down. Several years later, Eva is clean, free of her mother and stepfather, and getting involved in a dangerous but glamorous Harlem nightclub called The Bricks. Meanwhile, her cousin Fiyah is sent to prison for possession of an illegal firearm. A fellow inmate, King Brody, saves him from a vicious attack, but Fiyah knows that Brody will want something in return when he's back on the streets. The brutal, lyrical, and sensual tale has also been made into a movie with the same title.

Keywords: Abuse; Drug Addiction; Music Industry; New York; Prison

Similar Reads: *Hittin' the Bricks* is both an erotic story and a story of child abuse. Treasure E. Blue's *Street Girl Named Desire* describes a girl born to a drug-addicted mother and with a similarly painful childhood. Both Noire's novels *G-Spot* and *Candy Licker* also involve the music industry.

Core Collection: Adult

Hood: An Urban Erotic Tale. **New York: Atria Books, 2007. 340pp. ISBN 9781416553030, 1416553036.** ⟋⟋ ⟨⟨⟨

As an eleven-year-old boy, Lamont "Hood" Mason finds himself and his four-year-old brother Moo out on the streets of Brownsville, Brooklyn, on the coldest night of the year. From stepping up to take care of his brother, Hood learns to be a man. Noticed by Fat Daddy, a hustler based out of a barbershop, Hood finally sees life taking a turn for the better. Years later, he's a criminal on the meanest streets in New York City, stepping up to make a living, stay on top, and stay strong for the women who need him.

Keywords: Abuse; Brooklyn, NY; Drug Addiction; Mentors; Music Industry; Prison; Revenge; Teenagers

Similar Reads: *Hood* tells the story of a young boy supporting his family with the help of a mentor. Leondrei Prince's <u>Tommy Good</u> series also features a young boy whose mother cannot provide for him learning the ropes of the drug game with a mentor—his uncle—to guide him. Erica Hilton's *10 Crack Commandments* and T. Styles's <u>Hustler's Son</u> series also focus on boys learning to hustle and become men.

Thong on Fire: An Urban Erotic Tale. **New York: Atria Books, 2007. 291pp. ISBN 1416533028, 9781416533023.** ☞ ☞ ☞ ℂℂℂ

Half-black, half-Korean, and 100 percent hot, Seung Cee, aka Saucy Robinson, believes in survival by any means necessary. Whether she's smuggling drugs into prison, trading sex for cash, or plotting murder, Saucy is going to come out on top, with no regrets. As usual, Noire peppers her fast-paced street action with red hot sex scenes, each one wilder than the last.

Keywords: Abuse; Drug Addiction; New York; Prison; Sex Industry; Street Code; Women Hustlers

Similar Reads: *Thong on Fire* features a ruthless female character and steamy sexuality. For another erotic tale of a woman who kills with no regrets, try Cairo's *Kat Trap*. Relentless Aaron's *Triple Threat* and Dakota Knight's *Sola* also feature cold-blooded female killers.

Thug-A-Licious. **New York: Ballantine/One World, 2006. 352pp. ISBN 9780345486919.** ☞ ☞ ℂℂℂ

Andre "Thug-A-Licious" Williams is a well-known rapper and an NBA star who knows how to please the women in his life—and thanks to a habit of forgoing condoms, he is also the father of nine children. Raised in Harlem with beloved but drug-addicted guardians, Thug and his two cousins Smoove and Pimp learned to stick together and to make money by stealing, gambling, and, in Pimp's case, extreme violence. Thug heads to college and focuses on his basketball and rap careers, but he can't quite escape his past. In the meantime, Noire interjects plenty of skillfully written sex scenes, from Thug's perspective and the perspective of Thug's friend and lover Carmeisha. A sexy, fast-paced tale with prose that flows smoothly in and out of the bedroom.

Keywords: Music Industry; New York

Similar Reads: *Thug-A-Licious* is a lyrical, highly sexual story about a sports figure and rap artist told largely from a man's perspective. For more erotic stories from a male perspective, try Noire's *Hood*. For more about high-profile music careers, try Nikki Turner's *Ghetto Superstar* or the short story collection *Backstage*.

Storm.

Den of Sin. **Bellport, NY: Melodrama Publishing, 2007. 226pp. ISBN 9781934157084, 1934157082.** ☞ ℂℂℂ

Nadia is addicted to sex any way, any where. She goes to a deacon to get counseling for sex addiction and they're naked within the first five minutes, and thus begins a year-long relationship. When the deacon's wife shows up in his place for Nadia's regular "appointment," Nadia knows it's time to get her fix somewhere else. She and her fellow youth corrections officers, Aisha and The Prince, go to a place called The Den, a haven of no-holds-barred freaky sex. Plot takes a backseat to unbridled, raunchy eroticism.

Keywords: GLBTQ; Philadelphia

Similar Reads: *Den of Sin* is the highly sexual story of a woman who cheats shamelessly and enjoys a variety of sexual experiences. Allison Hobbs's *Bona Fide Gold Digger* features a similarly self-confident woman and a club where any fantasy can be fulfilled. Mirror Carter, the main character in Tiphani's *Expensive Taste*, is similarly shameless about cheating. Storm's *Eva, First Lady of Sin* and Anna J's *My Woman, His Wife* also feature bisexual encounters.

Eva, First Lady of Sin Series. ☞ ⟮⟮⟮

Freewheeling, self-possessed, sexually adventurous Eva has a series of erotic adventures in this series about cheating, secrets, and facing hard truths.

Keywords: GLBTQ; Philadelphia

Similar Reads: The <u>Eva</u> series focuses on a sexually charged bisexual woman using her body to get what she wants and deals with themes of infidelity and sexual repression. Chunichi's <u>California Connection</u> series also features a bisexual woman focused on getting sex and money. Noire's *G-Spot* features a sexually charged woman kept from her desire by a repressive man. For more bisexual erotica, try Storm's *Den of Sin* or Stephanie Johnson's *Lakeda: A Kiss of Erotica*.

Eva, First Lady of Sin. Bellport, NY: Melodrama Publishing, 2006. 232pp. ISBN 9781934157015, 1934157015.

> From the moment she discovered sex as a teenager, Eva was hooked. Raised by her repressive, religious grandmother, Eva was taught to say no to all boys' advances. Now she is saying yes, until her best friend teaches her to use her body to her own advantage and hold out for a man who is willing to pay. Money and pleasure rule Eva's carefree life until a doctor at an OB/GYN clinic diagnoses her with genital herpes. Now Eva has to face uncomfortable truths about her body and about the man she loves. Vivid sexual flashbacks make this one a steamy read.

Eva 2: First Lady of Sin. Bellport, NY: Melodrama Publishing, 2008. 263pp. ISBN 9781934157114, 1934157112.

> Freewheeling, self-possessed, and sexually adventurous Eva got unpleasant news about her sexual health in volume 1 of this erotically charged series. In this volume, Eva sorts out her relationship with the man she thought she loved, and her friends have sexual adventures of their own.

Warren, Mike.

A Private Affair Series. ☞ (((

In this steamy drama, a soldier explores his sexuality and struggles to accept his attraction to another man.

Keywords: GLBTQ, Middle Class Setting; Washington, DC

Similar Reads: *A Private Affair* is a steamy drama centering on a bisexual love triangle and a man struggling to come to terms with his attraction to another man. For another bisexual love triangle, try Clarence Nero's *Three Sides to Every Story*. For more on sexuality between men, try Reginald Hall's *In Love with a Thug*.

Core Collection: Adult

A Private Affair. Brandywine, MD: Life Changing Books, 2007. 240pp. ISBN 9781934230954 1934230952

Army private Sean lives on a military base, but he has a wife and child at home. He's sure he isn't gay, so why does he keep having sexual thoughts about other men? On the base, Sean befriends Cameron, a flamboyant gay private. When the two become roommates, Cameron confesses his love, but Sean insists he's not interested in another man. Sean's actions, however, speak louder than his words.

Sweet Swagger. Brandywine, MD: Life Changing Books, 2009. 240pp. ISBN 9781934230701, 1934230707.

Sean, a married army private, realized in *A Private Affair* that he had romantic and sexual feelings for Cameron, another male private living on his army base. Now Sean is finally ready to face his feelings for Cameron. But a variety of circumstances, including a police investigation, get in the way of Sean's intentions.

White Chocolate.

Sex in the Hood Series. ☞☞ (((

Deep in the underbelly of Detroit is a club called Babylon, where room upon room of willing women wait, ready to pleasure men any way they want, as long as the price is right. This series is full of steamy descriptions of the club itself and the numerous and varied sex acts performed within.

Keywords: Detroit; Sex Industry

Similar Reads: *Sex in the Hood* creates a fantasy of a sex club where anything is possible. For more settings like Babylon, try Anna J, Laurinda D. Brown and Brittani Williams's *Cat House* or Brittani Williams's *Sugar Walls*. For another sexually voracious female character like Victoria, try Noire's *G-Spot*.

Sex in the Hood. West Babylon, NY: Urban Books, 2005. 335pp. ISBN 1893196208, 9781893196209.

> In the first volume, Duke presides over Babylon. Victoria, a young biracial woman, has just lost her rich, white daddy and moved into her aunt's house in the ghetto. Victoria is afraid of sex but loves orgasms. When she meets up with Duke, the results are explosive.

Sex in the Hood 2. West Babylon, NY: Urban Books, 2006. 314pp. ISBN 1893196550, 9781893196551.

> In this volume, Knight, Duke's older brother, has taken control of Babylon and become involved with Victoria, and the two men are at war with each other.

Williams, Brittani.

Sugar Walls. **Jamaica, NY: Q-Boro Books, 2007. 223pp. ISBN 9781933967264, 1933967269.** ☞ (((

Unlike her sister Mya, Sugar has never been a fast girl. Repeatedly beaten by her mother, she leaves home at eighteen and finds herself working for a woman named Dyna. Dyna owns an escort service but employs Sugar as a promoter. But promoting an escort service gets Sugar a lot of attention, from men she approaches, from Dyna, and even from her little sister's man. Sugar's romantic and erotic adventures—as well as her business venture starting up a club of her own—comprise the bulk of this novel.

Keywords: Abuse; GLBTQ; Philadelphia; Sex Industry

Similar Reads: *Sugar Walls* is the story of a young woman working as an escort and discovering her own sexuality. For more young women who work in the sex industry, try Anna J, Brittani Williams, and Laurinda D. Brown's *Cat House* or Shannon Holmes's *Bad Girlz*. Storm's *Eva, First Lady of Sin* also focuses on a young woman exploring her own sexuality after living through a repressive family situation.

Zane.

Addicted Series. ☞ (((

These two companion volumes follow the lives and exploits of two women addicted to sex.

Keywords: Atlanta; Middle Class Setting

Similar Reads: *Addicted* is a highly sexual drama that takes place in a professional setting and contains themes of infidelity. Anna J's <u>My Woman, His Wife</u> series is another juicy erotic tale of a married couple struggling with infidelity. For more of Zane's trademark sexual prose, try her <u>Sex Chronicles</u> series

Classic

Core Collection: Adult

Addicted. New York: Atria Books, 2003 (1998). 326pp. ISBN 0743442849, 9780743442848.

> Zoe Reynard has an addiction to sex. As she begins work with a therapist, Dr. Marcella Spencer, to treat her condition, she recounts the story of her journey into sexual awakening, her eventual marriage, and the dalliances she's had apart from her husband. Juicy passages abound, but Zane also creates likable characters and compelling story lines.

Nervous. New York: Atria Books, 2004 (2003). 320pp. ISBN 0743476247, 9780743476249.

> In *Addicted*, we met Zoe Reynard, a woman with an addiction to sex. Zoe turned to a doctor to heal from her addiction and to give the reader juicy details of her sexual exploits. In *Nervous*, another of Dr. Spencer's patients struggles with her own sexual addiction.

Short Stories and Anthologies

These books contain erotic short stories and novellas. These are great suggestions for those looking for a quick read or to try a new author.

Brown, Laurinda D.

Walk Like a Man. Jamaica, NY: Q-Boro Books, 2006. 253pp. ISBN 0977624781, 9780977624782. ✐✐ (((

Brown's short story collection explores and celebrates various aspects of being a same-gender-loving woman. From lustful encounters and passionate romance to childhood abuse and domestic violence, Brown's words and characters sizzle.

Keywords: Abuse; GLBTQ; Short Stories

Similar Reads: *Walk Like a Man* is a steamy short story collection about a variety of lesbian, bisexual, and same-gender-loving women. For more erotic short stories about women's sexuality with each other, try Zane's *Purple Panties*. To learn more about Mo, who appears in one story in the collection, try Brown's novel *Strapped*, which explores Mo's first relationship as a teenager.

Core Collection: Adult

Flexin' & Sexin' Series. ✐✐ (((

This erotic series from Life Changing Books features sexually charged fiction by both well-known and newer names in street lit.

Keywords: Multiple Authors; Short Stories

Similar Reads: *Flexin' and Sexin'* showcases erotic writing by authors already known in the street lit universe. For more authors with name recognition writing about sexuality, try *From the Streets to the Sheets*, a collection edited by Noire.

Flexin' & Sexin': Sexy Street Tales, Volume 1. Brandywine, MD: Life Changing Books, 2007. 211pp. ISBN 9781934230961, 1934230960.

> This volume contains six erotic stories from across the street lit universe. Erick S. Gray tells a tale of forced prostitution, and Anna J spins a no-holds-barred tale of a hard-up woman willing to get cash any way she can. K'wan, Brittani Williams, Juicy Wright, and Aretha Temple also contribute

Flexin' & Sexin' Volume 2. Brandywine, MD: Life Changing Books, 2010. 248pp. ISBN-10: 1934230812, 9781934230817.

> This second installment features stories from Ashley and JaQuavis, Erick S. Gray, J. Tremble, Nakea, Derrick King, Nichelle Walker, and Dashawn Taylor.

Morrison, Mary B., and Noire.

Maneater. **New York: Kensington, 2009. 274pp. ISBN 9780758213204, 0758213204.** ☞ ☾☾☾

Two of the hottest writers of African American erotica contribute one novella each to this sizzling volume. In Morrison's *Character of a Man*, a self-proclaimed "maneater" is put to the test by her image-conscious fiancé. In Noire's *Sugar-Honey-Ice Tee*, three NFL stars meet three devious women, and sparks fly. Relationship drama and an impressive array of sexual acts are well-represented here. Best savored in private.

Keywords: Middle Class Setting; Multiple Authors

Similar Reads: The two novellas in *Maneater* deal with relationship drama and sexuality in upscale settings. For more upscale erotica, try Zane's *Addicted*. Noire's *Thug-A-Licious* is another erotic tale that involves a sports figure; "Thug-A-Licious" is the nickname of a college basketball star. For another combination of drama-laden novellas, try Wahida Clark and Kiki Swinson's *Sleeping with the Enemy*.

Noire, ed.

From the Streets to the Sheets: Urban Erotic Quickies. **New York: One World/ Ballantine Books, 2008. 337pp. ISBN 9780345508485, 0345508483.** ☞☞ ☾☾☾

Noire and a bevy of hot street lit authors team up for this anthology of twelve erotic short stories. Each entry is short—approximately twenty-five pages—steamy, and explicit.

Keywords: Multiple Authors; Sex Industry; Short Stories

Similar Reads: *From the Streets to the Sheets* is a collection of erotic stories with a street flavor. For more street-flavored erotica, try Noire's full-length novels, particularly *Hood* and *Hittin' the Bricks*. *Flexin' and Sexin'* is another collection of street-themed erotic stories.

Tyree, Omar.

Zane Presents . . . Dirty Old Men and Other Stories. Largo, MD: Strebor Books, 2009. 352pp. ISBN 9781593092733, 1593092733. ☞ ₵₵₵

> Tyree, known for mainstream fiction like *Flyy Girl* and *The Last Street Novel*, tries his hand at something steamier. The fourteen stories in this collection focus on older men attracted to younger women. In "The Bartender," Tyree's opener, an elderly gentleman is seduced by a twenty-five-year-old employee at a sports bar. In "Jail Bait," a divorced forty-seven-year-old newspaperman allows a flirtation with a girl who claims to be nineteen to turn into something a lot more dangerous. Some readers might wonder exactly how these "dirty old men" attract their mates, but those readers who identify with the men in question are in for enjoyable wish fulfillment.

> **Keywords:** Light Reads; Sex Industry; Short Stories

> **Similar Reads:** *Dirty Old Men* is a short story collection about older men and male fantasies about women. For more light stories about men's sexuality, try Dwayne S. Joseph's *Womanizers* or Dwayne S. Joseph, Roy Glenn, and Jihad's *Gigolos Get Lonely Too*. For more stories about men's fantasies, try Quentin Carter's *Stained Cotton* or White Chocolate's *Sex in the Hood*.

Zane

Sex Chronicles Series. ☞ ₵₵₵

> Now the inspiration for a television show on Cinemax's "After Dark," the Sex Chronicles were Zane's first book-length short story collection.

> **Keywords:** Middle Class Setting; Short Stories

> **Similar Reads:** Zane's Sex Chronicles are raw sensual and sexual stories by the queen of African American erotica. For more of Zane's trademark style, try her full-length novel *Addicted* or a short story collection in the Zane Presents . . . line, including Chocolate Flava and Purple Panties.

> **Core Collection:** Adult

The Sex Chronicles: Shattering the Myth. New York: Atria, 2003 (2000). 303pp. ISBN 074346270X, 9780743462709.

> Zane's original short story collection is divided into three sections: "Wild," "Wilder," and "Off Da Damn Hook." Students, professors, housewives, and an injured woman whose lover visits her in the hospital all make appearances in this sizzling, high-voltage collection that introduced Zane to a broad readership.

Gettin' Buck Wild: Sex Chronicles II. New York: Atria, 2004 (2002). 292pp. ISBN 0743457021, 9780743457026.

> Zane's Sex Chronicles are well known for their unabashed, raw, raunchy sexuality. This second volume from the erotica master is chock-full of wild, juicy, steamy sex.

Zane's Sex Chronicles. New York: Atria, 2008. 219pp. ISBN 1416584110, 9781416584117.

> Marketed as a tie-in to the Cinemax show, this compilation includes fifteen stories from the original two <u>Sex Chronicles</u> books.

Zane, ed.

Another Time, Another Place: Five Novellas. **Largo, MD: Strebor Books, 2006. 440pp. ISBN 1593090587, 9781593090586.** ☞ (((

A storm comes, and two women's emotional and erotic lives mysteriously overlap. An American in 1968 loses her husband and lover to the Vietnam War. In ancient Egypt, Raghaba, the Goddess of Desire, gives pleasure to gods and receives pleasure in return. The five novellas in Zane's collection remove us from the present in different ways. Some are historical fiction, some supernatural, and all deeply sensual. As usual with Zane, the focus is on sex and sexuality, and the imaginative twists make for an adventurous read.

Keywords: Historical Fiction; Middle Class Setting; Multiple Authors; Paranormal Fiction; Short Stories

Similar Reads: *Another Time, Another Place* is a sensual collection involving historical and supernatural elements. For another intersection between street fiction, history, and the supernatural, try Nane Quartay's *Badness*. For more erotica edited by Zane, try <u>Chocolate Flava</u>, <u>Caramel Flava</u>, <u>Honey Flava</u>, <u>Purple Panties</u>, or *Blackgentlemen.com*.

Honey Flava: The Eroticanoir.com Anthology. **New York: Atria Books, 2008. 268pp. ISBN 9781416548850, 1416548858.** ☞ (((

This anthology is Zane's attempt at collecting Asian-themed erotica. In the inaugural story, "The Meaning of *Zhuren*," a woman submits to pain, bondage, and instructions to call her partner by the Chinese word for "master." In "Geisha Girl," a Japanese mother sends her lesbian daughter for training as a geisha. In Zane's "Big Bang Theory," a car enthusiast enters a high-stakes race against two Asian brothers. As usual with Zane, the stories are frank, wild, and imaginative, though the content may represent American fantasies about Asian sexuality more than authentic experience.

Keywords: Middle Class Setting; Multiple Authors; Sex Industry; Short Stories

Similar Reads: *Honey Flava* explores Asian themes and experiences through a series of erotic short stories. For more Asian characters in street lit, try Noire's *Thong on Fire* or Kiki Swinson's <u>Playing Dirty</u> series. For more erotica collections curated by Zane, try <u>Chocolate Flava</u>, <u>Caramel Flava</u>, and <u>Purple Panties</u>.

<u>Caramel Flava Series</u>. ☞ (((

Edited by Zane, this series highlights Latino and Latina sexuality.

Keywords: Latino Characters; Multiple Authors; Short Stories

Similar Reads: <u>Caramel Flava</u> is an erotica collection with a Latino flavor. For more erotic short stories, try Zane's <u>Sex Chronicles</u> series or the *Flexin' and Sexin'* collections. For more Latino and Latina characters, try Black Artemis's *Explicit Content* or Daniel Serrano's *Gunmetal Black*.

Core Collection: Adult

Zane Presents . . . Caramel Flava: The Eroticanoir.com Anthology. New York: Atria, 2006. 337pp. ISBN 074329727X, 9780743297271.

> *La pasión es universal*, claims an author in this collection of erotic short stories with a Latino flavor. We all experience passion. In the opening story, a woman lets her wild side out at a masquerade ball, reconnecting with a piece of her history after ingesting a drink spiked with an aphrodisiac. In "Shameless," a blond American learns Spanish bedroom words and uses them liberally. And in "Open House," a couple visits a home for sale and tries out the master bedroom. Playful, sensual, and uncensored. An original story by Zane finishes off the collection.

Zane Presents . . . Sensuality: Caramel Flava II: The Eroticanoir.com Anthology. New York: Atria, 2009. ISBN 9781416548843, 141654884X.

> This second volume contains eighteen original stories, including another from erotica master Zane.

Chocolate Flava Series. 🖙 ⟨⟨⟨

More than twenty contributors to Zane's eroticanoir.com Web site get their voices heard in each volume of this steamy anthology focused on African American characters and sizzling sex.

Zane Presents . . . Chocolate Flava: The Eroticanoir.com Anthology. New York: Atria Books, 2004. 334pp. ISBN 0743482387, 9780743482387.

> Organized into three sections—"Ladies First," "Gentlemen Next," and "Zane Last"—this volume is full of raw sexuality from a variety of perspectives.

Zane Presents Succulent: Chocolate Flava II: The Eroticanoir.com Anthology. New York: Atria, 2008. 318pp. ISBN 9781416548836, 1416548831.

This second collection showcases a new set of authors.

Keywords: Multiple Authors; Short Stories

Similar Reads: Zane's Eroticanoir.com anthologies are collections of short stories from her Web site. For more collections edited by Zane, try the <u>Caramel Flava</u> series of erotica featuring Latino characters, *Honey Flava*, which focuses on Asian characters, or <u>Purple Panties</u>, a multiracial collection focusing on eroticism between women.

Classic

Core Collection: Adult

Purple Panties Series. ☞ (((

In this series, Zane and her contributors take on lesbian sexuality with the boldness, juiciness, and variety Zane's readers have come to expect from her anthologies.

Keywords: GLBTQ; Multiple Authors; Short Stories

Similar Reads: <u>Purple Panties</u> is a juicy exploration of lesbian, bisexual, and same-gender-loving orientations. For short stories on similar themes, try Laurinda D. Brown's collection *Walk Like a Man*. For other instances of bisexuality, try Anna J's <u>My Woman, His Wife</u>, or Storm's *Den of Sin*.

Zane Presents . . . Purple Panties: An Eroticanoir.com Anthology. Largo, MD: Strebor Books, 2008. 306pp. ISBN 9781593091651, 1593091656.

> Eroticism between women abounds in this collection. In Laurinda Brown's opener, "It's All or Nothing," two women take an impromptu train trip to New York in a sleeping car. In "Mom's Night Out," an African American mothers' group takes a break from talking about being mothers and wives and instead explores its members' sexuality hands on. "Miss Julidene's Sexy Items" tells the story of a sex shop proprietor who comes up with a new way to market her products. Many married women stray in this steamy anthology.

Zane Presents . . . Missionary No More: Purple Panties II: An Eroticanoir.com Anthology. Largo, MD: Strebor Books, 2009 (2008). 234pp. ISBN 1593092113, 9781593092115.

> This second anthology continues to explore sexuality between women.

Chapter 6

Thrillers

Thrillers in street lit are similar to thrillers in mainstream fiction. In fact, some street thrillers, like Solomon Jones's *C.R.E.A.M.*, are published by mainstream houses for a larger audience. Novels in this subgenre feature action-packed, suspenseful plots, often incorporating elements of political machinations, mystery, courtroom drama, or police investigation. Many street thrillers are told from multiple perspectives: from characters committing a crime or involved in a criminal operation and from members of a law enforcement agency such as the FBI, the DEA, or local police. The pleasure of the subgenre is often in uncovering the truth behind a set of events or in finding out who will outwit whom.

The illegal activities in street thrillers are often large-scale operations, such as the Reigns family's multi-billion-dollar drug enterprise in Teri Woods's <u>Deadly Reigns</u> series or the crooked rap label with mob connections in Mark Anthony's *Take Down*. Politics also come into play, and street thrillers are more likely to take place in middle-class or white-collar settings than most other subgenres.

Notable street thrillers include Miasha's *Chaser* and Teri Woods's *Alibi*.

Criminal Investigations

Novels in this section focus on police or other law enforcement agents trying to investigate, infiltrate, or take down criminal operations. Often the story is told from both the perspective of the law enforcement agents and the perspective of the investigation's target.

Anthony, Mark.

The Take Down. **New York: St. Martin's Griffin, 2006. 291pp. ISBN 0312340796, 9780312340797.** ☞ ☞ ₡₡

Her "government name" is Paula Winslow, but since she was sent to investigate Gun Clap Records, she has transformed herself into Jessica Jackson, head of New

York's White Chocolate modeling agency. Jessica is an FBI agent who's in it for the money, and getting sent to take down rap producer Tyrone "Horse" Hopkins and his mob connections is her big break. The novel starts with Horse's capture in an FBI raid, and Jessica looks back on how she caught him, how transforming herself into someone else has affected her psychologically, and where in her investigation she crossed the line.

Keywords: Abuse; Law Enforcement; Music Industry; New York; Street Code

Similar Reads: *The Take Down* is an action-packed story that mixes psychological drama with an FBI investigation into the music industry. For more on the dirty dealings behind the music industry, try K. Roland Williams's *Cut Throat* or Thomas Long's *Cash Rules*. For another FBI agent becoming emotionally invested in the group she's investigating, try Amaleka McCall's *Hush*.

Core Collection: Adult

Ashley and JaQuavis.

Diary of a Street Diva. **West Babylon, NY: Urban Books, 2009 (2005). 270pp. ISBN 9781601621412, 1601621418.** ⌕ ⌕ ((

Remy Morgan is dead, and Cease, the man she loved and lived with, is on trial for her murder. In the room Remy used as her own, Cease finds Remy's diary. Reading her words, Cease—and the reader—experience Remy's harsh life story firsthand. From getting kicked out of a group home, to becoming a stripper, to preparing cocaine, to a princess-like courtship with the kingpin from whom she was stealing, Remy is a survivor. Flashes to Cease's trial give the novel a courtroom drama flavor.

Keywords: Abuse; Flint, MI; Sex Industry; Street Code

Similar Reads: *Diary of a Street Diva* is a courtroom drama mixed with the story of a hard life. For more novels featuring courtroom scenes, try Darrell DeBrew's *Stacy* or Greg Mathis's *Street Judge*. Jason Poole's *Victoria's Secret* is another novel told through a found diary that details a woman's harsh life.

Debrew, Darrell.

Keisha. **Columbus, OH: Triple Crown Publications, 2005. 272pp. ISBN 0976789434, 9780976789437.** ⌕ ⌕ ((

A major hustler is murdered in a gambler's den. The next day two thugs, Clarence and Danny Boy, kill his wife. Their teenage daughter, Keisha, has a relationship with Clarence and doesn't know whether to give him up out of revenge or stand by her man. Investigating the murders is D.C.'s famous homicide detective, Sally Henderson. Also known as the "Pinstriped Bitch," Sally has two habits: seducing younger men and solving nearly every case that comes across her desk. The lives of Clarence, Danny Boy, Sally, and Keisha intersect in suspenseful and deadly ways.

Keywords: Law Enforcement; Revenge; Teenagers; Washington, DC

Similar Reads: *Keisha* is a fast-paced, suspenseful story set in two worlds—the streets and D.C.'s police force—featuring a hard-nosed detective and a teenage girl. For more tales told from both law enforcement and street perspectives, try Relentless Aaron's *Last Kingpin* or Amaleka McCall's *Hush*.

Stacy. **Columbus, OH: Triple Crown Publications, 2005. 185pp. ISBN 0976789442, 9780976789444.** ☞ ☞ (

Stacy Dee, mother, up-and-coming rapper, and self-proclaimed "Ultimate Gangsta Bitch," is being held hostage in a federal prison. The feds claim to have proof that Stacy is a high-ranking member of the Untouchables, a major crime organization in Philadelphia. Now she has a choice: rat out her fellow Untouchables or get slammed with five life sentences. While Stacy plans her approach on the inside, the other members of the organization plot their own survival.

Keywords: Music Industry; Noir; Philadelphia; Prison; Women Hustlers

Similar Reads: *Stacy* is a suspenseful, noir courtroom drama about a street-savvy woman who is considering snitching. For another story about a woman deciding whether to comply with the state and betray her friends and business partners, try *Imagine This*, the second book in Vickie Stringer's <u>Let That Be the Reason</u> series. For more fast-paced courtroom thrillers, try Ashley and JaQuavis's *Diary of a Street Diva* or Greg Mathis's *Street Judge*.

McCall, Amaleka G.

Hush. **West Babylon, NY: Urban Books, 2009. 229pp. ISBN 9781601622556, 1601622554.** ☞ ☞ ☞ ((

Deidre Aponte is a well-respected FBI agent from a family of FBI agents. A New York senator's daughter disappears, and Deidre is assigned to investigate. Her investigation gets her close to the F.A.B. crew, also known as Leticia, Chastity, and Tori—three dangerous, ruthless, and successful women drug dealers. But the closer she gets, the more Deidre becomes part of the F.A.B.'s operation. Deidre and the women of the F.A.B. all tell their own sides of the story in this brutal tale of friendship, power, and choosing sides.

Keywords: Law Enforcement; Middle Class Setting; New York; Prison; Women Hustlers

Similar Reads: *Hush* is a thriller told from multiple perspectives about an FBI investigation and an all-female crew. For another FBI agent getting emotionally invested in her assignment, try Mark Anthony's *Take Down*. For more about all-female crews, try Mikal Malone's *Pitbulls in a Skirt*, Nisa Santiago's *Cartier Cartel*, or Brandon McCalla's *Spot Rushers*.

Miasha.

Chaser. **New York: Simon & Schuster, 2009. 211pp. ISBN 9781416589860, 1416589864.** 𝒶𝒶𝒶 (

"Chaser" is the name given to tow truck operators who follow car accidents hoping to sell their services. Nasir is this kind of chaser, and cunning kingpin Kenny brings him in on a scheme to drive an old Range Rover into a wall for the insurance money. Leah is Kenny's girlfriend, and she's the one blamed for the scheme when the police arrive. Realizing that Kenny has behaved abusively toward her and has now manipulated her into taking the fall for his actions, Leah agrees to cooperate with the police in exchange for her freedom. The action that follows is fast-paced and always tense. Can Leah keep her cooperation a secret? What will happen if Kenny finds out?

Keywords: Abuse; Law Enforcement; Philadelphia; Prison; Street Code

Similar Reads: *Chaser* is a high-speed, high-stakes story about a mistreated woman risking her safety to cooperate with a federal investigation. For more about realizing a loved one has betrayed you, try Ashley and JaQuavis's *Dirty Money* or C. Stecko's *Brooklyn Brothel*. For another character secretly cooperating with the feds, try Relentless Aaron's *Last Kingpin*.

Poole, Jason.

Larceny. **Columbus, OH: Triple Crown Publications, 2004 (2003). 291pp. ISBN 0974789550, 9780974789552.** 𝒶 (

When Sonya and Jovan meet in the hallways of Washington, D.C.'s, Superior Court, both are well-dressed and working high-paying, white-collar jobs. Sonya agrees to have lunch with the attractive Jovan, and the two begin to get to know each other better. In the meantime, Jovan has something on his mind: he works as a paralegal, and a familiar name has just crossed the desk of the lawyer he works for. Bilal Davis, Jovan's childhood friend and partner in crime, is in trouble with the law again, and this time a guilty verdict could mean his life. Jovan vows to uphold the code of the streets and get Bilal free—and to kill any snitch who would dare tell "the cruelest lie told in silence."

Keywords: Middle Class Setting; Prison; Street Code; Washington, DC

Similar Reads: Though *Larceny* involves themes of street loyalty and the code against snitching, it also takes place within the professional white-collar world. Nurit Folkes's *Triangle of Sins* has a similar white-collar setting and also involves a male–female pair who are coming to know and trust each other. *Imagine This*, the second book in Vickie Stringer's Let That Be the Reason series, also deals with snitching, though Stringer's take is much more character-driven. Michael Evans's Son of a Snitch books explore the enforcement of the code against snitching and its effect on a young boy whose father is labeled a snitch.

Relentless Aaron.

The Last Kingpin. **New York: St. Martin's Paperbacks, 2007 (2000). 536pp. ISBN 9780312949679, 0312949677.** ☞ (

Brian "Freeze" Carter is a flashy, sexy, extravagant hustler who controls a cocaine empire. Cocky, proud, and in control, he is at first only mildly put out when Slim, the man he has transporting several kilos of cocaine up from Florida, tells him he had a flat tire and his shipment has been delayed. What Freeze doesn't know is that Slim is cooperating with the DEA, and Pat, an equally in-control officer for the DEA, has plans to topple the entire operation. A fast-paced thriller with a well-crafted plot.

Keywords: Florida; Law Enforcement; New York; Washington, DC

Similar Reads: *The Last Kingpin* is a taut, fast-paced story of a criminal organization and the investigators working to catch up. For more about determined and self-assured law enforcement officers, try Relentless Aaron's *Triple Threat*, Darrell DeBrew's *Keisha,* or Teri Woods's *Alibi.* Miasha's *Chaser* is another taut thriller about a character secretly cooperating with the feds.

Core Collection: Adult

Swinson, Kiki.

Playing Dirty Series. ☞ ((

Slick, conniving Yoshi Lomax is a high-priced defense attorney who is notorious for getting her way by hook or by crook. In this series, Yoshi is taken down, then tries to rise back up.

Keywords: Drug Addiction; Law Enforcement; Miami; Middle Class Setting; Street Code

Similar Reads: *Playing Dirty* takes place in a white-collar law enforcement setting and involves the FBI, the DEA, and a manipulative and highly successful woman. For another unstoppably powerful woman, try Janet Stevens Cook's *Black Skyy,* which stars a CIA-trained vigilante. For the maneuvers of high-profile drug lords and the law enforcement agents on their trail, try Teri Woods's <u>Deadly Reigns</u> series or Relentless Aaron's *Last Kingpin.*

Core Collection: Adult

Playing Dirty. West Babylon, NY: Urban Books, 2009. 281pp. ISBN 9780758228352, 075822835X.

Yoshi Lomax is a high-powered, high-priced defense attorney who believes in getting her clients off by any means necessary—including financial bribery and sexual favors. With ins at the DEA and the U.S. Attorney's office, Yoshi is at the top of her game. But she starts to lose control when she takes on two new clients at once: a sexy Haitian drug lord and a crime boss who reintroduces her to the pleasures and pitfalls of cocaine. Though Yoshi's power seems over the top, her exploits are delicious and her downfall more so.

Notorious. New York: Kensington, 2009. 281pp. ISBN 9780758228376, 0758228376.

Yoshi Lomax was once the most powerful and corrupt defense attorney in Miami. Then she made enemies who brought her down. Now, having fled Miami, Yoshi faces new troubles . . . and some familiar ones.

Williams, K. Roland.

Cut Throat. Columbus, OH: Triple Crown Publications, 2008. 226pp. ISBN 9780979951732, 0979951739. ☞☞ ⟨⟨

The music industry meets the drug game meets the FBI in the story of Quincy Williams, a regular R&B singer at D.C.'s Melody Room. Raymond, the club's owner and a major cocaine dealer, offers Quincy a new contract and forces him to sign it at gunpoint. In the meantime, an executive from Cut Throat Records scouts Quincy out at the Melody Room and offers him a deal of her own. Quincy finds himself torn between two prospects for his music career, various factions of the drug business, hordes of admiring women, and the unwanted attention of the FBI.

Keywords: Light Reads; Music Industry; Street Code; Washington, DC

Similar Reads: *Cut Throat* is a story of the sleazy music industry, interpersonal drama, and an FBI investigation. For more drama from a man's perspective, try *Chances* by Michael Covington or *Betrayed* by David Givens. For more about the music industry and its dirty dealings, try Thomas Long's *Cash Rules*, the story of three teenage hip-hop artists and their struggle with an unsavory producer. Black Artemis's *Explicit Content* explores the music industry from a more character-driven angle: the two main characters both seek music careers, but one is willing to sell out and the other stays true to her art.

Woods, Teri.

Deadly Reigns Series. ☞☞ ⟨⟨

The ruthless Reigns family controls a vast drug empire. Reading more like an over-the-top spy thriller than a street story, Deadly Reigns is full of bombs, double crosses, and ruthlessly efficient violence.

Keywords: Law Enforcement; Street Code

Similar Reads: The Deadly Reigns series is about a family drug business and the unwanted attention of the FBI. For more on families who run a drug business, try Rahsaan Ali's *Carmello* or Ashley and JaQuavis's Cartel series. For more on FBI investigations, try Relentless Aaron's *Last Kingpin* or Mark Anthony's *Take Down.*

Deadly Reigns: The First of a Trilogy. New York: Teri Woods Publishing, 2005. 333pp. ISBN 0967224977, 9780967224978.

The billionaire Reigns brothers run a larger-than-life drug enterprise with territory in Colombia and all over North America. But the FBI is on their trail, sending Agent Grace Moore to become Damian Reigns's girlfriend and infiltrate his life. Not only do the Reigns brothers have to steer clear of the feds, but their sister, Princess, has broken off from their organization and has deadly tricks of her own up her sleeve.

Deadly Reigns II: The Second of a Trilogy. New York: Teri Woods Publishing, 2006. 298pp. ISBN 0977323412, 9780977323418.

In this second volume, the Reigns family is still on top of their game.

Deadly Reigns III: The Third of a Trilogy. New York: Teri Woods Publishing, 2009. 215pp. ISBN 9780977323432, 0977323439.

Curtis Smith, Ginger Laine, and Jessica Tyler are additional authors for this final volume.

Heroes and Vigilantes

Demon hunters, real and fictitious heroes of the African American community, and powerful women taking the law into their own hands all appear in this section. The pleasure here is in watching goodhearted celebrities and preternaturally gifted civilians administer justice.

Cook, Janet Stevens.

Black Skyy. Largo, MD: Strebor Books, 2007. 296pp. ISBN 9781593091132, 1593091133. 🗡🗡 (

When Skyy was a child, she watched her heroin-addicted mother be killed by a vicious group of drug dealers. Now Skyy, aka The Lady in Black, is a CIA-trained vigilante, rescuing abuse victims everywhere and wreaking bloody vengeance on their abusers. During the day Skyy is regular Sandy, vice president of marketing for Bledsoe Communications, Inc., a Fortune 500 company that just happens to be run by the man who killed her mother. Jumping between settings and times, Cook tells a story of power, justice, and a black female superhero. A sequel, *Red Dawn*, is proposed but has not yet been published.

Keywords: Abuse; Middle Class Setting; New York; Revenge

Similar Reads: *Black Skyy* is the story of an extremely powerful vigilante, with themes of abuse and revenge. For more about abuse and revenge, try Treasure Hernandez's *Pimp's Life* or Jihad's *Baby Girl*. For more powerful women with questionable methods, try D. Mitchell's *Heroine* or Kiki Swinson's <u>Playing Dirty</u> series.

1

2

3

4

5

6

7

8

9

10

11

D.

Got Series. ⟋ (

In these crisp, short, and unusual noir thrillers, *you* are the hero.

Keywords: Atlanta; Brooklyn, NY; Noir; Street Code

Similar Reads: The <u>Got</u> series is a short, lyrical read about a college student caught up in crime. For more experimental prose, try Kenji Jasper's *Snow* or Hickson's free verse anthem *Ghettoheat*. For more about college students caught up in hustling, try Nisaa Showell's *Reign of a Hustler* or Anya Nicole's *Corporate Corner Boyz*.

Got. New York: Akashic Books, 2007. 171pp. ISBN 193335416X, 978-1933354163.

> In volume one, you are a college sophomore trying to pay the bills. One night at a strip club, a seductive woman distracts you while an accomplice gets away with a bag of cocaine and the money you owe your underhanded employer, Tony Star. Star beats you brutally, and the result is a whirlwind trip through Brooklyn in search of the perpetrators and the loot.

Cake. New York: Akashic Books, 2008. 139pp. ISBN 9781933354545, 193-3354542.

> In this lyrical follow-up, you move to Atlanta, but crime and difficult choices haunt you.

Gardner, T. L.

Demon Hunter Series. ⟋ ⟋ (

This Christian-themed fantasy stars Elijah, a man blessed with a guardian angel and the ability to fight supernatural evil.

Keywords: Christian Fiction; Paranormal Fiction; Philadelphia

Similar Reads: The <u>Demon Hunter</u> series is a Christian-inflected fantasy featuring supernatural elements. For more Christian-inflected fiction, try Joy's *Mama, I'm in Love . . . with a Gangsta* or the short story collection *Even Sinners Have Souls*. For more stories with supernatural elements, try Nane Quartay's *Badness* or Evie Rhodes's *Expired*.

Protector. Jamaica, NY: Q-Boro Books, 2007. 224pp. ISBN 9781933967134, 1933967137.

> The woman he loves is shot to death, and Elijah is also injured. Elijah, however, has a guardian angel—literally. Gabriel himself comes to heal Elijah in the hospital, shocking Elijah and his mother and sister when his head wound mysteriously disappears. This is the beginning of Elijah's journey, under the tutelage of the snarky, sarcastic Gabriel, through a world of demons, satanic cults, and Lucifer himself.

Sacrifice. Jamaica, NY: Q-Boro Books, 2008. 299pp. ISBN 9781933967387, 1933967382.

> In the first volume, Elijah came to understand his powers. In volume two, Elijah battles yet more demons and a vicious fallen angel.

Mathis, Greg.

Street Judge. **Largo, MD: Strebor Books, 2009 (2008). 316pp. ISBN 9781593091736, 1593091737.** ☞ ℭ

Author Judge Greg Mathis, a television judge, is known for coming up from street life and having been elected to a judgeship in Detroit. Mathis is also the protagonist in this mystery novel. A woman is found gruesomely murdered, and a man who has been arrested for selling drugs refuses to tell anyone but Judge Mathis what he knows about the crime. Mathis is known for being fair-minded and respectful—for instance, he insists on calling the murdered woman by her name, Sheila Morgan. Meanwhile, incriminating footage of Mathis's closest friend committing adultery is being used to blackmail him. Can the judge get to the bottom of what's going on? A suspenseful thriller with a message of empowerment and dignity for all.

Keywords: Detroit; Drug Addiction; Law Enforcement; Middle Class Setting; Mystery; Social Commentary

Similar Reads: *Street Judge* is a socially conscious mystery with a political celebrity at its center. For other socially conscious street lit set within local politics, try Solomon Jones's *C.R.E.A.M.* For another mystery, try Kane and Abel's *Diva* or Tony Lindsay's <u>David Price</u> series. For another character who stands in for the famous author, try Omar Tyree's *Last Street Novel*, in which a successful writer represents Tyree himself.

Mitchell, D.

Heroine. **Jamaica, NY: Q-Boro Books, 2008. 246pp. ISBN 9781933967639, 1933967633.** ☞ ℭ

Samara Brown is the Washington, D.C., black community's version of a superhero. Influenced by the Black Panthers and trained by her military assassin father, Samara uses her athletic skills and her weapons to rid the world of violent thugs. After graduating from Howard University, Samara opens a community center. But with her younger brother selling drugs, a very insistent man trying to get into her life, and her father far away, business is getting complicated.

Keywords: Assassins; Middle Class Setting; Overcoming Adversity; Social Commentary; Washington, DC

Similar Reads: *Heroine* is a socially conscious story with a critique of street life, focusing on an extraordinarily powerful protagonist fighting for justice. For more socially conscious fiction that critiques both street life and contemporary political institutions, try Greg Mathis's *Street Judge* or John Sibley's futuristic *Bodyslick*. For more preternaturally powerful characters fighting for justice, try Janet Stevens Cook's *Black Skyy* or T. L. Gardner's <u>Demon Hunter</u> series.

Sibley, John H.

Bodyslick. **New York: Vibe Street Lit/Kensington Publishing, 2008. 402pp. ISBN 9781601830043, 1601830041.** 🏃 🏃 (

The year is 2031, and Malcolm "Bodyslick" Steel is an underground organ harvester. An heir to the Vanderbilt fortune suffers heart failure, and after his first transplant fails, doctors turn to Bodyslick to supply a replacement heart. Descriptions of the setting—a future Chicago full of video-phones, U.S. government marijuana "seagarettes," laser guns, and robots that perform surgery and sense human arousal—make the book feel slower in pace than most street lit. Like mainstream street lit, however, the book is relentlessly race-conscious, both in the author's introduction and in textual moments—Bodyslick's parole hearing, for instance. The story also focuses on rival organ-harvesting gangs, whose turf wars resemble contemporary gang activity. An unusual story for readers willing to accept an unfamiliar future landscape.

Keywords: Chicago; Noir; Science Fiction; Social Commentary

Similar Reads: *Bodyslick* is a noir, socially conscious, experimental novel. For more street novels with a noir feel, try D's <u>Got</u> series, Tony Lindsay's <u>David Price</u> mysteries, or Charles D. Ellison's *Tantrum*. Kwame Teague's *Adventures of Ghetto Sam and The Glory of My Demise* also pairs experimental writing with race consciousness.

Tyree, Omar.

The Last Street Novel. **New York: Simon & Schuster, 2008 (2007). 401pp. ISBN 9781416541929, 1416541926.** 🏃 🏃 ((

Although the book opens with a man being tortured in an empty Harlem apartment, the overarching plot is fairly tame. Shareef Crawford, a wildly successful African American romance writer, comes back to his native Harlem on a book tour. He speaks to adoring fans and romances nearly every woman he meets. Then Coffee, a woman he meets at a reading, asks him to write a novel based on the life of a friend of hers in prison. Tyree uses the novel to prove that he can write street stories and to attack the street lit genre. Tyree has publicly criticized both writers and fans of contemporary street lit, and his characters here are mouthpieces for this view. A minor character, The Spear, is himself a street lit author, and his inability to sell his books or attract women surely reflects Tyree's feelings about typical street authors.

Keywords: Middle Class Setting; New York

Similar Reads: *The Last Street Novel* is a thriller featuring a male character who is both a famous entertainer and irresistible to women. For more powerful and seductive men, try Relentless Aaron's *Platinum Dolls* or Tyree's short story collection *Dirty Old Men*. For more settings within the entertainment industry, try Rahsaan Ali's *Backstabbers* or Wendy Williams's <u>Ritz Harper Chronicles</u>.

Core Collection: Adult

Mysteries and Suspense

Like mainstream mystery and suspense novels, novels in this subgenre focus on detectives, criminals, killers, and unexplained or mysterious circumstances. Individual actors rather than large-scale operations are the targets of investigation here, as in Relentless Aaron's *Triple Threat*, in which a police officer and a driven journalist pursue a serial killer.

Kane and Abel.

Diva. **Columbus, OH: Triple Crown Publications, 2004. 237pp. ISBN 0974789585, 9780974789583.** ⌐ (

Multi-platinum R&B star Delilah Brown is eighteen when a car accident claims her life. But this is no simple accident: everyone in the car also has a gunshot wound to the head. Two NYPD officers investigate: Detective Nico, a closet racist, and Detective Scott, a man with a past. We meet Delilah's grandmother Melinda; Big Rock, the rapper boyfriend who got her into the music game; and KB, an inmate in federal prison in Texas who may have been Delilah's stalker. The story is fast-paced, and like any good mystery novel, keeps you guessing until the very end.

Keywords: Law Enforcement; Music Industry; Mystery; New York

Similar Reads: *Diva* is a fast-paced mystery featuring police detectives and set within the music industry. To read more street lit from the point of view of investigators, try Relentless Aaron's *Last Kingpin* or Darrell DeBrew's *Keisha*. Mark Anthony's *Take Down* is another story of investigators that also takes place in the music industry.

Knight, Dakota.

Sola. **West Babylon, NY: Urban Books, 2007. 273pp. ISBN 1893196518, 9781893196513.** ⌐⌐ ((

Sola Nichols is better known as the Brown Recluse. Like the poisonous spider that is her namesake, Sola is a deadly assassin. She is notorious on the streets of Columbus, Ohio, for her cold, efficient contract kills. But Sola's actions draw attention from someone known as the Hunter. While Sola continues her assassin work, the Hunter is coming after her. Flashbacks to Sola's difficult childhood and abuse at the hands of her mother's boyfriend deepen this story of killing or being killed.

Keywords: Abuse; Assassins; Columbus, OH; Street Code; Women Hustlers

Similar Reads: *Sola* is a suspenseful tale about an unrepentant female murderer. For more female assassins, try Cairo's *Kat Trap* or Relentless Aaron's *Triple Threat*. For more about childhood abuse, try Noire's *Hittin' the Bricks* or Miasha's *Mommy's Angel*.

Lindsay, Tony.

David Price Series. ☞ ✆

Schooled on the streets of Chicago, David Price runs a security agency, but finds himself embroiled in mysteries.

Keywords: Chicago; Mystery; Noir

Similar Reads: The <u>David Price</u> books are true mysteries with a street flavor. For another street-inflected mystery, try Kane and Abel's *Diva* or Evie Rhodes's *Expired*.

One Dead Preacher: A David Price Mystery. Jamaica, NY: Q-Boro Books, 2007. 200pp. ISBN 1933967021, 9781933967028.

In volume 1, assertive and sexy Sugar Owens needs protection from her soon-to-be ex-husband, Brother Yazz, leader of a religious organization called the New Day Brothers. Referred by David's best friend Ricky, Sugar hires David, ostensibly to keep her safe. But there's more to the situation than meets the eye, as David realizes when Brother Yazz turns up dead. Tension—both emotional and sexual—builds slowly but steadily in this mystery with a street flavor.

One Dead Lawyer: A David Price Mystery. Jamaica, NY: Q-Boro Books, 2007. 223pp. ISBN 9781933967295, 1933967293.

In this volume, Price investigates again after a suspicious lawyer turns up murdered.

Relentless Aaron.

Platinum Dolls. **New York: St. Martin's, 2009 (2004). 248pp. ISBN 9780312949686, 0312949685.** ☞ ☞ ✆✆✆

Business and pleasure: that's how Stew Gregory, owner of the Platinum Dolls, views sex. He's a man in complete control, with attractive and sexually skilled women auditioning to work for his lucrative business. But just as a new "Doll" enters his plush life, Stew and the Platinum Dolls are in danger. Someone is shooting and killing women and threatening Stew's business. A sensual and suspenseful fantasy of male sexual power.

Keywords: Bronx, NY; Malibu, CA; Sex Industry

Similar Reads: *Platinum Dolls* is a suspenseful, highly sexual tale of a lushly powerful man who operates a sex business. White Chocolate's *Sex in the Hood* features a similarly decadent setting in which powerful men have unfettered access to women's sexuality.

Triple Threat. **New York: St. Martin's, 2008 (2004). 278pp. ISBN 9780312949662, 0312949669.** *ᴕ ᴕ* ((

A prolific, sexually charged serial killer is murdering men for her own pleasure and for the thrill of getting away with it. They call her the Pink Heart Murderer, and she is wreaking havoc on New York. Two women are in hot pursuit of the killer: Sissy Dickerson, a police officer, and April Davis, a journalist looking for a major story. With his usual fast-paced suspense, Relentless Aaron pushes the three women together and lets the sparks fly.

Keywords: Law Enforcement; Middle Class Setting; New York; Street Code

Similar Reads: *Triple Threat* is the story of a vicious female serial killer for whom killing is a sexual act, and of two investigators who are pursuing her. For more women who kill with sexual relish, try Cairo's *Kat Trap* or Dakota Knight's *Sola*. For more determined investigators, try Relentless Aaron's *Last Kingpin* or Darrell DeBrew's *Keisha*.

Rhodes, Evie.

Expired. **New York: Dafina, 2005. 292pp. ISBN 0758208707, 9780758208705.** *ᴕ ᴕ* (

In this spooky mystery, Randi, the youngest of Tracie Burlingame's four sons, is found dead on the sidewalk with no shoes and no blood. Someone—or something—is haunting Harlem and killing viciously. The cops are on the case, but it's Tracie and Harlem's resident psychic, Anita, who are closest to the truth.

Keywords: Drug Addiction; Mystery; New York; Paranormal Fiction

Similar Reads: *Expired* is a combination ghost story and mystery with an eerie feel. For another ghost story, try Nane Quartay's *Badness*. For more mysteries, try Kane and Abel's *Diva* or Tony Linsday's David Price series.

Smith, Méta.

Whip Appeal. **New York: Pocket Books, 2008. 273pp. ISBN 9781416551393, 1416551395.** *ᴕ* ((

Twenty-five-year-old Ebony Knight is found by the police, disoriented and shaken, in a room with two dead bodies. One body belongs to her fiancé, Jeff Cardoza. The other is Erik Johansen, a former client of Ebony's who stalked her. Ebony was making millions as a professional dominatrix who catered to an exclusive clientele. Now she's in a psychiatric hospital trying to reconstruct what happened the night Jeff and Erik died, prove her innocence, and escape. There to help her are her are her best friend and lawyer Carmelita, her overbearing mother, and a fellow patient who believes she was born on another planet. Ebony is not often shown in her role as a dominatrix here, but there is plenty of intrigue and suspense.

Keywords: GLBTQ; Miami; Sex Industry

Similar Reads: *Whip Appeal* is a suspenseful story set the morning after a crime that features a police investigation and a character who cannot remember the past. Amaleka McCall's *Myra: A Twisted Tale of Karma* has a similar structure in which a protagonist and investigators try to reconstruct the circumstances of a crime. Brandon McCalla's *Spot Rushers* focuses on three women reeling after a robbery gone wrong.

Woods, Teri.

Alibi. **New York: Grand Central, 2009. 257pp. ISBN 9780446581691, 0446581690.**
☞ ❢

In 1986 in Philadelphia, Simon Shuller is the only major player in the drug game. When Lance and Jeremy decide to rob his stash, they know they are attempting the nearly impossible. Nard, Shuller's loyal man, is guarding the stash when the would-be stickup artists arrive. A gunfight ensues, and only Nard is left standing. With two bodies on his hands, Nard needs an alibi. Enter Daisy Fothergill, a stripper and prostitute struggling to get by. For two thousand dollars, Daisy agrees to tell the cops she saw Nard at the Honey Dipper club on the night of the murders. But when the cops close in, everyone learns the true cost of Nard's alibi.

Keywords: 1980s; Law Enforcement; Philadelphia

Similar Reads: *Alibi* is a suspenseful crime drama set in the 1980s, focusing on a hustler evading a police investigation. For more suspenseful stories of evading the law, try Relentless Aaron's *Last Kingpin* or Miasha's *Chaser*. For more novels set in the 1980s, try Woods's *Predators* or Ed McNair's *My Time to Shine*.

Core Collection: Adult

Political Thrillers

In these thrillers, suspense and criminal investigations take place in a political context. Street action is connected to persons involved in politics or used for political ends, as in Charles Ellison's *Tantrum*, in which a journalist investigates the attempted murder of a Philadelphia city councilman, or Risqué's *Red Light Special*, in which a woman killed out of jealousy turns out to be connected to New York City's mayor.

Ellison, Charles D.

Tantrum. **New York: Ghettoheat, 2008. 240pp. ISBN 9780974298252, 0974298255.**
☞ ☞ ❢

Somewhere on the grimy streets of Philadelphia, Dread, a down and out homeless man, begs a local politician for money. At the same moment, an assassin lurks, aiming his weapon at the figure simply known as "Councilman." The assassin shoots, and Dread catches the bullet. The city—along with a frustrated journalist called Scribbles—is abuzz with theories about who wanted Councilman dead. But the appeal here is less in getting answers and more in savoring Ellison's stylized noir tone and his grim rendering of Philadelphia.

Keywords: Noir; Philadelphia; Street Code

Similar Reads: *Tantrum* is a noir political thriller with a stylized tone and a Philadelphia setting. For more novels with a stylized narrative voice, try Che Parker's *Tragic Flaw* or D's <u>Got</u> series. Solomon Jones's <u>C.R.E.A.M.</u> series is another crafted work that takes place within Philadelphia politics.

Jones, Solomon.

Pipe Dream. **New York: Villard/Strivers Row, 2001. 341pp. ISBN 0375756604, 9780375756603.** ⬘ ⬘ (

A Philadelphia city councilman known for his anticorruption stance is found murdered in a crack house, and Black, an addict, is under suspicion. Black and his crack addict associates band together to stay out of the reach of the law, but the police, under political pressure, are closing in.

Keywords: Drug Addiction; Philadelphia

Similar Reads: *Pipe Dream* is a crafted thriller that mixes street action with political intrigue. For other crafted works that mix street drama and politics, try Jones's *C.R.E.A.M.* or Charles D. Ellison's *Tantrum*. For another cop story featuring drug addicts, try Tony Lindsay's *Street Possession*.

<u>C.R.E.A.M. Series.</u> ⬘ ⬘ ((

This literary political thriller focuses on a young woman with a street past who gets involved in Philadelphia politics. Jones uses skillfully crafted dialogue and language to evoke tension, such as, "Twenty-fifth and Nicholas was eerily quiet, as if the streets were waiting for the other shoe to drop."

Keywords: Noir; Philadelphia; Prison; Revenge; Street Code

Similar Reads: *C.R.E.A.M.* is a crafted, noir political thriller. For another crafted, noir political thriller, try Charles D. Ellison's *Tantrum*. For more about drug dealers and turf wars, try Erick S. Gray's *Ghetto Heaven*.

C.R.E.A.M. New York: St. Martin's Griffin, 2007 (2006). 214pp. ISBN 0312361467, 9780312361464.

Karima, aka Cream, went to prison for six months to cover for the man she loved, a drug dealer named Duane Faison. Free again, Karima wants to leave the streets behind, but it's harder to leave Duane. With the help of her conniving aunt, president of the city council, Karima gets a job working for the mayor. What she doesn't realize is that her aunt is using Karima, her criminal past, and the mayor's fondness for young, attractive women to influence the mayoral election. Meanwhile, a vicious drug war heats up between Duane and the Twenty-Ninth Street crew, and Karima finds herself caught in the middle.

Payback: The Return of C.R.E.A.M. New York: Minotaur Books, 2009. 244pp. ISBN 9780312348380, 031234838X.

> In this second volume, Cream is on trial when a deranged killer murders her mother. Cream vows to track down the murderer and exact vengeance.

Risqué.

Red Light Special. **New York: One World/Ballantine Books, 2008. 256pp. ISBN 9780345504319, 0345504313.** ☛☛ ℭℭℭ

This steamy story of politics, jealousy, and revenge begins with a murder. An unnamed woman, hiding in a plush hotel room, watches her husband have sex with Eve, his favorite girl-on-the-side, then shoots Eve in cold blood. Eve turns out to be connected with Kenyatta Smith, the mayor of New York City, and the media frenzy is unrelenting. A fast-paced, upscale thriller full of suspense and raw sexuality.

Keywords: Assassins; Middle Class Setting; New York; Sex Industry; Street Code

Similar Reads: *Red Light Special* is an erotic thriller with an upscale setting in New York City politics. For other reads that combine sex and murder, try Cairo's *Kat Trap* or Relentless Aaron's *Triple Threat*. For other political scandals, try Solomon Jones's *C.R.E.A.M.* or Charles D. Ellison's *Tantrum*.

Chapter 7

Hard Times

Some street lit focuses on living large, but other novels deal with the pain of street life. Novels in the hard times subgenre explore the darker, sadder sides of street life and the struggle for survival. Common themes include abusive relationships, family violence, incest, drug addiction, poverty, and unwanted sex work.

Readers of hard times novels may be looking for inspiration in a character's rise above miserable circumstances, for the comfort of empathizing with someone else's pain, or for the relief of feeling that someone else—even if that someone is fictional— has it even worse. Teenagers, who are often drawn to dark, bleak stories, may be particularly interested in this subgenre.

Overcoming Adversity

Novels in this section are uplifting in tone, showing a character transcending difficult circumstances. Treasure E. Blue's *Street Girl Named Desire*, for example, shows the neglected daughter of a crack-addicted mother experiencing trials of her own but ending up a successful and well-loved singer.

Birch, Dywayne D.

Beneath the Bruises. **Largo, MD: Strebor Books, 2008. 242pp. ISBN 9781593092085, 1593092083.** 🐎 🐎 (

Author Dywayne D. Birch is a therapist who works with perpetrators of domestic abuse. This novel, which evolved from a poem Birch wrote three years earlier, focuses on Syreeta, a woman whose husband is abusing her. Through sessions with a therapist of her own, Syreeta learns to see her own value and free herself from her husband's control. Birch's original poem, also titled "Beneath the Bruises," ends the book on a note of hope.

Keywords: Abuse; Middle Class Setting; Overcoming Adversity

Similar Reads: *Beneath the Bruises* is an uplifting story about freeing oneself from domestic abuse. For a variety of stories about abusive relationships, try the short story collection *Breaking the Cycle*. For more stories of hardship that end on an uplifting note, try Treasure E. Blue's *Harlem Girl Lost* or *A Street Girl Named Desire*. Readers inspired by Syreeta's finding her own voice through poetry might be interested in Sapphire's *Push*, in which an abused teenager who cannot read learns to express herself through the written word.

Blue, Treasure E.

Harlem Girl Lost. New York: One World/Ballantine Books, 2006 (2004). 332pp. ISBN 0345492641, 9780345492647. ☞ ☞ (

Silver Jones grew up with two guardians: her drug-addicted mother Jesse and gay Auntie Birdie. As a child, Silver saw her mother experience several overdoses and sell sex for drug money. But Jesse also taught Silver to be kind and to believe in herself, repeating affirmations on their morning walks to school. Most of the novel tells Silver's story of triumph in the face of cruelty and violence. Chapters from Jesse's point of view describe how Silver was conceived and how drug addiction affects Jesse's life. Although Silver's ability to transcend her miserable circumstances with few consequences may seem unrealistic, the message of hope is compelling and clear.

Keywords: Drug Addiction; GLBTQ; New York; Overcoming Adversity; Sex Industry; Teenagers; Women Hustlers

Similar Reads: *Harlem Girl Lost* is an uplifting story about overcoming hardships and believing in oneself even when life is painful. For another story of healing against the odds, try Antoine "Inch" Thomas's *Flower's Bed*. Amaleka McCall's *Myra: A Twisted Tale of Karma* also stars a young girl who grows up with a drug-using mother and is driven to succeed.

Core Collection: Adult; School Libraries; Young Adult

A Street Girl Named Desire. New York: One World/Ballantine Books, 2007. 325pp. ISBN 9780345493286, 0345493281. ☞ ☞ ☞ ((

One a cold night in Harlem, tiny, pregnant, crack-addicted Nika is raped by a violent john. Covered in blood, she buys two vials of crack, gets high, and delivers a one-pound baby onto the snowy sidewalk. That baby is Desire Evans. Desire's life hits low points—rape, abuse, HIV infection, and her own addictions—as well as high points—adoption, a recording contract, and recovery. A brutal story of family, fame, and salvation.

Keywords: Abuse; Drug Addiction; Music Industry; New York; Overcoming Adversity; Sex Industry

Similar Reads: *A Street Girl Named Desire* is an uplifting but brutal story about abuse, addiction, and, ultimately, triumph. For more about abused children and teenagers, try Anna J's *Snow White* or Noire's *Hittin' the Bricks*. For more about succeeding against the odds, try Nikki Turner's *Ghetto Superstar* or *Riding Dirty on I-95*.

Core Collection: Adult

Brown, Tracy.

White Lines. **New York: St. Martin's Griffin, 2007. 497pp. ISBN 0312336489, 9780312336486.** 🖝🖝 ((

Jada is a teenager the first time she skips school and smokes a woolah—a joint laced with crack. A few lazy afternoons later and she is hooked, and not her mother, her sister, or her equally addicted best friend can break the bond between Jada and the drugs her body craves. Needing money to feed her habit, Jada falls in with an older man who at first seems supportive but then pushes her into prostitution against her will. At her lowest point, Jada meets Born, a respected Staten Island hustler. Is love enough to pull Jada away from her demons? Brown tells a story of love and survival that is both riveting and emotionally compelling.

Keywords: Abuse; Drug Addiction; Sex Industry; Staten Island, NY; Teenagers

Similar Reads: *White Lines* is an emotional, character-driven story about the pain of drug addiction. For more character-driven street lit, try Brown's *Black: A Street Tale* or Seven's *Gorilla Black*. For more about the devastating effects of drug addiction, try Y. Blak Moore's *Slipping* or Lisa Lennox's somewhat more sensational <u>Crack Head</u> series.

Core Collection: Adult; Young Adult; School Libraries

Camm, Meisha.

You Got to Pay to Play. **West Babylon, NY: Urban Books, 2009. 265pp. ISBN 9781601620859, 1601620853.** 🖝 ((

Though the title makes her sound conniving, Isabel Preston starts off a lonely child, missing her father and resenting her mother. Izzy's mother insists that she go to college, but Isabel refuses to listen to the woman she feels let her father leave. Involved with a drug dealer at age eighteen, Isabel leaves her mother's house for good. But the abusive man she moves in with is the first of many people to treat her roughly. Cynical and desperate, Isabel develops a new motto: you gotta pay to play. Embarking on life as a prostitute, Izzy has only her friends to count on. An emotional story of struggle and redemption with a compelling, sympathetic character at its center.

Keywords: Abuse; Norfolk, VA; Overcoming Adversity; Sex Industry

Similar Reads: *You Got to Pay to Play* is an emotional, triumphant story of a young woman's journey through loneliness, abuse, and the difficulty of surviving alone. For more on abusive relationships, try Azárel's *Bruised* or Nikki Turner's *Project Chick*. Treasure E. Blue's *Harlem Girl Lost* and *Street Girl Named Desire* both carry similarly uplifting messages of surviving against the odds.

Lennox, Lisa.

Crack Head Series. *ℴ ℴ* ((

This series stars privileged, naïve Laci Johnson, who learns more about street life than she had ever expected after a group of jealous girls tricks her into smoking crack.

Keywords: Drug Addiction; Bronx, NY; Teenagers

Core Collection: Adult; Young Adult; School Libraries

Crack Head. Columbus, OH: Triple Crown Publications, 2005 (2004). 222pp. ISBN 0974789534, 9780974789538.

> Laci Johnson is a privileged seventeen-year-old living with her white mother in the upscale Riverdale neighborhood in the Bronx. Her friends, a tough crew of girls who call themselves the South Bronx Bitches, are both jealous and resentful. To sabotage Laci, the SBB girls concoct a plan to trick her into trying crack. Suddenly Laci is hooked and debasing herself in ways she never thought possible. The love of a drug dealer named Dink and the caring attentions of her family help Laci heal from the horrors of addiction.

Crack Head II: Laci's Revenge. Columbus, OH: Triple Crown Publications, 2008. 271pp. ISBN 9780979951794, 0979951798.

> In this volume, Laci goes to college and struggles to heal from her addiction, while her beloved Dink tries to move away from drug dealing.

Long, Thomas.

Papa Don't Preach. **West Babylon, NY: Urban Books, 2006. 265pp. ISBN 1893196658, 9781893196650.** *ℴ ℴ* ((

A crack-addicted man examines his habit when he sees his son going down the same path. Nigel started smoking crack when his wife Lorraine turned him onto it in the eighties. He turned his friends, Fats and Pretty Ricky, onto the drug, and now the three of them do stickups, robberies, and petty crimes to pay for their next fix. But JR, Nigel's son with Lorraine, is suffering the ill effects of having an addicted mother. Hungry, beaten, and confused by his mother's behavior, JR turns to his father for help. Then Nigel goes to prison, and when he comes out, JR has learned more about the drug lifestyle than his father ever wished. Can Nigel overcome his own history to help his son?

Keywords: Abuse; Baltimore; Drug Addiction

Similar Reads: *Papa Don't Preach* is a grim story of addiction with themes of abuse and family relationships. For more bleak portraits of drug addiction, try Endy's In My Hood series or Donald Goines's classic *Dopefiend*. For another father stepping up to help his son, try Terra Little's romantic *Where There's Smoke*.

Santiago, Danielle.

Grindin': A Harlem Story. New York: Atria Book, 2007. 241pp. ISBN 0743277619, 9780743277617. 🖝🖝 ❪❪

A heroin addict, then a hustler, Nina is killed by her abusive boyfriend, leaving behind her son Taylor and her cousin Kennedy Sanchez. Still missing Nina, Kennedy goes out to a nightclub and meets Chaz, a hip-hop artist and, as it turns out, a man worth keeping. Drugs and robberies take a backseat to relationships and life's big questions in this emotional story. How do you say good-bye to your best friend? How do you raise a boy to treat women right? How do you feel safe in your country after a terrorist attack? Santiago, who has created the Mischievous Girls Foundation to help battered women, tackles these questions and ends on a note of hope.

Keywords: Abuse; Charlotte, NC; Drug Addiction; Music Industry; New York

Similar Reads: *Grindin'* is an emotional, uplifting tale about moving on after a tragedy. For more emotional street stories, try Ana'Gia Wright's *Lil' Sister* or Keisha Ervin's *Torn*. Tracy Brown's *White Lines* is another emotional street story that deals with addiction and ends with hope.

Sapphire.

Push. New York: Alfred A. Knopf, 1996. 141pp. ISBN 0679446265, 978-0679446262. 🖝🖝🖝 ❪❪

Though *Push* was published by a literary imprint and uses crafted language, it nonetheless speaks to fans of street lit. Poet Sapphire takes on the voice of Precious, a sixteen-year-old girl in 1980s Harlem who wants to grow, learn, and heal, but is hindered by brutal circumstances. Pregnant with her second child by her father, physically and sexually abused by her mother, held back twice in school and unable to read, Precious moves through the world with her defenses up. Then she is kicked out of school and sent instead to an alternative program, where she learns to read, write, and tell her own story. This novel was made into the film *Precious*.

Keywords: Abuse; Character-Driven; GLBTQ; New York; Overcoming Adversity; Teenagers

Similar Reads: *Push* is a brutal but ultimately uplifting story of a teenage girl experiencing physical and sexual abuse, told in crafted but conversational language. To read about other children subjected to abuse, try Anna J's *Snow White*, Miasha's *Mommy's Angel*, or K'wan's *Street Dreams*. Poetry plays a central role in *Push* and in Sapphire's language. Readers looking for more poetry can try Crystal Lacey Winslow's *Up Close & Personal* or Hickson's *Ghettoheat*.

Classic

Core Collection: Adult; Young Adult; School Libraries

Sidi.

Fatou Series. ⟨⟨

In this thoughtful series, a young girl from West Africa is sold overseas to marry a man in New York. The cultural differences between Fatou's home country and the United States, as well as her consciousness of being an undocumented immigrant, give this book a different flavor than most street lit.

Keywords: Abuse; New York; Sex Industry; Social Commentary

Similar Reads: *Fatou* is an emotional, socially conscious story of a child sold into sexual slavery, with themes of abuse and revenge. For more about young women sold into sexual slavery, try Miasha's *Sistah for Sale* or Keith Lee Johnson's Little Black Girl Lost series. For more young women coming of age and becoming street savvy while encountering adversity, try Keisha Ervin's *Chyna Black* or Antoine "Inch" Thomas's *Flower's Bed*.

Core Collection: Adult; Young Adult; School Libraries

Fatou, an African Girl in Harlem. New York: Harlem Book Center, 2005. 287pp. ISBN 0976393905, 9780976393900.

> Raised in West Africa, twelve-year-old Fatou La Princesse had no idea her parents had sold her to be the wife of a middle-aged man named Lama. Raped by her father, then sent overseas to America, Fatou initially struggles. Lama expects her to be sexually receptive, and the other women in the household are jealous of the attention Lama gives Fatou. As she grows older and more experienced, Fatou makes a place for herself braiding hair at Fifi's, and then she becomes involved in more dangerous—and more illegal—pursuits.

Fatou: Return to Harlem. New York: Harlem Book Center, 2006. 287pp. ISBN 097639393X, 9780976393931.

> In the first *Fatou*, a West African girl was sold as a child bride to Lama, a man in Harlem, then found herself involved in dangerous and illegal pursuits. In this volume, after losing the one person she cared about most, Fatou seeks revenge against the parties responsible.

Swinson, Kiki.

The Candy Shop. New York: Dafina, 2010 (2007). 288pp. ISBN 0758238916, 978-0758238917. ⟨⟨

Faith was gainfully employed at an elementary school when she got her first taste of "candy." Her best friend and secretary Teresa snorted a mix of heroin and cocaine in Faith's office, and against her better judgment, Faith gave it a try. Caught by a drug test, Faith was forced to leave her job, and the drugs became even more tempting. Years later, she's homeless, strung out, and desperate. The story of Faith's path from the middle class to the streets is grim but ends with a small note of hope.

Keywords: Drug Addiction; Norfolk, VA

Similar Reads: *The Candy Shop* is a gritty and sensationalistic tale of the horrors of drug addiction. For another middle-class character taken down by drugs, try Lisa Lennox's *Crack Head*. For more on drugs' painful effects, try Endy's <u>In My Hood</u> series or Tracy Brown's *White Lines*.

Thomas, Antoine "Inch".

<u>Flower's Bed Series.</u> 𝒶 𝒶 ⟨⟨

Though perhaps didactic, <u>Flower's Bed</u> deals with incest, abuse, and healing and is particularly popular with teenage readers.

Keywords: Abuse; New York; Overcoming Adversity; Sex Industry; Teenagers

Similar Reads: *Flower's Bed* is a dramatic tale about incest, healing, and the redemptive power of friendships. For more stories of children subjected to abuse, try K'wan's *Street Dreams* or Anna J's *Snow White*. For more healing relationships between teenagers, try Seven's *Gorilla Black* or Sherrie Walker's *Mistress of the Game*. Readers interested in Flower's healing through therapy may also be drawn to Dywayne D. Birch's *Beneath the Bruises*, in which an adult woman goes to therapy to deal with her abusive relationship.

Core Collection: Adult; Young Adult; School Libraries

Flower's Bed: The Most Controversial Book of This Era. New York: Amiaya Entertainment, 2003. 199pp. ISBN 9780974507507.

On her ninth birthday, Flower Abrams's father molests her for the first time. This abuse begins a brutal pattern that continues for several years, until her father is killed in what seems to be a robbery. With the help of a close friend, Flower struggles to make ends meet. Flower works as a stripper; at the same time, a counselor at school helps her understand and come to terms with her own abuse.

Flower's Bed the Sequel: Black Roses. New York: Amiaya Entertainment, 2007. ISBN 9780977754489, 0977754480.

In this sequel another young woman, Rose, is being abused by her foster family. Flower, now engaged in the healing process herself, mentors Rose through the pain of abuse and what comes after.

Turner, Nikki.

A Project Chick. **Columbus, OH: Triple Crown Publications, 2004. 274pp. ISBN 0970247265, 9780970247261.** 𝒶 𝒶 ⟨⟨

Tressa met Lucky through her big brother Taj. Taj was in prison and Lucky was his right-hand man. Tressa and Lucky's romance began as a fairy tale: extravagant gifts, status, and an emotional connection. But as time went on, Lucky became violent and controlling. Now Tressa is a single mother with two children and a psychotic, abusive man. She struggles to keep herself and her children safe and happy, and to fight off Lucky any way she can.

Keywords: Abuse; Richmond, VA

Similar Reads: *A Project Chick* is a chilling story of a woman and her violent abuser. Mark Anthony's *Reasonable Doubt* is another frightening story about the mechanics of domestic abuse. For other women attached to manipulative, violent men, try Azárel's *Bruised* or Danette Majette's *Good Girl Gone Bad*.

Riding Dirty on I-95. New York: One World/ Ballantine Books, 2006. 306pp. ISBN 9780345476845. ⚐⚐ ⟮⟮

When Mercy Jiles was seven years old, her beloved father was killed for gambling debts. He left her with a respect for the streets and the words of songwriter Kenny Rogers: "You gotta know when to hold 'em, know when to fold 'em." Emancipated from the foster care system at seventeen, Mercy makes ends meet with legal jobs and by transporting drugs up and down I-95, the only way to bring contraband in or out of Richmond, Virginia. In a side plot, gentle gangster C-Note transforms himself into brutal killer Cleezy and gets away with a series of murders. Mercy's charm is her character: she is an average woman with an average body who dreams big and has no qualms about standing up for herself. Mercy's ups and downs are engaging, even if her eventual fortune is a bit too good to be believable.

Keywords: Film Industry; Overcoming Adversity; Richmond, VA; Teenagers

Similar Reads: *Riding Dirty on I-95* is an uplifting, episodic story with a strong father–daughter connection. Turner writes more about characters who triumph after years of hardship in *Ghetto Superstar* and *Black Widow*, and Treasure E. Blue's *Street Girl Named Desire* is another uplifting tale about a woman with a hard life who finds success. Other strong father–daughter relationships appear in Shannon Holmes's *Dirty Game*, Mallori McNeal's *Down Chick*, and Divine G's *Baby Doll*.

Core Collection: Adult

Williams, Karen.

Harlem on Lock. Jamaica, NY: Q-Boro Books, 2008. 259pp. ISBN 9781933967349, 193396734X. ⚐⚐ ⟮⟮

The daughter of Aja, a gifted singer who is addicted to heroin, seventeen year-old Harlem knows pain, desperation, and hunger. A gifted student and warmhearted daughter, Harlem loves Aja despite her failings and is even willing to do sexual favors for their lecherous landlord to spare her mother the pain of withdrawal. When Aja dies of an overdose, Harlem's father allows men in the neighborhood to rape her to fund his own addiction. Harlem is eventually rescued by Chief, a drug kingpin who takes her as his kept woman. Longing for Savior, the goodhearted drug dealer she has loved for years, Harlem is not satisfied living under Chief's rules. When her will clashes with that of the powerful kingpin, Harlem finds herself in soul-crushing danger.

Keywords: Abuse; Drug Addiction; Los Angeles; Overcoming Adversity; Teenagers

Similar Reads: *Harlem on Lock* is the emotional, sympathetic story of a kindhearted teenage girl forced to endure cruel treatment. For more about the children of drug addicts, try *Hittin' the Bricks* by Noire or *Snow White* by Anna J. For more mistreated characters with hearts of gold, try Williams's *People vs. Cashmere* or Miasha's *Mommy's Angel*.

Core Collection: Young Adult; School Libraries

Rock Bottom

Novels in this section are relentlessly bleak, showing the pain and brutality of staying alive in difficult circumstances. One of the bleakest novels in the subgenre appears in this section: Tanika Lynch's *Whore*, in which a teenage girl desperate to support her siblings takes a job as a sex worker but becomes dependent on drugs to numb the pain of letting strangers use her body.

Anthony, Mark.

Lady's Night. **New York: St. Martin's Griffin, 2005. 324pp. ISBN 0312340788, 9780312340780.** ⚔ ⚔ ❨❨

At age fifteen, Tina is raped by her stepfather. Worse, her mother tells her she should have "closed her eyes and enjoyed it." So Tina leaves home for the streets. Working at a donut shop in Queensbridge, she meets a thug named Cream. She commands so much respect from Cream with her attitude that he nicknames her Lady. When Cream returns to the donut shop, he has a business proposition for her: join his "team" and become a prostitute. But between her jealous fellow prostitutes, Cream's constant surveillance, and the violence required to keep the operation intact, Lady finds that the work is more trouble than she imagined.

Keywords: Abuse; Queens, NY; Sex Industry; Street Code; Teenagers

Similar Reads: *Lady's Night* is an emotional story of a young woman who faces abuse from her family and finds herself unwillingly involved in prostitution. For more teen girls who face abuse and end up in the sex industry, try Shavon Moore's *Ecstasy* or Dejon's *My Skin Is My Sin*. For another story of a fearsome pimp and a woman working to escape his cruelty, try Erica Hilton's *Dirty Little Angel*.

Core Collection: Young Adult

Reasonable Doubt. **New York: St. Martin's Griffin, 2008. 327pp. ISBN 9780312340803, 031234080X.** ⚔ ⚔ ⚔ ❨

Katrina was a naïve freshman at NYU when she went on her first date with abusive, manipulative Snipes. Now Snipes is on the run from the feds. Katrina wants to get away, but Snipes has shown her what happens to snitches: he murders them. A believable and frightening depiction of an abusive relationship and its aftermath.

Keywords: Abuse; New York

Similar Reads: This book explores the emotional and psychological mechanics of an abusive relationship. For another dark look inside a violent relationship, try Nikki Turner's *A Project Chick* or Azárel's *Bruised*.

Core Collection: Adult; Young Adult; School Libraries

Azárel.

Daddy's House. **Brandywine, MD: Life Changing Books, 2007. 230pp. ISBN 9781934230916, 193423091X.** *ⱥ ⱥ ⱥ* ((

Candice, a former drug dealer, is on the run from her mother, a drug kingpin. Her mother, known as Big V on the streets, has been after Candice ever since she agreed to cooperate with the feds. When thugs break down the door of her Witness Protection Program apartment in Hamilton, New Jersey, Candice flees out the window in a nightgown. She calls her cousin Tracey for help, but when she gets to Tracey's place in Harlem, a pimp called Daddy is waiting to take her in. Can Candice survive the stress and humiliation of working in Daddy's House?

Keywords: Abuse; New York; Sex Industry

Similar Reads: *Daddy's House* is a suspenseful, brutal story of a woman coerced into prostitution. For more stories of unwilling prostitutes and their unpleasant working conditions, try C. Stecko's *Brooklyn Brothel* or Erica Hilton's *Dirty Little Angel*. Iceberg Slim's classic *Pimp* and Treasure Hernandez's *Pimp's Life* explore prostitution from the point of view of the pimp.

Core Collection: Adult

Bruised Series. *ⱥ ⱥ ⱥ* ((

This series follows Carlie, a woman being emotionally and physically abused by her lover Devon.

Keywords: Abuse; New York

Similar Reads: The <u>Bruised</u> series is about a woman caught in an abusive relationship and the friends and family who support her. For more about abusive relationships, try Mark Anthony's *Reasonable Doubt* or Nikki Turner's *Project Chick*. The short story collection *Breaking the Cycle* explores abuse from a variety of perspectives.

Core Collection: Adult

Bruised. Brandywine, MD: Life Changing Books, 2005. 284pp. ISBN 0974139424, 9780974139425.

When Carlie met Devon, she fell for him hard. Now, still young, Carlie finds herself constantly beaten and attacked by the man she loves. Her family, her friends, and the doctors and nurses who treat her after a particularly brutal incident all want the best for her, but it's hard to leave someone you love, especially if that someone is violent and dangerous.

Bruised 2: The Ultimate Revenge. Brandywine, MD: Life Changing Books, 2006. 232pp. ISBN 0974139475, 9780974139470.

In this second volume, Carlie has moved on to a new lover, but Devon is still determined to get her back, by violent means if necessary.

Coleman, JaQuavis.

The Dopeman's Wife. **West Babylon, NY: Urban Books, 2009. 230pp. ISBN 9781601621597, 1601621590.** *🖝 🖝* **⟮⟮**

Nautica and her cousin Khia hustle together. They work as strippers in the same club in Flint, Michigan, and plan together to seduce men and rob them. Then Nautica becomes involved with a devious, controlling man, Zion, who claims to be a drug dealer but is actually a thief. Zion crosses Khia, and in revenge for his transgression and his mistreatment of Nautica, the two women drug him and attempt to murder him. When Zion survives and kills Khia in retaliation, Nautica flees to New York. Can she start life anew, or will her past follow her?

Keywords: Abuse; Drug Addiction; Flint, MI; Sex Industry

Similar Reads: *The Dopeman's Wife* is a bleak, sexual, and violent tale of women out for money and men out for blood. For more women willing to drug men to rob them, try Anna J's *Get Money Chicks*. Tonya Ridley's *Talk of the Town* also explores what happens when a woman who hopes to seduce a man out of his money meets with violent retaliation. For another sexual but bleak tale about abusive relationships, try Noire's *G-Spot*.

DeJon.

My Skin Is My Sin. **Jamaica, NY: Q-Boro Books, 2007. 260pp. ISBN 9781933967202, 193396720X.** *🖝 🖝 🖝* **⟮⟮**

Pumpkin leaves home at age seventeen. Her mother has fallen prey to drug addiction, and at first Pumpkin gets sent to her aunt, but then her aunt's girlfriend molests her and steals her belongings. Without a dollar to her name, Pumpkin starts staying with her friend Dallisha and Dallisha's older sister. Known as Goldmine, Dallisha's sister got her name at the Atlanta strip club where she still rakes in money. Needing money, Pumpkin lets Goldmine bring her into the world of stripping for cash. In the meantime, a drug dealer called White Boy Danny is taking his racist hatred out on his clients. Scenes of brutal violence pepper this story of a teenage girl surviving the streets.

Keywords: Abuse; Atlanta; Sex Industry; Teenagers

Similar Reads: *My Skin Is My Sin* is a violent story of a teenage girl who becomes a stripper to survive. For more about teenage girls who become strippers, try Marlon McCaulsky's *Pink Palace*, Karen Williams's *People vs. Cashmere*, or Shannon Holmes's *Bad Girlz*.

Endy.

Deal with Death. **Bellport, NY: Melodrama Publishing, 2008. 350pp. ISBN 9781934157121, 1934157120.** 🚗🚗🚗 ⟮⟮

Nina is a high-functioning drug addict who manages to keep a job, be a mother to two teenage sons, and get high regularly. Then she sees Death, a sadistic heroin dealer with whom she has a past, brutally murder a rival gangster with a lethal injection. Disturbed and afraid, Nina becomes more dependent on heroin and less able to cope with the rest of her life. Meanwhile, her sons are getting into the game from the other side—as dealers. Complex family relationships and secrets from the past keep this longer read engaging.

Keywords: Drug Addiction; Newark, NJ; Prison

Similar Reads: *Deal with Death* is a longer read with themes of family relationships and drug addiction. For more close relationships between parents and their teen or adult children, try 50 Cent and Mark Anthony's *Harlem Heat* or Nikki Turner's *Black Widow*. For more about heroin addiction, try Kiki Swinson's *Candy Shop* or Donald Goines's classic, gritty *Dopefiend*.

In My Hood Series. 🚗🚗 ⟮⟮

This series about drug addiction and drug dealing is bleak and told from a variety of perspectives.

Keywords: Drug Addiction; Newark, NJ; Prison

Similar Reads: The In My Hood books are bleak stories of drug addiction from a variety of perspectives. For more on drug addiction, try Endy's *Deal with Death* or Tracy Brown's *White Lines*. For more bleakly rendered images of addiction and the living conditions of homeless drug addicts, try Donald Goines's *Dopefiend* or Treasure E. Blue's *Harlem Girl Lost*.

Core Collection: Adult

In My Hood. Bellport, NY: Melodrama Publishing, 2006. 219pp. ISBN 097-1702195, 9780971702196.

Desiree "Rae-Rae" Johnson is addicted to crack, and her childhood friend Bilal is addicted to heroin. Hoping for easy money, they try to rob a bank, but their efforts land them both in prison. Bilal commits suicide in prison, and Rae-Rae comes out sober but changed. She hooks up with a gangster named Ishmael, but she doesn't realize just how intimately her past and Ishmael's are connected. Short chapters and switches in perspective give the novel a fast-paced, almost jumpy feel.

In My Hood II. Bellport, NY: Melodrama Publishing, 2007. 256pp. ISBN 193-4157066, 9781934157060.

In this volume, a new cast of characters shakes up Newark, New Jersey, starting with Nettie rounding up her own crew.

In My Hood 3. Bellport, NY: Melodrama Publishing, 2009. 295pp. ISBN 9781934157626.

> Wahida Clark contributes an introduction to this third volume in this bleak series about drug addiction and drug dealing. In this installment, the son of Ishmael and Desiree struggles to make a life of his own, but his parents' legacy is stacked against him.

Goines, Donald.

Dopefiend. **Los Angeles: Holloway House, 2007 (1971). 319pp. ISBN 0870679384, 9780870679384.** 🖋🖋🖋 ((

In this gruesome, sensationalistic slice of life story from Detroit, a man named Porky runs a house where heroin users snort, shoot up, and degrade themselves for more hits. Terry and Teddy are a young couple. Teddy uses heroin regularly, and Terry only uses on occasion. But Porky has ulterior motives for wanting Terry to become addicted to heroin. He is attracted to her and hopes she will become dependent on his drug supply. As Terry's need for heroin grows, she becomes less and less in control of her life. Watch her hit rock bottom in Goines's classic.

Keywords: Abuse; Detroit; Drug Addiction

Similar Reads: *Dopefiend* is a brutal, sensationalistic story of a drug dealer who manipulates and degrades his clients. For more sensationalistic books about the cruelty shown to drug addicts, try Ace's *Predators* or Lisa Lennox's *Crack Head*. For more images of heroin-induced squalor, try Endy's *In My Hood* or Treasure E. Blue's *Harlem Girl Lost*.

Classic

Core Collection: Adult

Hernandez, Treasure.

Flint Series. 🖋🖋 ((

One of the closest series to a soap opera in the street lit genre, Flint is published in short installments that leave readers clamoring—sometimes with frustration—for more. Halleigh and Malek's love for each other, Halleigh's naïveté, and Malek's devotion to the woman he loves form the center of this series.

Keywords: Abuse; Flint, MI; Prison; Sex Industry; Teenagers

Similar Reads: The Flint series is a melodramatic saga featuring teenage lovers, prostitution, prison, and drug addiction. For more teenagers in love sticking up for each other, try Solomon Jones's *Ride or Die*, J. M. Benjamin's *Ride or Die Chick*, and Tracy Brown's *Black: A Street Tale*. For more brutal stories of prostitution, try C. Stecko's *Brooklyn Brothel*, Erica Hilton's *Dirty Little Angel*, or Azárel's *Daddy's House*.

Core Collection: Adult

Choosing Sides: Flint, Book 1. West Babylon, NY: Urban Books, 2009 (2008). 250pp. ISBN 9781601621719, 160162171X.

High schoolers Halleigh and Malek have a bright future together. Malek is the most talked about high school basketballer since LeBron James. Halleigh has been dating him for two years and is ready to take their relationship to the next physical level. Unfortunately, Halleigh's mother lost her job when Flint's General Motors plant closed and has become a drug addict who can barely fund her habit. The night Halleigh plans to have sex with Malek for the first time, her mother has run out of money and allows two drug dealers to rape her daughter instead. Hoping to put Halleigh up in a hotel for the night, Malek attempts to rob a convenience store. Malek is arrested and sent to prison, while Halleigh becomes involved with a dangerous pimp who promises to help her, for a price.

Working Girls: Flint, Book 2. West Babylon, NY: Urban Books, 2008. 227pp. ISBN 9781601620798, 1601620799.

In this volume, lovers Halleigh and Malek struggle to find each other as each ends up in a desperate situation.

Back to the Streets: Flint, Book 3. West Babylon, NY: Urban Books, 2008. 184pp. ISBN 9781601620804, 1601620802.

In this volume, Malek returns to his drug hustling, and Halleigh escapes Manolo, her ruthless pimp.

Resurrection: Flint, Book 4. West Babylon, NY: Urban Books, 2008. 178pp. ISBN 9781601620835, 1601620837.

In volume 4, high school sweethearts Halleigh and Malek are reunited, but life is still no fairy tale.

Back in the Hood: Flint, Book 5. West Babylon, NY: Urban Books, 2008. 199pp. ISBN 9781601621474, 1601621477.

Picking up after a cliffhanger ending in volume 4, volume 5 finds Halleigh pregnant and Malek hoping to pull off one big stunt to provide for her.

A King Is Born: Flint, Book 6. West Babylon, NY: Urban Books, 2009. 186pp. ISBN 9781601621696, 1601621698.

In this sixth installment, Halleigh is kidnapped by her enemies. Can Malek rescue her in time?

A Girl from Flint: Flint, Book 7. West Babylon, NY: Urban Books, 2010. 288pp. ISBN 9781601622617, 1601622619.

This seventh volume delivers all the action, betrayals, and romance that readers have come to expect.

Hilton, Erica.

Dirty Little Angel. **Bellport, NY: Melodrama Publishing, 2008. 283pp. ISBN 9781934157190, 1934157198.** ☞ ☞ ☞ 〔〔

Danielle Chaos Mitchell was born in a rat-infested, abandoned building in the Bronx while her mother turned a trick. Left to foster care at age five, Chaos grew up fast. Now, at nineteen, she is one of the top moneymakers for a ruthless pimp called Crown. Believing that whores are "like livestock," Crown keeps his women dependent on and obedient to him, while hustling the customers at his Philadelphia club into paying extra for their premium services. Chaos sees a way out in YB, a drug dealer and one of the few men who isn't afraid of Crown. What neither Chaos nor YB realizes is that Crown is not easily escaped.

Keywords: Abuse; Philadelphia; Sex Industry

Similar Reads: *Dirty Little Angel* is the story of a brutal pimp and a woman determined to survive and escape his cruelty. For more cruel pimps, try Treasure Hernandez's *Pimp's Life* or the classics *Pimp* by Iceberg Slim and *Whoreson* by Donald Goines. For more about trying to escape prostitution, try C. Stecko's *Brooklyn Brothel* or Miasha's *Sistah for Sale*.

Holmes, Shannon.

Bad Girlz Series. ☞ ☞ 〔〔

The first *Bad Girlz* was one of the first street novels to be picked up by a major publisher. The series stars Tonya, better known as Tender, a teenage girl who becomes a stripper after running away from an abusive home situation.

Keywords: Abuse; Philadelphia; Sex Industry; Street Code; Teenagers; Women Hustlers

Similar Reads: The Bad Girlz series is about abuse, betrayal, and the ins and outs of working as a stripper. For more on teen girls who become strippers out of necessity, try Shavon Moore's *Ecstasy* or Marlon McCaulsky's *Pink Palace*. For more about devious business partners, try Dejon's *My Skin Is My Sin* or Tonya Ridley's *Talk of the Town*.

Core Collection: Adult; Young Adult

Bad Girlz. **New York: Atria Books, 2003. 208pp. ISBN 074348620X, 9780743486200.**

Bad Girlz begins with a horrific act of abuse. The stepfather of teenage Tonya gives her a laced joint and then repeatedly violates her nearly unconscious body. When Tonya comes to, her mother refuses to believe Tonya's story and kicks her daughter out of the house. Kat, a stripper, finds Tonya and gives her a place to stay, a job in a strip club, and a new name: Tender. Kat teaches Tender the ins and outs of working as a stripper, but she has a few tricks of her own up her sleeve.

1

2

3

4

5

6

7

8

9

10

11

Bad Girlz 4 Life. New York: St. Martin's Griffin, 338pp. ISBN 9780312359027, 0312359020.

In the first volume of *Bad Girlz*, innocent Tonya became street-savvy stripper Tender. In this sequel, a hardened Tender is back, and though she wants to quit stripping, she finds herself once again in the business.

Johnson, Keith Lee.

Little Black Girl Lost Series. ⚓⚓ ((

Growing up in 1950s New Orleans, fifteen year-old Johnnie is a devout Christian. Her mother Marguerite, however, is a business-minded prostitute. Marguerite inducts Johnnie into the family business by selling her virginity to a white man when Johnnie is only fifteen. At first miserable, Johnnie learns to cope with her circumstances and make her own way in life.

Keywords: 1950s; New Orleans; Sex Industry; Teenagers

Similar Reads: Little Black Girl Lost is a multi-installment series set in 1950s New Orleans with themes of abuse and prostitution. For another story set in the 1950s, try Jihad's *MVP*. For more about young women unwillingly sold into prostitution, try Miasha's *Sistah for Sale* or Azárel's *Daddy's House*. For another multi-volume series about teenagers in painful situations, try Treasure Hernandez's Flint series.

Little Black Girl Lost. West Babylon, NY: Urban Books, 2005. 371pp. ISBN 0974702552, 9780974702551.

> This series, set in the 1950s, stars Johnnie, a young black woman sold into prostitution at age fifteen. In this first volume, Johnnie's mother sells her virginity to the notorious Earl Shamus, and Johnnie attracts the attention of the dangerous Napoleon Bentley.

Little Black Girl Lost 2. West Babylon, NY: Urban Books, 2006. 372pp. ISBN 1893196399, 9781893196391.

> In this volume, Johnnie's affections are caught between two dangerous men.

Little Black Girl Lost 3. West Babylon, NY: Urban Books, 2007 (2006). 294pp. ISBN 189319678X, 9781893196780.

> In this volume, a hardened Johnnie faces criminal intrigue and a police investigation.

Little Black Girl Lost 4: The Diary of Josephine Baptiste. West Babylon, NY: Urban Books, 2009. 245pp. ISBN 9781601621498, 1601621493.

> In its first three volumes, the series starred Johnnie, a young black woman sold into prostitution at age fifteen. Subtitled *The Diary of Josephine Baptiste*, this volume focuses on Johnnie's grandmother, a Nigerian girl captured and sold into slavery in New Orleans.

Jolie, Chantel.

In Those Jeans. Brandywine, MD: Life Changing Books, 2008. 229pp. ISBN 9781934230848, 1934230847. ☞ ☞ ☞ ❨❨

Chanel is a woman with expensive taste . . . and a few fake credit cards to fund her clothing habit. When she gets arrested in a department store in Detroit, Chanel flees to Atlanta in search of a way to make a living, and to avoid jail . . . not a good place for a woman like her, she tells the reader. In Atlanta, Chanel finds work in the Magic City strip club. But there's tension between the strippers and among the clientele. Chanel becomes involved with a client named Samuel, but both lovers have something to hide. When their secrets are revealed, the fallout is explosive.

Keywords: Abuse; Atlanta; Detroit; GLBTQ; Sex Industry; Street Code; Women Hustlers

Similar Reads: *In Those Jeans* is a chatty story of a materialistic, image-conscious woman and competition at a strip club. For more brand-name conscious female characters, try Tiphani's *Expensive Taste* or Miasha's *Secret Society*. For more behind-the-scenes competition at strip clubs, try Marlon McCaulsky's *Pink Palace* or Shannon Holmes's *Bad Girlz*.

Lynch, Tanika.

Whore. Columbus, OH: Triple Crown Publications, 2006. 263pp. ISBN 0976789469, 9780976789468. ☞ ☞ ☞ ❨❨

In this relentlessly bleak tale, fourteen year-old Kamone is responsible for Paul and Ivory, her two little siblings. Their mother, Suga, is a prostitute working for a madam called Mama Cookie. Suga, a drug addict, doesn't keep enough food in the house and sometimes lets her tricks touch Kamone too, for the right price. Then Suga tests positive for HIV, and Kamone reveals her diagnosis to the other prostitutes who work for Mama Cookie. Suga flees, and Kamone is left to provide for her siblings. Unable to make money legally and unwilling to let the state split up the family, Kamone turns to prostitution. The other prostitutes turn her onto drugs as a way of making sex with strangers bearable, and a new cycle of violence, addiction, and misery is born.

Keywords: Abuse; Detroit; Drug Addiction; Sex Industry; Street Code; Teenagers

Similar Reads: *Whore* is a brutal, harsh story of the desperation of a teen girl providing for her two younger siblings. For more about teenagers forced into harsh situations to support their families, try Miasha's *Mommy's Angel* or Anna J's *Snow White*.

Madlock, Felicia.

Back on the Block. **West Babylon, NY: Urban Books, 2007 (2005). 202pp. ISBN 1893196267, 9781893196261.** ☞ ☞ ((

After a few years away from Chicago, the town where she and her sister Tracey grew up with an abusive, alcoholic mother, Reese is home. Clean after a drug treatment program, she's come to reach out to her sister, who's still smoking crack and turning tricks. But not everyone's thrilled about Reese's return—not Tracey; not Jamal Winters, the pimp for whom Reese would have done anything in the old days; and definitely not David Davenport, the cop who believes Jamal and Reese are responsible for his brother's murder. Interpersonal relationships and looming suspense dominate this street thriller.

Keywords: Abuse; Chicago; Drug Addiction; Revenge; Sex Industry

Similar Reads: *Back on the Block* is a suspenseful story about rival sisters, cops, and drug addiction. For more pulpy, drug-related action set in Chicago, try Tony Lindsay's *Street Possession*. For more suspenseful takes on addiction, try Endy's *Deal with Death* or Kiki Swinson's *Candy Shop*.

Sins of the Father. **West Babylon, NY: Urban Books, 2006 (2004). 283pp. ISBN 1893196623, 9781893196629.** ☞ ((

The death of Samuel "Street" Jamieson sends the lives of his many family members in very different directions. Terrance and Malik, the two adult sons Street abandoned, continue to be angry. Nadine, the woman whose life he ruined, grieves for Street anyway. Sammie Junior, Street's child who is in sixth grade, is sent to live with his aunt Crystal, a woman with a drug addiction who lives in a notorious housing project on Chicago's South Side. Each family member copes with the past and the present in a different way.

Keywords: Chicago; Drug Addiction; Teenagers

Similar Reads: *Sins of the Father* is a family saga dealing with themes of death, abuse, and absent fathers. For another son struggling with his father's abandoning him, try Leo Sullivan's *Innocent*. For another boy sent to live with relatives in a housing project, try C-Murder's *Death Around the Corner*.

McCaulsky, Marlon.

The Pink Palace. **Columbus, OH: Triple Crown Publications, 2008. 247pp. ISBN 9780979951756, 0979951755.** ☞ ☞ ((

Janelle Taylor never intended to be a stripper. But when her cop stepfather took advantage of her, she realized she had to leave home. After two years of staying with friends, Janelle makes her way to Atlanta to live with her cousin Nikki. Nikki introduces her to stripping at a club called the Pink Palace, and Janelle's sexy alter ego Mo'Nique is born. In the meantime, Jayson Harper, an undercover cop who goes by the name Tommy, is trying to infiltrate an Atlanta drug operation. A dealer, Damien, brings Tommy to the Pink Palace, and he and Mo'Nique hit it off. Their relationship heats up, but what will happen when the truth about Tommy's identity comes out? Told from multiple characters' points of view, this well-spun tale includes sex, drama, drug dealing, and going undercover.

Keywords: Abuse; Atlanta; Multiple Perspectives; Sex Industry; Teenagers

Similar Reads: *The Pink Palace* is the story of a likable teenager who unwillingly becomes a stripper. For more kind, sympathetic teenage characters, try Cynthia White's *Queen* or Karen Williams's *People vs. Cashmere*. For more about teenage girls becoming strippers to support themselves, try Shannon Holmes's *Bad Girlz* or, for a more brutal take, Dejon's *My Skin Is My Sin*.

Core Collection: Adult; Young Adult

Miasha.

Mommy's Angel. **New York: Simon & Schuster, 2007. 211pp. ISBN 978-1416542483, 1416542485.** ☞ ☞ ☞ ((

After her older brother Curtis is shot and killed, fifteen year-old Angel's family falls apart. Her mom becomes addicted to heroin. Her stepfather molests Angel and her twelve-year-old sister Naja. There is never money for food. Angel takes the money situation into her own hands by getting her brother's former best friend to get her a job as a stripper. The money is good, but the cost is high. A quick, bleak read about family, desperation, and the devastating effects of drug addiction.

Keywords: Brooklyn, NY; Drug Addiction; Sex Industry; Teenagers

Similar Reads: *Mommy's Angel* uses a smooth narrative voice similar to that in Miasha's *Sistah for Sale*. More stories of teenage girls fending for themselves in the face of drug-addicted family members include Karen Williams's *Harlem on Lock* and Tanika Lynch's *Whore*.

Core Collection: Adult; Young Adult

Moore, Y. Blak.

Slipping. **New York: One World/Ballantine Books, 2005. 273pp. ISBN 0345475941, 9780345475947.** ☞ ☞ ☞ ((

Don-Don Haskill is a seventeen-year-old growing up with his mother and older sister in Chicago. At age four, he found his father's body on the roof of his building, dead by suicide. Now Don-Don hangs out with his friends, playing basketball and smoking weed. Don-Don's downfall begins one day on the courts when he meets sexy Juanita and takes her to a party. Juanita smokes premos—weed laced with crack—and convinces Don-Don to smoke one with her. From that day on, Don-Don is hooked. Getting crack at any cost becomes the number one goal of his grim and desperate life.

Keywords: Chicago; Drug Addiction; Teenagers

Similar Reads: *Slipping* is a grim cautionary tale about the devastating effects of drug addiction. For more on teenagers becoming dangerously addicted to hard drugs, try Tracy Brown's emotional *White Lines* or Lisa Lennox's sensationalistic <u>Crack Head</u> series.

Core Collection: Young Adult

Poole, Jason.

Victoria's Secret. **Owings Mills, MD: The Cartel Publications, 2008. 224pp. ISBN 9780979493140, 0979493145.** ☞☞ ❨❨

Victoria is in the hospital in a coma, and her man and pimp Babyface comes to visit her. In the hospital room, he finds Victoria's diary, which provides the frame for the novel. Looking back, we learn about Victoria's childhood, her abuse, and her time in a group home. We learn how Babyface rescues her from an attempted rape, and how Victoria becomes a high-end prostitute in Washington, D.C. Reconnecting with her friends from the group home, Victoria works alongside them for a while, until disagreements cause them to part ways and set in motion a quest for revenge, with deadly consequences.

Keywords: Abuse; Sex Industry; Street Code; Washington, DC

Similar Reads: *Victoria's Secret* tells the story of the abuse and ill treatment of a child through a woman's diary. For more on childhood abuse, try Jihad's *Baby Girl* or Antoine "Inch" Thomas's *Flower's Bed.* Sherrie Walker's *Mistress of the Game* also deals with children living in a group home. Readers who enjoy the diary conceit might enjoy other stories told through diaries, including Ashley and JaQuavis's *Diary of a Street Diva* and Miasha's *Diary of a Mistress.*

Quartay, Nane.

The Badness. **Largo, MD: Strebor Books, 2005. 218pp. ISBN 1593090374, 9781593090371.** ☞☞ ❨

Just after the Civil War, Jefferson Browne made the mistake of telling his aunt Ruby-Ruby that he didn't believe in voodoo. Ruby-Ruby cursed him and all the firstborn sons in his line. Now, in the year 2000, that curse has fallen on Alias. Alias imbues dollar bills with the power of the curse, and those bills find Doin, who has just fallen in love with the compelling Joozy. Finally D. Wayne, driven mad by the syphilis he got from his alcoholic, abusive mother, becomes a ruthless killer who thinks he's following the will of his god. Flashes back to the Civil War and between these unhappy characters give the book an eerie and disturbing feel.

Keywords: Abuse; Historical Fiction; Paranormal Fiction

Similar Reads: *The Badness* is an eerie, supernatural story with themes of haunting and child abuse. For other characters haunted by ghosts or visions, try Kenji Jasper's *Snow* or C-Murder's *Death Around the Corner.* For more stories of boys suffering from child abuse, try Noire's erotic *Hood* or Iceberg Slim's classic *Pimp.* Evie Rhodes's *Expired* is another eerie ghost story.

Raye, Sasha.

From Hood to Hollywood. **Brandywine, MD: Life Changing Books, 2009.** 249pp. ISBN 9781934230800, 1934230804. ☞ ☞ ⟨⟨

Once upon a time, Demi had a posh apartment in New York's Chelsea neighborhood and access to all the fancy clothes, jewelry, and cars she could ever want. Then her drug-dealing boyfriend Perry got arrested, and Demi and her five-year-old daughter moved back in with her family in the projects. Between her mother, who does sex work in the house; her brother, who spends his days smoking weed and watching porn; and her daughter, who might be autistic and always needs a babysitter, Demi has her hands full. Then one night at a club, she meets Jorel, a film producer who tells her she might have what it takes to be in the movies. Will Demi finally get a break?

Keywords: Film Industry; Los Angeles; New York

Similar Reads: *From Hood to Hollywood* is a story of being broke, family tension, and the seedy entertainment industry. For more families living together and arguing, try Alastair J. Hatter's *It's On and Poppin'* or Allison Hobbs's *Bona Fide Gold Digger.* For more on the sleazy entertainment business, try K. Roland Williams's *Cut Throat* or Thomas Long's *Cash Rules.*

Stecko, C.

Brooklyn Brothel. **Brandywine, MD: Life Changing Books, 2009.** 227pp. ISBN 9781934230787, 1934230782. ☞ ☞ ⟨⟨

Chantel is twenty-three but feels more like an eighteen-year-old girl than an independent woman. When Bo, the man she believes loves her, sends her to New York to make money as a prostitute, Chantel does as she is told. She is taken to an "in-house" run by a ruthless madam named Betty. Chantel, who takes the name Co-Co, learns the rules of sex work the hard way. She has sex with men who smell, men who hurt her, and men who give her crabs, while Betty mistreats her, Bo betrays her, and the man who has custody of her children keeps her apart from the family she loves most. A grim cautionary tale and introduction to the unglamorous side of the sex trade.

Keywords: Brooklyn, NY; Prison; Sex Industry; Street Code

Similar Reads: *Brooklyn Brothel* is the gritty, painful story of a naïve woman coerced into prostitution by a loved one. For more stories of women forced into the sex trade against their will, try Azárel's *Daddy's House* or Miasha's *Sistah for Sale.* Sidi's <u>Fatou</u> series features a similar story of a girl entering a house of women and being forced to learn the rules.

1

2

3

4

5

6

7

8

9

10

11

Short Stories and Anthologies

The lone title in this section contains short stories in the hard times subgenre.

Zane, ed.

Breaking the Cycle. **Largo, MD: Strebor Books, 2005 (2004). 229pp. ISBN 159-3090218, 9781593090210.** ☞ ☞ ℂℂ

Zane is the editor of this collection, but rather than focus on the sexual pleasure of the reader, this anthology collects stories of abuse at the hands of intimate partners and family members. Readers are invited to break the cycle and find ways to stand strong against the forces that allow people to be victimized. Men, women, parents, and children all face abuse and cruelty in these eight painful stories. Zane contributes a heartfelt introduction and a list of resources for anyone facing similar situations.

Keywords: Abuse; Multiple Authors; Overcoming Adversity; Short Stories

Similar Reads: Street lit is full of portrayals of abuse and victimization, including Antoine "Inch" Thomas's *Flower's Bed*, Azárel's *Bruised*, and Nikki Turner's *Project Chick*. For more on how it feels to "break the cycle," try Dywayne D. Birch's *Beneath the Bruises*, which focuses on a woman's therapeutic journey to healing from abuse.

Chapter 8

Prison

Arrest, incarceration, the justice system, and returning home after a prison term are common themes in street lit, but in the prison subgenre, these concerns take center stage. Some novels in this subgenre focus on life inside prison, while others show characters returning home from a prison term and rebuilding their lives.

Main characters in the prison subgenre are often male, but the subgenre also features notable female characters, including Candy, the transsexual heroine forced into a men's prison in Damon "Amin" Meadows and Jason Poole's *Convict's Candy*, and Eve, the revenge-driven leader of a fearsome clique in K'wan's *Eve*.

Well-known novels in the prison subgenre include K'wan's *Road Dawgz* and Asante Kahari's *Homo Thug*.

Life on the Inside

Novels in this section focus on the shape of daily life within a prison, including political or religious beliefs acquired in prison, homosexuality in prison, or the dangerous situations of characters targeted for abuse because of their sexuality or gender.

50 Cent and Relentless Aaron.

Derelict. **New York: Pocket Books, 2007. 227pp. ISBN 9781416549499, 1416549498.** ☞ ⟨⟨

Jamel Ross used to have it all: a multi-million-dollar music business, multiple women, and celebrity status. Now he's behind bars, caught writing bad checks. As a prisoner, Jamel has designs on the prison psychologist, Dr. Kay Edmonson. Switching between Jamel's and Dr. Edmonson's perspectives, Relentless Aaron shows the psychologist's seduction at the hands of a former playboy—a series of events that may be unrealistic but are extremely satisfying for Jamel and the readers who sympathize with him.

Keywords: Fort Dix, NJ; Multiple Perspectives; Music Industry; Prison

Similar Reads: *Derelict* is a novella about a man seducing a woman from the perspective of both parties. For more fantasies about men's sexual influence over women, try Quentin Carter's Hoodwinked series or Victor L. Martin's *Hood Legend*. For more about romance from both parties' perspectives, try T. N. Baker's *Dice* or Erick S. Gray's *Booty Call *69*.

Brandie.

The Clique. **West Babylon, NY: Urban Books, 2008. 264pp. ISBN 9781601620330, 1601620330.** ☞ ☞ ☞ ❨❨

Atlanta hustler Spencer was there for Mo when her own mother abandoned her. Only problem is, he was there for a lot of other women, too. Spencer has children all around the city, and each of their mamas wants a piece of Spencer's love, attention, and money. Finally a fight breaks out among four women, with Mo and her best friend Royal on one side and Spencer's one-time lover Emil and her weak friend Pepper on the other. Someone gets stabbed, and that's when the police show up. In jail, the former enemies realize the only way to survive is to "clique up" and look out for each other. But how long will their alliance last?

Keywords: Atlanta; Prison

Similar Reads: *The Clique* is a high-drama tale featuring a crew of women, but the joy is in watching the women fight over their man. For more women fighting over men, try Wahida Clark and Kiki Swinson's *Sleeping with the Enemy* or Tu-Shonda L. Whitaker's *Ex Factor*. For more women who become a crew after first being enemies, try Erick S. Gray's *Nasty Girls* or Eyone Williams's *Hell Razor Honeys*.

Gray, Erick S.

Money Power Respect. **Jamaica, NY: Q-Boro Books, 2008 (2005). 244pp. ISBN 1933967366, 9781933967363.** ☞ ☞ ❨❨

At just fifteen, Ricky Johnson is on top of his game. Ushered into a position of power in the Queens drug trade by an older hustler called Fat Tony, Ricky runs a tight organization and spends his money on sneakers, chains, and good clothes. Then his partner Kinko warns him that a rival dealer, Heavy, is moving in on their territory. Ricky and Kinko go an a mission to Far Rockaway to take out Heavy. The police get wind of their plan, and Ricky is arrested and sent to jail. A teacher, Mr. Jenkins, tries to help Ricky get his GED and go down a legitimate path, but the lure of money, power, and respect may just be too tempting.

Keywords: Queens, NY; Social Commentary; Teenagers

Similar Reads: *Money Power Respect* is a coming-of-age story about a teenage hustler, told in a narrative voice that critiques street life. For more teenage boys becoming successful hustlers, try Erica Hilton's *10 Crack Commandments* or Ed McNair's *My Time to Shine*. For more critiques of street life, try Gray's *Crave All, Lose All* or Shannon Holmes's *Never Go Home Again*.

Core Collection: Young Adult

Jihad.

Riding Rhythm. **West Babylon, NY: Urban Books, 2006. 303pp. ISBN 1893196488, 9781893196483.** 🖝 (

It's the 1960s, and young Moses is speaking up for freedom and Black Power. He founds a gang called the Disciples, which is intended to serve Chicago's black community but instead turns violent. Then racist cops arrest Moses and convict him of a crime he did not commit: the murder of a congressman and the rape of his wife. In prison, Moses continues to fight for justice with the help of fellow inmates and a student named Rhythm Azure, whom he comes to know spiritually through letter writing.

Keywords: 1960s; Chicago; Historical Fiction; Social Commentary

Similar Reads: *Riding Rhythm* is a contemplative, socially conscious, historical novel. For more books that explore racism and Black Power, try Ace's *Predators*, Leo Sullivan's *Life*, or Nathan McCall's memoir *Makes Me Wanna Holler*. For street fiction set in the 1950s and 1960s, try Donald Goines's classic pulp novels, Keith Lee Johnson's <u>Little Black Girl Lost</u> series, or Jihad's *MVP*.

Joy.

Dollar Bill. **Columbus, OH: Triple Crown Publications, 2003. 267pp. ISBN 097024729X, 9780970247292.** 🖝🖝 ((

Dareese, aka Dollar Bill, is an eighteen-year-old stickup artist. Working with his two partners, tomboyish Tommy and white Ral Kennedy, who likes to joke that he's related to JFK, Dollar decides to decides to move up from stealing cars to stealing cash and jewelry from Cartel, the man he steals cars for. The robbery goes awry, and Dollar kills three men. He is arrested and put in prison, where he learns the true meaning of not getting caught slipping. An action-packed story of staying alert and staying one step ahead, both in and out of jail.

Keywords: Gary, IN; Street Code

Similar Reads: *Dollar Bill* is an action-packed, plot-driven story of overconfident teenage hustlers and the necessity of watching your back in prison and on the streets. For more arrogant hustlers, try 50 Cent and K'wan's *Blow* or Erica Hilton's *10 Crack Commandments*. For more about the dangers of life inside prison, try Asante Kahari's *Homo Thug* or Damon "Amin" Meadows and Jason Poole's *Convict's Candy*.

Classic

Kahari, Asante.

Homo Thug. **Brooklyn, NY: Black Print Publishing, ISBN 0974805165, 9780974805160.** 🖝🖝 ((

Homo Thug is an underground classic story of a male prisoner discovering his sexuality and questioning his manhood. Michael Fraser is a teenager when he first gets sent from Sparford juvenile facility to Sing Sing prison in upstate New York. He's never been with a woman but thinks he would like to, and he's both fascinated and horrified when he sees a sexual and romantic relationship between two men at Sparford. At Sing Sing, an older Muslim inmate named Mustafa takes Michael under his wing and asks only that he never give into the temptation of having sex with another man. At the same time, Michael is consumed with lust for Dee Dee, an inmate who looks like a woman and just might give Michael what he wants, for a price. Though currently out of print, this novel is a classic in its subgenre. Emotional, keen observations of prison life and deep uncertainty about homosexuality and manhood keep the story real and intense.

Keywords: GLBTQ; New York

Similar Reads: *Homo Thug* is a story of a young man questioning his sexuality and the dynamics inside prison walls. For another young man finding love inside prison walls, try Clarence Nero's Three Sides to Every Story series. For more about the hardships of being in prison, try Joy's *Dollar Bill* or Damon "Amin" Meadows and Jason Poole's *Convict's Candy*.

Meadows, Damon "Amin," and Jason Poole.

Convict's Candy. New York: Ghettoheat, 2007 (2006). ISBN 0974298220, 9780974298221. *&r &r* ((

In this harrowing but sympathetic tale, a transsexual woman navigates life inside a men's prison. One week before she is scheduled for surgery that would confirm her as a woman in the eyes of the law, Candy Sweets is arrested for credit card fraud and sent to prison . . . a men's prison. Behind bars, homophobia and transphobia abound, as do the threat of rape and the fear of HIV infection. Candy is a strong-willed, sensitively portrayed character, and readers will empathize with her chatty, conversational narrative voice.

Keywords: Abuse; GLBTQ; Teenagers

Similar Reads: *Convict's Candy* is a conversational story about a transsexual woman and the struggles of prison life. For more about feminine characters surviving men's prisons, try Clarence Nero's *Three Sides to Every Story*. For other GLBTQ transsexual women heroines, try Miasha's *Secret Society* or Chantel Jolie's *In Those Jeans*.

Core Collection: Adult

Nero, Clarence.

Three Sides to Every Story Series. *&r &r* ((

Two strong themes dominate this character-focused series: love, both romantic and among family; and shattering stereotypes about sexuality, HIV, and being a man.

Keywords: GLBTQ; Multiple Perspectives; New Orleans; Sex Industry; Washington, DC

Similar Reads: The <u>Three Sides to Every Story</u> series is a character-driven exploration of male bisexuality, family, and life inside prison. For more about homosexuality inside prison walls, try Asante Kahari's *Homo Thug*. For another story of a man trying to make sense of his family and his attraction to other men, try Mike Warren's <u>Private Affair</u> series.

Core Collection: Adult

Three Sides to Every Story: A Novel. New York: Harlem Moon, 2006. 332pp. ISBN 0767921364, 9780767921367.

> In the Ninth Ward of New Orleans, each member of a bisexual love triangle tells his or her story. Johnny tries to save his high school girlfriend Tonya from her violent ex-boyfriend and ends up sentenced to five years for assault at the notorious Sierra Leone prison in rural Louisiana. Tonya gets work as a stripper but stops writing to Johnny after a sleazy but rich hip-hop star makes her his girl and pays her to dance in videos. James, an effeminate gay man and member of the House of Craft—an alternative gay family headed by fierce drag queen Pandora Craft—meets Johnny in prison, and the two form an intellectual and emotional friendship. Although Johnny at first tries to deny his attraction to James, the relationship soon becomes physical.

Too Much of a Good Thing Ain't Bad. New York: Broadway Books, 2009. 235pp. ISBN 9780767929721 0767929721.

> In the first volume, *Three Sides to Every Story*, Johnny found himself caught in a love triangle between his high school girlfriend Tonya and James, a man he met in prison. In this volume, after Hurricane Katrina wreaks havoc on New Orleans, Johnny and James move to Washington, D.C., where Johnny's family try to steer Johnny away from James and toward heterosexuality.

Sullivan, Leo.

Innocent. **Columbus, OH: Triple Crown Publications, 2009. 298pp. ISBN 9780982099643, 0982099649.** 🖝 🖝 ❨❨

This saga of wrongful imprisonment and interpersonal drama centers on two characters, I.C. Miller and Tamara Jenkins. I.C., whose first initial stands for Innocent, fathered Tamara's child in high school but refused to take responsibility or even admit that the child was his. At just shy of eighteen, I.C. gets arrested by racist cops and convicted of a crime he did not commit, a rape and murder at a Dairy Queen. Tamara, now a single mother struggling for money and willing to get it by any means necessary, except for a minimum wage job, gets involved with Pharoah, a sexy but dangerous man. When I.C. and Tamara's paths cross once again, the stakes are high. Can they save each other from a deadly fate?

Keywords: Atlanta; Contemplative; Multiple Perspectives; Social Commentary

Similar Reads: *Innocent* is a story told from two contrasting perspectives, one contemplative, the other full of drama and attitude. For another contemplative take on fatherhood, try Felicia Madlock's *Sins of the Father*. For more characters with attitude like Tamara's, try K'wan's *Hood Rat* or Erick S. Gray's *Nasty Girls*.

Core Collection: Adult

Life After Prison

Novels in this section focus on life after prison: characters getting revenge on the parties they believe are responsible for their imprisonment, struggling to deal with the changes that have happened in the outside world while they were away, or joyously returning home to a warm, loving welcome.

Ashley and JaQuavis.

The Trophy Wife. West Babylon, NY: Urban Books, 2008. 216pp. ISBN 9781601620514, 1601620519. 🖋🖋 ((

Once a top-of-the-line hustler, Kalil gets out of prison to find himself at the bottom of the food chain. Fatboy, whom Kalil never respected, is on top. Fatboy's selling weak drugs, and worse, Kalil's cousin is working for him. Worse still, Kalil comes home to find his former wifey, Destiny, sleeping with Fatboy. Despite his anger, Kalil wants to stay on the straight and narrow to stay in his young daughter's life. But when Fatboy crosses a line, Kalil vows to retaliate. Meanwhile London, a sexy dance instructor, is being abused by her husband, and Kalil thinks he can help, but his two goals have more in common than he knows. In a fresh twist, Ashley and JaQuavis themselves appear as characters.

Keywords: Abuse; New York; Revenge; Street Code

Similar Reads: *The Trophy Wife* is a violent story about coming back to the outside world after being in prison, with themes of abuse and revenge. For more about reentering the world after prison and finding that things have changed, try Lena Scott's *O. G.* For more about revenge, try 50 Cent and Noire's *Baby Brother* or Y. Blak Moore's *Triple Take*. Michael Covington's *Chances* and Danette Majette's *Good Girl Gone Bad* also feature characters who are being abused.

Black, Sonny F.

Gangsta Bitch. Newark, NJ: Black Dawn Books, 2008. 198pp. ISBN 1599713241, 9781599713243. 🖋🖋🖋 ((

In the first novel from prolific author K'wan's Black Dawn Books, Duce, aka D-Murder, is out of jail and back on the streets of New York. He comes home to a large cast of characters, most notably Frankie Five-Fingers, an ice cold female hustler and self-proclaimed gangsta bitch. Raw violence, drama, and sex abound.

Keywords: Multiple Perspectives; New York

Similar Reads: *Gangsta Bitch* features a ruthless, street-savvy female hustler and a wide array of characters. For more women like Frankie Five-Fingers, try Teri Woods's *Angel* or Joy King's <u>Stackin' Paper</u> series. For more novels with a wide variety of characters and perspectives, try Kevin Bullock's *In the Cut* or Mike Sanders's *Thirsty*.

Bullock, Kevin.

In the Cut. **Charlotte, NC: Urban Lifestyle Press, 2006. 228pp. ISBN 0971769737, 9780971769731.** 🖋🖋 ((

When he leaves prison before his buddy Manus, Brad promises he'll keep in touch. But once Brad gets out, there's enough drama—and enough women—to keep him busy. High for the first time on ecstasy, Brad has sex with Gloria, the woman who helped put him in prison, and the next night a gunfight breaks out between Brad and L, Gloria's main man. Brad is killed, and Manus and his hustling take center stage in this outrageous—if sometimes clumsy—drama.

Keywords: Durham, NC; Light Reads; Multiple Perspectives

Similar Reads: *In the Cut* is a high-drama story featuring a variety of characters and comically inept men. For more inept hustlers, try 50 Cent and K'wan's *Blow*. For more novels featuring a wide variety of characters, try Sonny F. Black's *Gangsta Bitch* or Mike Sanders's *Thirsty*.

Covington, Michael.

Chances. **Columbus, OH: Triple Crown Publications, 2007. 240pp. ISBN 9780976789475, 0976789477.** 🖋🖋 ((

Released after five years in prison, DeAndre comes back to his old Chicago neighborhood. A few of the girls he used to see are still there and ready to welcome Dre home. Dre's sister Dee Dee is waiting for him too, but she's now involved with a violent hustler. Dre's reentry into the free world is full of women and parties but also protecting Dee Dee, no matter what the cost.

Keywords: Abuse; Chicago; Light Reads

Similar Reads: *Chances* is drama from a male perspective with themes of abuse, family, and returning home after prison. For more lighter drama featuring male characters, try Rahsaan Ali's *Selfish Intentions* or David Givens's *Betrayed*. For more on domestic abuse, try JaQuavis Coleman's *Dopeman's Wife* or Azárel's *Bruised*.

Freeze.

Against the Grain. **New York: One World/Ballantine Books, 2008. 279pp. ISBN 9780345503619, 0345503619.** 🖋 (

After a bank robbery, Kay spent almost ten years in prison with his best friend's death on his conscience. Finally free, he comes back to Baltimore to a warm welcome, a son he's never met, and a place ready for him in the drug game. Kay is a kindhearted gangster who once helped a pair of sisters who were starving while their addicted mother spent the last of the family's money on heroin. Now he's sucked into yet more high-stakes crime. And with the feds on his organization's tail, it's only a matter of time before he's called in to make one of the hardest choices a gangster—and a friend—can make.

Keywords: Baltimore; Street Code; Washington, DC

Similar Reads: *Against the Grain* is a novel about warm friendships, the joy of returning home after prison, and trying to stay ahead of the FBI. For more on returning home to friends after prison, try K'wan's *Road Dawgz* or Leondrei Prince's *Bloody Money*. For more organizations under FBI scrutiny, try Relentless Aaron's *Last Kingpin* or Danette Majette's *Deep*.

Holmes, Shannon.

Never Go Home Again. **New York: Atria, 2006 (2004). 336pp. ISBN 0743496167, 9780743496162.** ⌨ (

Corey Dixon is a smart sixteen-year-old who could have a bright future. Instead, he gets locked up for selling crack. When he gets out of prison, a teacher warns him to stay free, but he slips easily back into his old ways. Holmes's cautionary tale shows the hold of the drug game and prison life on a young man. Can Corey escape before it's too late?

Keywords: Bronx, NY; Mentors; Social Commentary; Street Code; Teenagers

Similar Reads: *Never Go Home Again* is a cautionary tale about a teen boy drawn to street life and the mentor who tries to steer him straight. For more about teenagers and the mentors concerned for their future, try Dana Dane's *Numbers* or Divine G's *Baby Doll*. For another cautionary tale warning teenage boys away from street life, try Erick S. Gray's *Money Power Respect*.

Core Collection: Young Adult; School Libraries

K'wan.

Eve. **New York: St. Martin's Griffin, 2006. 326pp. ISBN 0312333102, 9780312333102.** ⌨ ⌨ ((

Eve Panelli is eighteen years old and freshly released from prison. When she gets out, her grudges, memories, and prior allegiances come with her. Eve returns to her "click" of scandalous women, the Twenty Gang; to Felon, the player who has always wanted to be with her, even though her going to jail was his fault; and to Cassidy, the best friend with whom she has a warm, playful relationship. Eve is a practical but strong-willed character who will stop at nothing to stand up for the people she cares about.

Keywords: New York; Revenge; Teenagers; Women Hustlers

Similar Reads: *Eve* is a high-drama story about a crew of female hustlers and a quest for revenge. For more all-female crews, try Nisa Santiago's *Cartier Cartel*, Allysha Hamber's *Northside Clit*, or Amaleka McCall's *Hush*. For more on revenge, try Reign's <u>Shyt List</u> series or Wahida Clark's *Payback Is a Mutha*.

Road Dawgz. **Columbus, OH: Triple Crown Publications, 2003. 278pp. ISBN 0970247249, 9780970247247.** ⌐⌐ ((

It's 1995, and KeShawn, aka K-Dawg, is back home after five years on prison. New York has changed. Some of his friends have come up, and others have gone way down. Now that he's out, K-Dawg plans to put together a drug empire and crown himself emperor. The one thing he knows for sure is, he is never going back to prison.

Keywords: New York; Street Code

Similar Reads: Although *Road Dawgz* is about the thrill of making it big, the relationships between K-Dawg and his family and childhood friends are as compelling as the action. Try *Death Around the Corner* for another story of boys coming up in the drug game together. For more crews warmly welcoming a character home from prison, try Freeze's *Against the Grain* or Leondrei Prince's *Bloody Money*.

Martin, Victor L.

For the Strength of You. **Columbus, OH: Triple Crown Publications, 2005. 217pp. ISBN 0976234971, 9780976234975.** ⌐⌐ ((

Anshon is a small-time drug dealer who thinks he's on the come-up. He did time in prison for his sister Tammy, but now he's out and ready to make money. This novel follows Anshon and the people in his life: Tammy, the sister who's getting out of the drug game; Fe-Fe, a neighborhood girl who is addicted to drugs; and Constance, the white prison guard Anshon's been sleeping with.

Keywords: Drug Addiction; Selma, NC; Street Code

Similar Reads: *For the Strength of You* is a slice of life story about a midlevel player in the drug game. For more about mediocre hustlers, try 50 Cent and K'wan's *Blow* or 50 Cent and K. Elliott's *Ski Mask Way*. For more slice of life stories, try Blaine Martin's *Hustle Hard* or Gregory Dixon's *Sugar Daddy's Game*.

Moore, Y. Blak.

Triple Take. **New York: Strivers Row, 2003. 230pp. ISBN 0375760660, 9780375760662.** ⌐⌐⌐ ((

After ten years in prison, JC comes back to Chicago, bent on taking revenge on the three former partners who cooperated with the cops and testified against him. His first week home, he meets Champagne, a woman with a luscious body and a job both having sex with elite politicians and extorting them. The two discover that they share an intense physical and emotional connection, but nothing can sway JC from his ultimate goal: bringing his traitorous ex-friends down in a triple take.

Keywords: Chicago; Revenge

Similar Reads: *Triple Take* is a gritty, violent story about revenge and a high-class scheming woman. For more about brutal revenge, try Wahida Clark's <u>Thugs</u> series. For more women who seduce the rich and powerful for their own gain, try Risqué's *Red Light Special* and Crystal Lacey Winslow's *Life, Love & Loneliness*.

Prince, Leondrei.

Bloody Money Series. ☞☞☞ ⟮⟮

This series gives us a raucous, joyous, violent story of friendship and crime.

Keywords: Stick-up Artists; Street Code; Wilmington, DE

Similar Reads: *Bloody Money* is a story of male camaraderie and friends and business partners who have each other's backs. For another story of male friendship and welcoming a hustler back from prison, try K'wan's *Road Dawgz*. For more about stickup artists, try Randy Thompson's *Ski Mask Way* or Dejon's *Ice Cream for Freaks*.

Core Collection: Adult

Bloody Money. Wilmington, DE: Street Knowledge Publishing, 2003. 314pp. ISBN 0974619906, 9780974619903.

> In this tale of stickups, riches, and male camaraderie, Dog, Pretty E, and Hit Man reconnect with their best friend Rasul when he returns from eight years in prison. After a series of bloody robberies, the three stickup artists have enough money to buy Rasul an expensive condo, a Benz, and a closet full of designer clothes. They have just two problems: a police detective who's a little too curious about their whereabouts, and a mob connection that came from Rasul's former cellmate but might be more trouble than it's worth.

Bloody Money 2: The Game Ain't Fair! Wilmington, DE: Street Knowledge Publishing, 2005. 281pp. ISBN 0974619922, 9780974619927.

> In the first volume Dog, Pretty E, and Hit Man reconnected with their best friend Rasul when he returned from eight years in prison. In this volume, the game still ain't fair for Rasul and his buddies.

Bloody Money 3: The City Under Siege. Wilmington, DE: Street Knowledge Publishing, 2007. ISBN-10: 0979955645, ISBN-13: 978-0979955648.

> In this volume the Bloody Money crew faces yet another setback.

Relentless Aaron.

Push Series. ☞☞ ⟮⟮

This pair of books by street pulp master Relentless Aaron follows street vigilante Reginald "Push" Jackson.

Keywords: Law Enforcement; New York; Revenge

Similar Reads: *Push* is a suspenseful thriller about a kindhearted gangster, avenging wrongs done to one's family, and receiving the FBI's unwanted attention. For more about righteous revenge, try Evie Rhodes's *Street Vengeance* or 50 Cent and Noire's *Baby Brother*. To read more about eluding the FBI, try Relentless Aaron's *Last Kingpin*. Freeze's *Against the Grain* also features a kindhearted hustler trying to avoid FBI attention.

Core Collection: Adult

Push. New York: St. Martin's Paperbacks, 2007 (2001). 307pp. ISBN 9780312949693, 0312949693.

> Reginald "Push" Jackson is a gangster with good intentions. Orphaned at twelve when home intruders murder his parents, Push starts hustling to support his siblings. He ends up in a federal penitentiary for fifteen years. There, he meets his parents' killers and exacts his revenge. When he gets out, revenge and family loyalty influence him once again: finding out that a lover is beating his sister Crystal, Push finds the man and murders him, only to find out that a player named Roy Washington has witnessed his crime. The book becomes a battle of wits and wills between Push, Washington, and the lawyers, police, and federal investigators who take an interest in the crime.

To Live and Die in Harlem. New York: St. Martin's, 2007 (2005). 374pp. ISBN 9780312949624, 0312949626.

> In the sequel, Push is back, and this time his target is a criminal network in Harlem. The cops are investigating, but only one man can get to the bottom of New York's worst crime.

Scott, Lena.

O. G. West Babylon, NY: Urban Books, 2007. 263pp. ISBN 9781601620132, 1601620136.

After twenty years in prison, Abel Diggs comes back to Oakland to a changed world. His baby sister is grown up. The girl he got pregnant at sixteen is now a mother of two, married to another man. The man who really pulled the trigger has left town and come back again. Abel comes back to town with a melancholy air, scribbling poems in his journal, wondering at the ways the world has changed. In the meantime, his two children, Jamie and Melena, are growing up in their own hard way and making many of the same mistakes he did.

Keywords: Contemplative; Oakland, CA; Social Commentary

Similar Reads: *O. G.* is a slower-paced, contemplative novel about an older, thoughtful male protagonist. For more slower-paced novels, try Daniel Serrano's *Gunmetal Black* or Nisaa A. Showell's *Reign of a Hustler*. For other contemplative pieces, try Theo Gangi's *Bang Bang* or Deborah Mayer's *Love & Loyalty*.

Serrano, Daniel.

Gunmetal Black. New York: Grand Central Publishing, 2008. 498pp. ISBN 9780446194136, 0446194131. ☞ (

Eddie Santiago leaves prison ready to start over. He's saved up over $40,000 from dealing weed, and he and another former inmate have plans to start a record label for old school salsa music. But when his old friend Tony meets him on his first day out of prison, Eddie gets played. Two crooked cops take his savings, and Tony and his underhanded friend Pelón are all too eager to line him up with a job, a high-stakes job that jeopardizes his freedom all over again. The tone is character-driven and thoughtful, and the language—both poetic descriptions and abundant Spanish phrases—is carefully crafted.

Keywords: Character-Driven; Chicago; Latino Characters; Music Industry; Street Code

Similar Reads: *Gunmetal Black* is a thick, character-driven story with crafted language and themes of police corruption and the temptations of street life. For more character-driven street lit, try Gregory Dixon's *Sugar Daddy's Game* or Tracy Brown's *Criminal Minded*. For more thick, slower-paced novels, try Lena Scott's *O. G.* or Danette Majette's *Deep*.

Sullivan, Leo L.

Life. Columbus, OH: Triple Crown Publications, 2005. 328pp. ISBN 0976234998, 9780976234999. ☞ ☞ ((

Fresh out of prison, Life Thugstin has the misfortune of trying to commit robbery in the presence of an undercover cop. Life flees the scene and, after a high-speed car chase, asks a young woman in a clothing store to help hide him. That woman, a college student named Hope Evans who believes in Black Liberation, makes the split-second decision to help, and the two of them take off for Tallahassee in a tense and occasionally comic drive. Once at their destination, Hope returns to school and Life tries to establish himself in the local drug trade. But despite their differences, the two of them find that their lives continue to intertwine.

Keywords: Social Commentary; Street Code; Tallahassee, FL

Similar Reads: *Life* is a socially conscious novel about black liberation and an unlikely pair thrown together. For more explorations of Black Liberation and resisting racism, try Sullivan's *Dangerous*, Jihad's *Riding Rhythm*, or Nathan McCall's memoir *Makes Me Wanna Holler*. For more couples thrown together while one flees the police, try 50 Cent and Nikki Turner's *Death Before Dishonor* or Treasure E. Blue's *Keyshia and Clyde*.

Core Collection: Adult

Chapter 9
Family

Family is a theme in many street novels, but in the family subgenre, relationships between blood relatives are at the center of the story. The types of stories in this subgenre vary: some are action-oriented, some focus more on characters and their relationships, and some are all about the emotional drama between family members.

There are three common types of family relationships in the family subgenre. In some family novels, such as Nikki Turner's *Ghetto Superstar*, family members have warm, close-knit relationships with each other. In others, there is tension between family members, as in Tu-Shonda Whitaker's *Ex Factor*, in which three adult sisters and their mother scheme, fight, and go behind each other's backs. In a third type of family novel, drug dealing or another illegal enterprise is a family business. Works of this kind include K'wan's *Hoodlum* and Ashley and JaQuavis's <u>Cartel</u> series.

Family Drama

The novels in this section feature family members who just can't get along. In both Azárel's *Carbon Copy* and Tiphani's *Millionaire Mistress*, conniving women scheme against their cousins. Other themes covered in this section include parents' divorce, cruelly overprotective brothers, and one sister sleeping with another sister's man.

Azárel.

Carbon Copy. **Brandywine, MD: Life Changing Books, 2009. 248pp. ISBN 9781934230671, 1934230677.** ⚓ ⚓ ❨❨

Monique and Dominique are identical twins, but their lives are quite different. Monique always comes out ahead: she gets the man both twins want, gets pregnant first, and is the one their mom likes better. Dominique is jealous and wants everything her sister has, including her husband Raphael. Ruthless and over the top, Dominique would do anything to get ahead of her sister. Unrealistic? Sure, but the fun is in guessing what outrageous stunt Dominique will pull next.

Keywords: Atlanta; Multiple Perspectives

Similar Reads: *Carbon Copy* is about sibling rivalry and outrageous drama. For another pair of siblings in vicious competition, try Tu-Shonda L. Whitaker's *Ex Factor*. Characters whose behavior is as outrageous as Dominique's include Mirror from Tiphani's *Expensive Taste* and Red from Vickie Stringer's *Dirty Red*.

Core Collection: Adult

Fletcher, Michele A.

Charge It to the Game: An Urban Novel Based on a True Story. **Greenbelt, MD: La'Femme Fatale, 2007. 231pp. ISBN 9780979265600, 0979265606.** ☞☞ ⟨⟨

Erica grew up in a "ghetto fabulous" home in Fort Greene, Brooklyn. Her father was a notorious gangster who abused her mother. Watching her mother suffer at her father's hands, Erica vowed she would never become dependent on a man. At twenty-three, Erica is involved with Victor, another Brooklyn hustler. But Erica's got a scheme of her own: credit card fraud—and another man involved in the operation. As her scheme heats up, Erica tries to avoid making the same mistakes as her mother and getting caught. A guide at the end advises readers on keeping safe from identity theft.

Keywords: Abuse; Brooklyn, NY

Similar Reads: *Charge It to the Game* stars an independent, determined young woman and explores themes of abusive relationships. For more on abusive relationships, try Azárel's Bruised series or KaShamba Williams's *Blinded*. Meisha Camm's *You Got to Pay to Play* also features a young woman coming of age and choosing the wrong man.

Hatter, Alastair J.

It's On and Poppin'. **Jamaica, NY: Q-Boro Books, 2007 (2005). 312pp. ISBN 9781933967158, 1933967153.** ☞☞ ⟨⟨⟨

Dee Dee is twenty-three years old, but her two brothers still take it upon themselves to "protect" her by attacking any men she brings home. Jay and Bee, her brothers, are drug dealers who sell a potent "Texas Tea." The drama heats up when Jay and Bee start working with someone new, and Jay's girl Meika starts stealing his money.

Keywords: Memphis; Prison; Street Code

Similar Reads: *It's On and Poppin'* is a steamy drama focusing on tension between siblings. For another steamy drama about brothers, try 50 Cent and Noire's *Baby Brother*. For more strife between brothers and sisters, try Rahsaan Ali's *Carmello*.

Hobbs, Allison.

Double Dippin'. **Largo, MD: Strebor Books, 2006. 284pp. ISBN 159309065X, 9781593090654.** ☞☞ ⟨⟨

Twin brothers Shane and Tariq Baptista are close but couldn't be more different. Their mentally ill mother was shot to death by a police officer when the boys were four, and since then they've been moving from foster home to foster home together. Tariq is shy and sensitive, while Shane is brash, cruel, and manipulative. Shane gets sent to reform school after being caught with drugs, and when the two brothers reunite, their differences have only intensified. Shane's sinister manipulation of those around him is both fascinating and repulsive.

Keywords: Abuse; Philadelphia; Teenagers

Similar Reads: *Double Dippin'* is about two brothers growing up together, but the underhanded actions of master schemer Shane are at the heart of its appeal. To watch another master manipulator in action, try 50 Cent and Relentless Aaron's *Derelict*, in which a playboy prisoner seduces a female prison psychologist.

Jihad.

MVP (Murder Vengeance Power). **Conyers, GA: Envisions Publishing, 2007. 285pp. ISBN 9780970610218, 0970610211.** ☞ ☞ (

Jihad goes back to the 1940s and 1950s to begin this family story. We meet two families, the Parkers and the Jones, then ultimately focus on the families' sons. Jonathon Parker and Coltrane Jones find themselves on opposite sides of the law. Jonathon, white, obsessed with comic books, and viciously manipulative, becomes a lawyer; Coltrane deals drugs and initially turns to Jonathan for his defense. Though the number of characters, generations, and pages may be off-putting for many readers, fans of Jihad will want to experience this dark saga.

Keywords: 1940s; 1950s; Abuse; Atlanta; Historical Fiction; Revenge; Street Code

Similar Reads: *MVP* takes readers back to the 1940s and 1950s and pits a lawyer against a drug dealer. For another 1950s setting, try Keith Lee Johnson's <u>Little Black Girl Lost</u> series. For more battles between drug dealers and law enforcement, try Jason Poole's *Larceny* or Relentless Aaron's *Last Kingpin*.

McCall, Amaleka.

Myra: A Twisted Tale of Karma. **Bellport, NY: Melodrama Publishing, 2009. 273pp. ISBN 9781934157206, 1934157201.** ☞ ☞ ☞ (

A crime has been committed, and when the police arrive, Myra Danford is in the bathtub, apparently having attempted suicide. The next morning, she wakes up in a straitjacket at a mental institution. She can't remember what happened, but she does remember growing up and rising above her circumstances. Her mother fell prey to heroin addiction after her father left them, and she let men abuse ten-year-old Myra in exchange for drugs. Determined to make a better life, Myra graduated as valedictorian of her high school and received a prestigious college scholarship. Then Milton—a sports star with a checkered past and an equally checkered present— entered her life, and Myra got on the road to disaster. A foreword by *Wifey* author Kiki Swinson warns readers against becoming a "ride or die chick" for a man.

Keywords: Abuse; Brooklyn, NY; Drug Addiction; Teenagers

Similar Reads: *Myra* is a suspenseful cautionary tale about childhood abuse and getting involved with dangerous men. For another child subjected to abuse by her drug-addicted mother, try *Snow White* by Anna J or *Whore* by Tanika Lynch. For another woman who takes the fall for a man, try KaShamba Williams's *Driven*. Méta Smith's *Whip Appeal* has a similar narrative structure: the main character wakes up in a mental institution and must piece together how she got there.

Core Collection: Adult; Young Adult

Moore, Shavon.

Ecstasy. Columbus, OH: Triple Crown Publications, 2009. 270pp. ISBN 9780982099667, 0982099665. ⚘⚘ ((

Ava Marseille doesn't want to be a stripper. She started at Spelman College but came home when her mother's drug addiction meant no one else could take care of Ava's little sister Simone. Now she works nights in the Sugar & Spice club doing private dances for men she can't stand. Just when she thinks she can quit, her home life erupts again, and Ava is kicked out of her mother's house. She moves in with her rich and judgmental aunt and uncle, only to find that her uncle is dangerous and abusive. Then she meets Bryce Carter, a friendly and attractive FBI agent. As she comes to know Bryce and his work, she realizes that her world and his have more in common than she realized.

Keywords: Abuse; Atlanta; Teenagers

Similar Reads: *Ecstasy* is a Cinderella story in which a kindhearted, compassionate young woman is forced into stripping and an abusive living situation by circumstances beyond her control. For another kindhearted heroine providing for her family, try Karen Williams's *People vs. Cashmere*. Marlon McCaulsky's *Pink Palace* also features a gentle heroine who reluctantly becomes a stripper in the face of limited options.

Core Collection: Adult; Young Adult

Tiphani.

Millionaire Mistress Series. ⚘⚘ ((

This series follows two very different cousins: level-headed Oshyn and desperate, scheming Chloe.

Keywords: Abuse; Raleigh, NC; Revenge

Similar Reads: The <u>Millionaire Mistress</u> series features a high-drama competition between two very different cousins. Azárel's <u>Carbon Copy</u> is another series featuring two female relatives, one scheming to get what the other has. For more dramatic competition and scheming between two women, try Mark Anthony's *Queen Bee* or Tonya Ridley's *Talk of the Town*.

Core Collection: Adult

The Millionaire Mistress. Brandywine, MD: Life Changing Books, 2006. 249pp. ISBN 0974139467, 9780974139463.

> Chloe and Oshyn are cousins, but the only thing they have in common is Chloe sleeping with Oshyn's man. That incident was in 2001, and now, in 2007, both cousins are in Raleigh, North Carolina. Oshyn is making a name for herself in the real estate business. Chloe is sleeping with married men and extorting money from them in increasingly audacious ways. Then a new man, Brooklyn, comes into the cousins' lives. He prefers Oshyn, but Chloe is determined to make him hers, whatever the cost.

Still a Mistress: The Saga Continues. Brandywine, MD: Life Changing Books, 2007. 242pp. ISBN 9781934230893, 1934230898 .

> In this volume, Oshyn tries to separate herself from her cousin, but Chloe is still scheming.

Millionaire Mistress: Part 3, Chloe's Revenge. Brandywine, MD: Life Changing Books, 2009. 227pp. ISBN 9781934230725, 1934230723.

> In this third installment, Chloe is out to hurt her cousin in any way possible, including killing her.

Tyson, Alex.

A Compton Chick. **West Babylon, NY: Urban Books, 2007. 200pp. ISBN 1893196771, 9781893196773.** ☞ (

It's 1983, and sixteen-year-old Jackie Smalls is coming to realize that she has become pregnant. Her parents have just divorced, and she lives at home with her mom and several siblings. Worse, the baby's father denies that the baby is his. This is the story of how Jackie finds love and loses it, then finds and loses love again. A warm but slight family drama.

Keywords: 1980s; Compton, CA; Drug Addiction; Prison; Teenagers

Similar Reads: *A Compton Chick* is a warm, episodic family drama set in the 1980s. For another episodic story about a teenage girl, try Nikki Turner's *Hustler's Wife*. For more 1980s, try Ed McNair's *My Time to Shine*, Erica Hilton's *10 Crack Commandments*, or Omar Tyree's classic *Flyy Girl*.

Whitaker, Tu-Shonda L.

The Ex Factor. **New York: One World/Ballantine Books, 2007. 354pp. ISBN 9780345486660, 0345486668.** ☞ ((

Three adult sisters and their mother deal with love, pregnancy, children, cheating men, and each other in this high-drama read. Imani is faithful to her man Walik, who's locked up, until she discovers he's been cheating on her. Prudish Celeste thinks she has the perfect marriage until she begins to suspect that her husband Sharief has been straying. Monica knows exactly where Sharief is—he's in her arms, giving her the best sex of her life. And Starr, their mother, can't help but intervene on her grown children's behalf. Sexy, funny, and over the top.

Keywords: Middle Class Setting; New York; Prison

Similar Reads: *The Ex Factor* is an over-the-top drama full of betrayal and family tension. Azárel's <u>Carbon Copy</u> and Tiphani's <u>Millionaire Mistress</u> series both feature relatives scheming against each other. Allison Hobbs's *Bona Fide Gold Digger* also involves a mother and two sisters whose fighting and power plays are juicy and outrageous.

Williams, KaShamba.

Driven Series. ⚓⚓ (

This series stars Nasir, the son of a drug-dealing man and a woman in prison. Nasir's childhood with his grandmother and a rocky romantic relationship take a central role in these two volumes.

Keywords: 1980s; Prison

Similar Reads: *Driven* is an intergenerational story of a woman taking the fall for her man and a teenage boy learning to navigate relationships and street life. For more about female characters taking risks for the men in their lives, try Amaleka McCall's *Myra: A Twisted Tale of Karma* or Keisha Ervin's *Chyna Black*. For more about teenage boys coming of age with relationship troubles, try T. Styles's *Hustler's Son* or Leo Sullivan's *Innocent*.

Driven. West Babylon, NY: Urban Books, 2007 (2005). 266pp. ISBN 1893196860, 9781893196865

> In the early 1980s, slick pimp Marv and seventeen-year-old Loretta have fallen in love. Loretta is pregnant with Marv's son. When she gives birth, Marv is drunk and high, but he loves his son Nasir as soon as he sees the baby. Marv is a drug dealer, but his men are nervous and inexperienced and send Loretta alone on the highway with enough heroin to put her in jail for ten years minimum. She gets caught, and Marv is later killed in a fight, so Nasir grows up with his gossipy grandmother, Mom Flossy. With origins like that, it's no wonder Nasir ends up with family troubles of his own.

At the Court's Mercy. West Babylon, NY: Urban Books, 2007. 270pp. ISBN 9781601620309, 1601620306.

> In this installment, Nasir continues to battle the women in his life for custody of his child and much, much more.

Family Love

In these novels, family members love and support one another. Themes covered here include a father avenging the death of his child in Trustice Gentles's *Rage Times Fury* and a caring father trying unsuccessfully to keep his daughter off the streets in Shannon Holmes's *Dirty Game*.

50 Cent and Noire.

Baby Brother: An Urban Erotic Appetizer. **New York: Pocket Books, 2007. 153pp. ISBN 9781416532026, 1416532021.** ⌐⌐ ((

Zabu Davis, the youngest of seven brothers in Queens, New York, is the only one in the family with aspirations beyond the streets. While his brothers hustle and beef with other dealers, Baby Brother is on his way to Stanford University. Then something happens to disrupt his plans in a big way: Baby Brother's girl is shot, and he's arrested for her murder. A short, steamy tale of family and revenge.

Keywords: Prison; Queens, NY; Revenge

Similar Reads: *Baby Brother* is a steamy tale starring a young man who has aspirations outside the streets. 50 Cent and Derrick R. Pledger's *Diamond District* and Anya Nicole's *Corporate Corner Boyz* also star college students who fall into hustling. Noire's *Thug-A-Licious* is a more overtly erotic take on a young hustler in college and his family.

Gentles, Trustice.

Rage Times Fury. **Columbus, OH: Triple Crown Publications, 2004. 261pp. ISBN 097478950X, 9780974789507.** ⌐ (

Malik lives in the hood, but he doesn't mess with drug dealers—he's a family man. Malik has a wife, Soraya, and two young sons, Malik Junior and Brian. Then a couple of men from the neighborhood disrespect Yvette, the woman who is involved with a player who calls himself Drugs. This incident starts a chain reaction that leads to someone pulling a gun, and Malik Junior gets caught in the crossfire. How do you stay out of the game when someone in the game shoots your son? Malik doesn't—he's out for revenge.

Keywords: Brooklyn, NY; Revenge

Similar Reads: *Rage Times Fury* is a tender family drama about revenge and the high cost of street violence. For more tender relationships between romantic partners, try Tracy Brown's *White Lines* or Terra Little's *Where There's Smoke.* For more stories of avenging wrongdoing, try Relentless Aaron's *Push* or 50 Cent and Noire's *Baby Brother*.

Holmes, Shannon.

Dirty Game. **New York: St. Martin's Griffin, 2007. 304pp. ISBN 978-0312359010.** ⌐⌐ ((

Single father Ken-Ken Greene knows firsthand the cost of playing the game. He lost his wife and partner-in-crime Maria in a botched robbery and would do anything to keep his daughter Destiny off the streets. But Destiny has ideas of her own and soon becomes every bit the player her father was. Stiff prose and exaggerated dialect may turn off some readers, but the father and daughter relationship is unique.

Keywords: New York; Teenagers; Women Hustlers

Similar Reads: *Dirty Game* is a teenage girl's coming-of-age story with a strong father–daughter relationship. For more stories of teenage girls learning to hustle, try Sha's *Harder* or Tonya Ridley's *Takeover*. For more loving father–daughter relationships, try Nikki Turner's *Riding Dirty on I-95* or Karen Williams's *People vs. Cashmere*. *Baby Doll*, by Divine G, also features a strong bond between a teen girl and the man who mentors her.

Core Collection: Adult; Young Adult

Jihad.

Baby Girl. **West Babylon, NY: Urban Books, 2005. 259pp. ISBN 1893196232, 9781893196230.** ☞ ☞ ❨❨

Babygirl grew up in luxury with a high-powered real estate agent mother. But after Momma came home to catch her husband in the act of abusing their six-year-old child, both Momma and Babygirl fled to the streets. Years later, Babygirl is willing to do whatever it takes to protect herself and to survive. She learns love from her Momma but gets her street smarts from her heroin-addicted Uncle Shabazz. Babygirl's exploits are typical street lit fare, but the warmth between family members is unique.

Keywords: Abuse; Atlanta; Drug Addiction; Los Angeles; Sex Industry

Similar Reads: *Baby Girl* is a story of street-smart women, warmth between a mother and a daughter, and child abuse. For another mother and daughter who navigate street life together, try 50 Cent and Mark Anthony's *Harlem Heat*. For more street-smart teenage girls, try Noire's *Hittin' the Bricks* or Tonya Ridley's *Takeover*.

Core Collection: Young Adult

Turner, Nikki.

Ghetto Superstar. **New York: One World/Ballantine Books, 2009. 260pp. ISBN 9780345493897, 0345493893.** ☞ ❨

Fabiola—whose name combines her mother Viola's first name and the word "fabulous"—is a rising star in the music industry, despite having little money and hailing from Richmond, Virginia. When the story begins, Fabiola beats out semi-pros from New York to win a $50,000 recording contract from Hot Soundz records. Then, overnight, her luck changes. Hot Soundz's assets are seized, and her family goes home to find themselves evicted from their house. At the last minute, a wealthy local gangster, Casino, steps in on behalf of the family and gives them a place to live. From then on, Fabiola feels indebted to Casino, no matter how high she rises in the music business. Like Turner's *Black Widow* and *Riding Dirty on I-95*, this is a hopeful story of love and success against the odds. Tension within the music industry and between the women in Casino's life adds drama to Fabiola's climb.

Keywords: Music Industry; Overcoming Adversity; Richmond, VA

Similar Reads: *Ghetto Superstar* is an uplifting story of a young woman finding success in the music industry and support in the arms of a hustler. Several of Turner's novels have a similarly uplifting feel, particularly *Black Widow* and *Riding Dirty on I-95*. Treasure E. Blue's *Street Girl Named Desire* is also an uplifting tale of finding success and acceptance, though heroine Desire's path to happiness is much rockier than Fabiola's. For more on the music industry, try the short story collection *Backstage*.

Core Collection: Adult; Young Adult; School Libraries

Family Business

The novels in this section feature families who hustle together. Some families run large-scale operations, as in Ashley and JaQuavis's *Cartel*. Other novels, like 50 Cent and Mark Anthony's *Harlem Heat* or Ed McNair's *My Time to Shine*, feature mothers and daughters, or brothers, who get into the business of drug dealing together.

50 Cent and Mark Anthony.

Harlem Heat. **New York: Pocket Books, 2007. 180pp. ISBN 9781416549093, 1416549099.** ☞ ☞ (

Teenage Chyna and her thirty-two-year-old mother are close: they work together running the gun-smuggling organization Harlem Heat. When Panama Pete, a onetime drug kingpin, returns to Harlem after years in prison, he wants to take over the organization. But Chyna and her mom are keeping Harlem Heat for themselves, no matter what the cost.

Keywords: New York; Sex Industry; Teenagers; Women Hustlers

Similar Reads: *Harlem Heat* is an action-oriented novella about strong women and a mother–daughter relationship. For more no-nonsense women who hustle, try Vickie Stringer's *Let That Be the Reason*, in which inexperienced Pamela strikes out on her own to make a living, or Nikki Turner's *Death Before Dishonor*, which pairs a man on the run from police with an assertive woman who is no stranger to the long arm of the law. For another story of a close mother–daughter relationship, try *Baby Girl* by Jihad.

Core Collection: Young Adult

Ali, Rahsaan.

Carmello: A Family Affair. **West Babylon, NY: Urban Books, 2008. 282pp. ISBN 9781601620576, 1601620578.** ☞ ☞ ((

A drug lord has murdered their parents, and Carmello, China, and Caine are ready to get revenge and get rich. They approach Colombian drug lord Santiago, who sets them up to deal on the streets of Queens. The three siblings are on their way to getting everything they want, as long as they can stay out of trouble and not fight with each other. Short chapters are told in alternating voices. In a subplot, China and her best friend have a lesbian affair.

Keywords: GLBTQ; Multiple Perspectives; Queens, NY; Revenge

Similar Reads: *Carmello* involves siblings working together in illegal business. For more families hustling together, try Ashley and JaQuavis's <u>Cartel</u> series or Teri Woods's *Deady Reigns*. For other instances of lesbian sexuality, try Chunichi's <u>Gangster's Girl</u> series or Amaleka McCall's *Hush*.

Ashley and JaQuavis.

The Cartel Series. ☞☞ ((

This slower-paced series explores the lives and dealings of Miami's top drug family.

Keywords: Miami; Revenge

Similar Reads: <u>The Cartel</u> series focuses on a drug-dealing family. For more stories in which drug dealing is a family business, try *Marked* by Capone, *Carmello* by Rahsaan Ali, or Teri Woods's <u>Deadly Reigns</u> series.

Core Collection: Adult; Young Adult

The Cartel. West Babylon, NY: Urban Books, 2009. 278pp. ISBN 9781601621429, 1601621426.

> The Diamonds—also known as the Cartel—are Miami's number one crime family. Brothers, sisters, wives, and husbands are all part of the drug organization and all reap the benefits of the money that comes from their business. When a Haitian gang attempts to take over Miami's drug trade, the family patriarch, Carter, is murdered. Young Carter, his illegitimate son, comes to town for the funeral, and Carter's best friend Polo convinces Young Carter to become a true part of the family. But his role becomes much more complicated when he becomes involved with Miamor, a young woman who, unbeknownst to him, is a ruthless killer.

The Cartel 2. West Babylon, NY: Urban Books, 2009. 236pp. ISBN 9781601622563, 1601622562.

> In the second installment of this slower-paced series, a snitch threatens the Cartel's operations.

Capone.

Marked. **Brandywine, MD: Life Changing Books, 2008. 246pp. ISBN 9781934230855, 1934230855.** ☞☞ (

A trained marine, Deluxe wants to use his sniper skills in the service of his country. But his uncle Gator wants to place him in a high position in the family's drug organization. When a cop stops Gator's car and seems likely to discover the twenty-five kilos of cocaine in the trunk, Deluxe reluctantly kills him. As he gets deeper into the family business, he still can't escape the pangs of conscience he feels for killing the cop. Will he get away squeaky clean, or pay the ultimate price?

Keywords: Detroit; Revenge

Similar Reads: *Marked* is a story about revenge, a family business, and an unwilling hustler. For more stories of hustlers who feel that the life chose them, try Trustice Gentles's *Rage Times Fury* or Erick S. Gray's *Crave All, Lose All*. For more families who hustle together, try Rahsaan Ali's *Carmello* or Ashley and JaQuavis's *Cartel*.

Evans, Michael.

Son of a Snitch Series. ☞☞☞ ❨❨

This violent, shocking series follows the life of a family disgraced after its father figure cooperates with law enforcement.

Keywords: Fashion Industry; New York; Prison

Similar Reads: *Son of a Snitch* is a story of a teenage boy becoming a hustler, and *The Bastard* is about the misadventures of a pair of twins. Gregory Dixon's *Cake Man* is another story of a teenage boy learning to hustle while his father is in prison. For another story of twins who could not be more different, try Allison Hobbs's *Double Dippin'*.

Son of a Snitch. Brooklyn, NY: MonteMe, 2006. 271pp. ISBN 0974277517, 9780974277516.

> Once head of the SSJ crew, one of New York's most feared drug crews, Lorenzo lost his reputation when he cooperated with the feds to save his wife. For seven years, his son Jessie paid the price on the streets. Now Jessie's out to prove himself. Corrupt cops, graphic torture, and an incestuous brother–sister relationship keep this story fresh and shocking.

The Bastard. Brooklyn, NY: MonteMe, 2008. 255pp. ISBN 9780974277523, 0974277525.

> In the first volume of Evans's violent, shocking series, Jessie, the son of a drug lord who cooperated with the police, made a name for himself. Nine years later, Jessie's sister Crystal has a pair of twin boys, one destined for the streets, the other gentler and bound for the fashion industry. But who is the father, and what will happen when Crystal's secrets are revealed?

Hendricks, James.

A Good Day to Die. **New York: Augustus Publishing, 2007. 302pp. ISBN 0975945327, 9780975945322.** ☞☞☞ ❨

James Hendricks, known as Bay Bay in his youth in Gary, Indiana, wrote this story about rival gangs in Gary while in federal prison. In 1993, thirteen-year-old twins Don and Jon are initiated into the Vice Lords, one of the Midwest's two major gangs, and are given guns. The twins use their new powers—and new weapons—liberally, until a full-scale gang war erupts between the Vice Lords and their enemies, the Gangster Disciples. Though the bodies pile up and retaliation gets more and more severe, neither side is willing to back down.

Keywords: Gangs; Gary, IN; Revenge; Street Code

Similar Reads: *A Good Day to Die* is a story of gang warfare with a strong critique of gang life. For another story of a young person joining a gang and regretting it, try Rochan Morgan's *Crossroads*. For a true story of life in a gang, try Reymundo Sanchez's memoir *My Bloody Life: The Making of a Latin King*.

Core Collection: Young Adult

K'wan.

Hoodlum. **New York: St. Martin's Griffin, 2005. 326pp. ISBN 9780312333089, 0312333080.** 🐄🐄 ((

In K'wan's longest volume to date, the youngest son of a drug family comes home to New York after quitting college basketball at N.C. State. Shai falls right into the family business, a highly coordinated and efficient mix of Mafia connections, protection rackets, and drugs. A "Godfather"-like mix of organized crime and family saga.

Keywords: New York; Street Code

Similar Reads: *Hoodlum* is the story of a family in the drug business. For more novels in which drug dealing is a family affair, try Capone's *Marked* or Ashley and JaQuavis's <u>Cartel</u> series. Both *The Cartel* and Rahsaan Ali's *Carmello* also involve high-level organized crime.

McNair, Ed.

Turning Point. **West Babylon, NY: Urban Books, 2008. 309pp. ISBN 9781601620408, 1601620403.** 🐄🐄🐄 ((

Shots are going off and gangsters are getting paid in Norfolk, Virginia. Russ, better known as Truck in the streets, returns home from a juvenile detention facility and is back to his old ways within the day. Working with his brother Cadillac, Truck runs a vicious, efficient, and lucrative operation. A vast array of characters vie for power in this sprawling shoot-'em-up.

Keywords: Norfolk, VA; Street Code

Similar Reads: *Turning Point* is an action-packed shoot-'em-up about young brothers hustling together and a ruthless gangster. For more stories of brothers working together in the drug business, try McNair's *My Time to Shine* or Alastair J. Hatter's *It's On and Poppin'*. Sonny F. Black's *Gangsta Bitch* is another violent shoot-'em-up with a wide variety of characters.

My Time to Shine Series. ⚐⚐ ((

This series focuses on Dee, Junie, and Black, three brothers in Norfolk, Virginia, who move from poverty to kingpin status when they start selling crack in the 1980s.

Keywords: 1980s; Norfolk, VA; Teenagers

Similar Reads: *My Time to Shine* explores the pain of growing up in poverty as well as the joy of coming into money, and the setting of Norfolk, Virginia, in the 1980s plays a significant role. For more about young people who begin hustling to support themselves, try Leondrei Prince's *Tommy Good Story* or Noire's *Hood*. For more about teenage boys becoming crack dealers in the 1980s, try Erica Hilton's *10 Crack Commandments*.

Core Collection: Adult; Young Adult

My Time to Shine. West Babylon, NY: Urban Books, 2006. 254pp. ISBN 1893196720, 9781893196728.

> It's 1986, and Dee and his mother and brothers are struggling to make ends meet. Being poor is one thing for Dee, but he hates to see his little brother Black, who's still in high school, get ragged on for his clothes. One night at a club called the Big Apple, Dee sees two men who have a profound impact on him: they're driving fancy cars, getting the attention of beautiful women, and buying their drinks with fat knots of cash. Dee knows he wants to live that kind of life, and soon enough, he and Black are selling crack, spending money, and living a dream. But the brothers' dream could easily become the family's nightmare.

Black Reign. West Babylon, NY: Urban Books, 2006. 254pp. ISBN 1893196755, 9781893196759.

> In McNair's first entry in the series, Black was the youngest brother in a family of up-and-coming crack dealers. Now he's a dangerous kingpin, and Angela, a student at Hampton University, becomes involved with him.

Black Reign 2. West Babylon, NY: Urban Books, 2008. 254pp. ISBN 9781601620583, 1601620586.

> Years later, the three brothers are determined to keep up the family business no matter what it takes to stay on top.

Parker, Che.

The Tragic Flaw. Largo, MD: Strebor Books, 2007. 299pp. ISBN 978-1593091262, 1593091265. ⚐⚐ ((

In elevated language, Parker sets the scene in Kansas City, Missouri, in a neighborhood with dirty sidewalks, children playing jump rope, and men outside drinking liquor from plastic cups. The center of his story is Cicero, the half-black, half-Italian son of a cruel mobster. Raised to be cold and merciless, Cicero comes to rule the neighborhood with an iron fist. But how long can he ride high before his evil deeds catch up with him?

Keywords: Kansas City, MO; Street Code

Similar Reads: *The Tragic Flaw* is a stylized, evocative story of a particular Kansas City neighborhood and the heir to a powerful crime family's business. For more novels that evoke a sense of place, try Mikal Malone's *Pitbulls in a Skirt* or Erick S. Gray's *Ghetto Heaven*. For more on inheriting an illegal family business, try K'wan's *Hoodlum* or Capone's *Marked*.

Short Stories and Anthologies

The titles in this section contain short stories and anthologies in the family subgenre.

Streets of New York Series. ☞ ☞ ⟨⟨

Street lit's big names each tell a piece of this story of street life and family from a male perspective.

Keywords: Multiple Authors; New York; Revenge; Street Code

Similar Reads: The <u>Streets of New York</u> series tells a story of male camaraderie, shoot-'em-up action, fatherhood, and conflict between former partners. Ashley and JaQuavis's *Trophy Wife* features a similar conflict between being a father and being a gangster. For more about conflict between former partners, try Thomas Long's *Thug's Life*.

Streets of New York, Volume 1. New York: Augustus Publishing, 2009 (2004). 228pp. ISBN 9780979281679, 0979281679.

> Promise, a member of a successful stickup crew, lost his wife to a shooting a few months before the action begins. Now he is responsible for their three-year-old daughter Ashley. But the members of his old crew still call on him to do high-risk work. To complicate matters, Promise develops a relationship with Ashley's preschool teacher, Audrey. Gray narrates from Promise's point of view and Anthony narrates from Audrey's. Whyte writes as Pooh, another member of Promise's crew.

Streets of New York, Volume 2. New York: Augustus Publishing, 2009. 231pp. ISBN 9780979281686, 0979281687.

> K'wan contributes a forward to this second volume, in which Promise's former partners are running a successful nightclub without him, prompting Promise's jealousy and rage.

Streets of New York, Volume 3. New York: Augustus Publishing, 2009. 223pp. ISBN 9780979281693, 0979281695.

> Treasure E. Blue contributes a foreword in this volume, in which the streets are shaken after a vicious gang war among the three former partners.

Turner, Nikki, ed.

Nikki Turner Presents . . . Street Chronicles: Christmas in the Hood. **New York: One World/Ballantine Books, 2007. 302pp. ISBN 9780345497802, 0345497805.** ☞ ☞ ￼

How do you afford Christmas presents for your children when you're broke? How do you celebrate your loved ones when the streets are calling your name? A mix of known and unknown authors, including K. Elliott, Seth "Soul Man" Ferranti, and J. M. Benjamin, contribute to this holiday-themed collection with attitude.

Keywords: Multiple Authors; Sex Industry; Short Stories

Similar Reads: *Christmas in the Hood* is a short story collection that mixes the holiday spirit with street attitude. For more street-themed short stories, try *Tales from Da Hood*, the original entry in the Nikki Turner Presents . . . line. Readers intrigued by the religious aspects of Christmas can try *Even Sinners Have Souls*, a street-themed short story collection with a Christian flavor.

1

2

3

4

5

6

7

8

9

10

11

Chapter **10**

Friendship

In some street novels, a group of friends forms the center of the story. Friendship novels explore the relationship between two or more characters who are close but not family or romantic partners.

Novels in this subgenre are character-driven stories. These novels usually center on three or four friends, and narrative perspective often alternates among the friends. In some friendship novels, the relationships between friends are warm and supportive. In others, the so-called friends connive, backstab, or otherwise betray each other. The appeal of friendship novels is often in experiencing each friend's take on the events that unfold. Classic friendship novels include T. N. Baker's *Sheisty* and Shannon Holmes's *B-More Careful*.

Friends 'til the End

Novels in this section describe true friendships, in which friends support each other through hard times and take pleasure in each other's happiness.

Anthony, Mark.

Paper Chasers. Jamaica, NY: Q-Boro Books, 2007 (2003). 320pp. ISBN 978-1933967301, 1933967307. ☞ ☞ (

Holz and his buddies make up a group called Fourth Crew. They stick together, but unlike a gang, their vibe is positive. Fourth Crew live in Laurelton, Queens, and hang out in Harlem on Wednesdays. They're middle-class kids and can't compete with the cars and jewelry the big players throw around, but they're okay with that until the summer they decide they're getting paid. As soon as Fourth Crew enters the drug business, things get very serious. Holz gets involved and learns the ins and outs of the drug business. At the same time, his narration points out the ways racism and other social problems lead to violence against black men.

Keywords: 1990s; Queens, NY; Street Code

Similar Reads: *Paper Chasers* is a reflective, socially conscious story about male friends who become hustlers and reap the consequences. For more stories of young men going into hustling together and getting in over their heads, try 50 Cent and Derrick R. Pledger's *Diamond District* or Randy Thompson's *Ski Mask Way*. For another socially conscious look at the pressures facing young black men, try *Life* or *Innocent* by Leo Sullivan.

Core Collection: Adult; Young Adult; School Libraries

Ashley and JaQuavis.

Dirty Money. West Babylon, NY: Urban Books, 2008 (2006). 286pp. ISBN 9781601620774, 1601620772. ☞ ((

Although she was once a goody two-shoes, Anari's life changed when she caught the bag of dope Maurice threw in the bushes when the police caught him. She caught Maurice's eye and became his baby girl for years. Then a rival drug dealer killed him, and Anari was left with a baby and the knowledge that Maurice had had a secret life and another lover. On her own, Anari has to fend for herself with the help of her bisexual best friend Tanya; an attentive man, Von; and Shawna, a slick girl who might not be everything she claims.

Keywords: Abuse; GLBTQ; New Jersey

Similar Reads: *Dirty Money* is about betrayal and a woman fending for herself after losing the man who provided for her. For other women getting by on their own, try Nikki Turner's *Hustler's Wife* or Ashley and JaQuavis's *Supreme Clientele*. For other characters struggling with a lover's betrayal, try Nikki Turner's *Glamorous Life* or Keisha Ervin's *Torn*.

Core Collection: Adult

Brandie.

Don't Hate the Player . . . Hate the Game. West Babylon, NY: Urban Books, 2008 (2006). 509pp. ISBN 9781601620453, 1601620454. ☞ ☞ ((

Chocolate, Money, and Taeko are three guy friends with three very different approaches to life. Money is all about living fast and banking on a football scholarship. Chocolate, who watched his Uncle Bee die of AIDS after unprotected sex, tries to live cautiously. Taeko's got more heart—and basketball skills—than common sense. The three friends attract plenty of drama with women and between themselves. But things get serious when Chocolate encounters a mystery woman—who happens to be named Brandie—and Money falls for the girlfriend of an abusive drug dealer. Warm moments between friends and family abound, as do steamy sex scenes.

Keywords: Abuse; Atlanta; Light Reads

Similar Reads: *Don't Hate the Player . . . Hate the Game* is a lighthearted drama featuring warm friendships between men. For more lighthearted drama starring men, try Dwayne S. Joseph's *Womanizers* or David Givens's *Betrayed*. For more warmth between male friends, try K'wan's *Road Dawgz*, Leondrei Prince's *Bloody Money*, or Capone's *Marked*.

Brickhouse, Linda.

Jealousy: The Complete Saga. Bellport, NY: Melodrama Publishing, 2009. 309pp. ISBN 9781934157138, 1934157139. ☞ ☞ ((

Back in grade school, Chaka and his friends made up a crew, the Baker Boys 5. Later they grew into the Dirty Dozen, named after a crew in a movie. But when Chaka gets shot and killed, the crew is also blown apart. This slower-paced novel jumps back and forth between past and present and explores the effects of Chaka's death on a variety of characters, including Buck, who took the rap for a crime in which Chaka was involved; Petra, the mother of Chaka's children; and Eve, the mistress who might have been responsible for setting Chaka up to die.

Keywords: New York; Prison

Similar Reads: *Jealousy* is a slower-paced novel that explores relationships between boys who grew into street life together. For more slower-paced novels, try Danette Majette's *Deep* or Lena Scott's *O. G.* For more about teenage boys learning to hustle together, try Randy Thompson's *Ski Mask Way*.

Gray, Erick S.

Nasty Girls. New York: St. Martin's Griffin, 2006. 312pp. ISBN 0312349963, 9780312349967. ☞ ☞ ((

Though they started out as enemies, Camille, Jade, and Shy are friends who stick together: they go to clubs together, stick up for each other in fights, and give each other support when the men in their lives behave badly. When a fight erupts in a club, both Shy's man Roscoe and Jade's man James get involved. After the dust settles, Roscoe is arrested for murder, and Shy and Jade can see that there's something James isn't telling. Who will Shy and Jade side with—the men they love, or the friends they trust?

Keywords: Prison; Queens, NY

Similar Reads: *Nasty Girls* is a story about brash, high-drama women who stick up for each other. For more women who defend themselves at the least provocation, try Shannon Holmes's *B-More Careful* or Deja King's <u>Bitch</u> series. Eyone Williams's *Hell Razor Honeys* also features a crew of female friends who started out as each other's enemies.

Hamber, Allysha.

The Northside Clit. Wilmington, DE: Street Knowledge Publishing, 2007. 243pp. ISBN 9780974619996, 097461999X. ☞ ☞ ((

Queen and her girls have named their clique after the North Side of St. Louis and the most sensitive and powerful part of their bodies. The five of them, including timid Pebbles and lesbian couple Trey and Butter, go in together on a robbery. But Xavier, the drug dealer whose home the crew

1

2

3

4

5

6

7

8

9

10

11

is robbing, catches them in the act and calls the police. What follows is a whirlwind of drama in and out of court.

Keywords: GLBTQ; Prison; St. Louis; Women Hustlers

Similar Reads: *The Northside Clit* is the story of a clique of female stickup artists and what happens after a botched robbery. For more about all-female crews, try K'wan's *Eve*, LaShonda DeVaughn's *Hood Chick's Story*, or Nisa Santiago's *Cartier Cartel*. Brandon McCalla's *Spot Rushers* tells a grimmer story of what happens after four female stickup artists attempt one too many robberies and one of their crew gets killed.

J, Anna.

Get Money Chicks. **Jamaica, NY: Q-Boro Books, 2007. ISBN 9781933967172, 193-396717X.** ☞ ☞ ☾

Mina, Shanna, and Karen are longtime friends who know what's important: cash. Their latest trick is to go home with a man and slip him an "el"—a joint laced with embalming fluid—then make off with his wallet while he's knocked out. The game goes too far when Mina gives an "el" to her old friend Black Ron, and Black Ron never wakes up. Mina is initially afraid she'll be sent to prison, but the coroner rules the death an accident, and the friends go back to their scheming ways. What will it take to set these "get money chicks" on the right track?

Keywords: Philadelphia; Sex Industry

Similar Reads: *Get Money Chicks* is the story of three scheming women looking to get money from hapless men. For more female friends with similar goals, try J. M. Benjamin's *Down in the Dirty* or A. J. Rivers's *Cash Money*.

King, Deja.

Trife Life to Lavish. **Collierville, TN: A King Production, 2009. 266pp. ISBN 9780975581179, 0975581171.** ☞ ☾

Nichelle has lived in the projects in Queens with her mom ever since she saw her mother kill her father in self-defense as a child. Her first friend in the projects is Tierra Thompson, who is four years older than Nichelle and takes her on as a little sister and eventually best friend. At twenty-one, Tierra is frustrated by being involved with men who promise her money and support but don't follow through. Just as she is getting fed up with her man Radric, Radric's friend and associate Renny takes an interest in Nichelle. A story of friendship between women, relationship troubles between women and men, and the difference between a life of poverty and a life that is lavish. Lessons about "the life" begin most chapters.

Keywords: Queens, NY; Teenagers

Similar Reads: *Trife Life to Lavish* is a story about warm friendship and two young women who grew up together. For more stories of warm friendships, try Keisha Seignious's *Boogie Down Story* or Willie Dutch's *Day After Forever*. For more characters growing up together and staying friends, try Seven's *Gorilla Black* or Sherrie Walker's *Mistress of the Game*.

Core Collection: Adult

Long, Thomas.

Cash Rules. West Babylon, NY: Urban Books, 2005. 265pp. ISBN 978-1893196193. ⚐⚐ ⟨⟨

The hip-hop industry is raunchy and cutthroat, as Takeisha, Latrell, and Danita, aka T-Love, Luscious, and D-Boogie learn firsthand. Taking on the name KS (short for Killin 'em Softly) Crew, the three high school best friends hook up with an unscrupulous rap producer to move their careers forward. The story follows the group's rise to stardom, with each step crazier and more sexually adventurous than the next. Will the struggle for success come between three friends in the end? Be prepared for frank and wild sexual content and a truly gritty look at the rap industry.

Keywords: Baltimore; Music Industry

Similar Reads: *Cash Rules* is a gritty, raunchy tale of three friends navigating the rap industry. For more about how entering the music business changes friendships, try Black Artemis's *Explicit Content*. For more about the underhanded behavior of music producers, try Mark Anthony's *Take Down* or K. Roland Williams's *Cut Throat*.

Majette, Danette.

Good Girl Gone Bad. Brandywine, MD: Life Changing Books, 2009. 235pp. SBN 9781934230664, 1934230669. ⚐⚐ ⟨⟨

Money makes the world go round, and Jazmine, Alyse, and Roslynn know that all too well. Jazmine lives under the thumb of her abusive husband Vince, fearing that she will be unable to support herself and her son if she leaves him. Alyse works a grueling, degrading job cleaning hotel rooms and still struggles to pay doctor's bills for her sick daughter's care. Roslynn, a social climber, spends her husband's money liberally on clothes, jewelry, and a car, even though her habits risk bankrupting him. With money tight, the three women are desperate and ready to risk everything.

Keywords: Abuse; Multiple Perspectives; New Jersey

Similar Reads: *Good Girl Gone Bad* is a story about three adult women's friendship, with themes of domestic abuse and the need for money. *Rich Girls* by Kendall Banks focuses on three women with a similar set of aspirations and obstacles. For more about abuse at the hands of a loved one, try Azárel's *Bruised* or Dywayne D. Birch's *Beneath the Bruises*.

McCalla, Brandon.

Spot Rushers. New York: Augustus Publishing, 2007. 229pp. ISBN 978-0979281624, 0979281628. ⚐⚐⚐ ⟨⟨

Rayne, Sabrina, Bernadette, and Dora Dean are spot rushers: one of them gains a man's trust, and then the four pounce, robbing him blind with guns, razor blades, and a machete if necessary. But when the spot rushers hit a crack house belonging to South Philly's notorious Steve Stunner, everything falls apart. Dora Dean is killed, and the other three make it to the hospital with gunshot wounds. With psychological realism and brutal violence, McCalla shows how the survivors deal with the police, grief, anger, and each other.

Keywords: New York; Philadelphia; Street Code; Women Hustlers

Similar Reads: *Spot Rushers* is a violent, emotional story of four women hustlers traumatized after the death of a partner. For more women who hustle together, try Allysha Hamber's *Northside Clit* or Mikal Malone's *Pitbulls in a Skirt*. Both Méta Smith's *Whip Appeal* and Amaleka McCall's *Myra: A Twisted Tale of Karma* have similar plot structures in which characters come to grips with reality after a devastating incident.

McGill, Caroline.

A Dollar Outta Fifteen Cent Series. 🖝🖝 ((

This high-drama, episodic series stars Portia, a stripper who wants to make "a dollar outta fifteen cent," and the friends who help her through life's struggles.

Keywords: New York; Sex Industry; Street Code

Similar Reads: The <u>Dollar Outta Fifteen Cent</u> series is an episodic story featuring action, drama, and warm friendships. For more episodic series with cliffhanger endings, try Treasure Hernandez's <u>Flint</u> series or Kiki Swinson's <u>Wifey</u>. For more warm friendships, try Deja King's *Trife Life to Lavish* or Anthony Whyte's <u>Ghetto Girls</u> series.

A Dollar Outta Fifteen Cent: An Urban Love Story of Sex, Money, and Murda. New York: Synergy Publications, 2004. 375pp. ISBN 0975298003, 9780975298008.

> Well-dressed, fly, and in it for her own gain, Portia works at a local strip club, in the persona of red hot stripper Mystique. Between tips and the extra she gets from private sessions, she's making enough to get by and keep wearing Gucci. She doesn't tell her friends everything about her job, but she isn't ashamed either—her relations with men are strictly business. But when one of her regulars starts finding a way into her heart, things start changing. Though Portia's story is at the center of the novel, her friends' lives and troubles also get airtime: an affair with a boss, a cheating husband, and potential exposure to HIV.

A Dollar Outta Fifteen Cent 2: Money Talks . . . Bullsh*t Walks. New York: Synergy Publications, 2007. 368pp. ISBN 9780975298022, 097529802X.

> Picking up where the original left off, this sequel again focuses on Portia and her friends as they navigate new challenges in their relationships and on the streets.

A Dollar Outta Fifteen Cent III: Mo' Money . . . Mo' Problems. New York: Synergy Publications, 2008. 363pp. ISBN 9780975298046, 0975298046.

> Picking up after volume 2's cliffhanger ending, this volume follows Portia, Fatima, Khalil, and Laila as they deal with the aftermath of a fatal shootout.

A Dollar Outta Fifteen Cent IV: Money Makes the World Go 'Round.
New York: Synergy Publication, 2009. ISBN 0975298054, 978-0975298053.
In the fourth installment, author McGill delivers even more twists and
turns in Portia's story.

Rivers, A. J.

Cash Money. **Columbus, OH: Triple Crown Publications, 2005. 286pp.
ISBN 0976234939, 9780976234937.** ☛ ☛ ❨❨

Three young people star in this "urban love story" about cold hard
cash. Nita and Free, two recent high school graduates, have sex with an
unattractive hustler for money, then rob him when he tries to rip them off.
B.J., a twenty-year-old, up-and-coming drug dealer, puts the game first,
family second, and women way below. The action begins at a 50 Cent
concert and continues through a shopping mall, hotel rooms, clubs, and a
series of fancy cars.

Keywords: Teenagers

Similar Reads: *Cash Money* is a breezy, brand-name-studded story of teenage girls
looking for easy money. For more name brands and materialistic characters, try
Sister Souljah's *Coldest Winter Ever*, Tiphani's *Expensive Taste*, or Danielle Santiago's
Grindin'. Erica K. Barnes's *I Ain't Saying She's a Gold Digger* also features a teenage
girl looking to hustle money from the men in her life.

Seignious, Keisha.

A Boogie Down Story. **New York: Augustus Publishing, 2007. 247pp. ISBN
9780979281600, 0979281601.** ☛ ❨❨

It's a hot summer afternoon in the Bronx in 1985, and sixteen-year-
olds Forster and Cash have been best friends since the second grade.
Coincidentally, so have the two sixteen-year-old girls they meet that day:
fast Keya and cautious Dawn. Fast forward to 1991, and the four are still in
each others' lives. Forster supplements his day job with a drug hustle, and
Cash is dealing full time with a reputation for emotional instability. Dawn
is a secretary who wants to stay away from street life, and Keya has a child
and a drug habit. As Forster, Cash, Keya, and Dawn's lives progress, can
their friendships stay strong? Is there a chance for love?

Keywords: 1990s; Bronx, NY; Drug Addiction; Sex Industry

Similar Reads: *A Boogie Down Story* is a tale of two men and two women staying
in each other's lives with a setting in the 1980s and early 1990s. For more stories of
long-term, warm friendships try Deja King's *Trife Life to Lavish* or Brandie's *Don't
Hate the Player . . . Hate the Game*. For more stories set in the 1980s and 1990s, try
Mark Anthony's *Paper Chasers*, Alex Tyson's *Compton Chick*, or Omar Tyree's classic
Flyy Girl.

Turner, Nikki.

The Glamorous Life. **New York: One World/Ballantine Books, 2005. 293pp. ISBN 0345476832, 9780345476838.** ☞ ((

Bambi comes from a two-parent, middle-class family, but something about street life calls to her. She gets involved with Reggie, a drug dealer, and falls head over heels in love with both him and the luxurious lifestyle his cash flow provides. Then, at what is supposed to be their engagement party, she finds out Reggie has someone on the side—a man. Heartbroken, Bambi swears never to let emotions stop her in the pursuit of cold, hard cash. Though the main focus is on Bambi's involvements with men and her ways of making money, her relationships with her mother and with her best friend Egypt also play a role.

Keywords: Revenge; Richmond, VA

Similar Reads: *The Glamorous Life* features warm relationships and a woman who shuts down her emotions in favor of money. For more women focused on money rather than love, try Keisha Ervin's *Hold U Down* or Michele A. Fletcher's *Charge It to the Game.* Willie Dutch's *Day After Forever* features another scorned woman who turns to a friend for comfort.

The Urban Griot.

Capital City. **West Babylon, NY: Urban Books, 2008. 452pp. ISBN 9781601621344, 1601621345.** ☞ (

The Urban Griot uses this slice of life story as a platform to talk about the hardships that young black men face in a white supremacist society. The story focuses on three young men in Washington, D.C., in the early 1990s. Butterman deals drugs, Shank does stickups, and Wes, a student in political science, debates the state of African Americans in politics. Social and cultural details of the 1990s—including references to Bill Clinton, *The Bodyguard,* and *Waiting to Exhale*—make this read enjoyable for its nostalgia as well as its reflections on race in the United States.

Keywords: 1990s; Washington, DC

Similar Reads: *Capital City* is a socially conscious, slice of life story with a 1990s setting. Mark Anthony's *Paper Chasers,* which takes place in 1991, also explores issues of race and the struggles of young black men in America. For more reflections on American racism, try Leo Sullivan's *Life* or Judge Greg Mathis's *Street Judge.*

Whyte, Anthony.

Ghetto Girls Series. ☞☞ ((

Coco, Danielle, and Josephine are better known as Da Crew, three teenage girls who have gotten started dancing in music videos. When they meet DeeDee, niece of music producer Eric Ascot, the four become inseparable in friendship and in business.

Keywords: Abuse; Drug Addiction; Music Industry; New York; Revenge; Teenagers

Similar Reads: The Ghetto Girls series features the music industry and themes of revenge, but warm friendships between young women are at the heart of the stories. For more stories of warm friendships between teenage girls and young women, try Deja King's *Trife Life to Lavish* or Eyone Williams's *Hell Razor Honeys*. For more about the dangerous music industry, try Thomas Long's *Cash Rules* or Black Artemis's *Explicit Content*.

Core Collection: Adult; Young Adult

Ghetto Girls. New York: Augustus Publishing, 2005 (2002). 266pp. ISBN 0975945319, 9780975945315.

> One night at a club, Coco, Danielle, and Josephine, better known as Da Crew, meet DeeDee, a well-dressed girl driving her uncle's Benz, and they stick together for the night. In the morning, they learn two things: that DeeDee was carjacked and raped leaving the club, and that DeeDee's uncle is well-connected music producer Eric Ascot. Three threads are set in motion: Ascot's thoughtless push for revenge, in a plot involving two ruthless and clownish hit men; the tentative friendship between DeeDee and Coco; and the two hit men's vulgar, hedonistic pursuit of sex, drugs, and violence.

Ghetto Girls Too. New York: Augustus Publishing, 2004. 327pp. ISBN 0975945300, 9780975945308.

> In this volume, music producer Eric Ascot gets involved with the mob, and the girls' music career heats up.

Ghetto Girls 3. New York: Augustus Publishing, 2006. 236pp. ISBN 0975945351, 9780975945353.

> In this third volume, the four members of music group Da Crew make different choices about their music careers and their romantic lives.

Ghetto Girls IV: Young Luv. New York: Augustus Publishing, 2009. 241pp. ISBN 9780979281662, 0979281660.

> Teenage friends, Coco, Danielle, Josephine, and DeeDee, make their way through the music business and street drama in this series. In this fourth volume, Coco's career is threatened, and the police close in on music producer Eric Ascot.

Williams, Eyone.

Hell Razor Honeys. **Owings Mills, MD: The Cartel Publications, 2008. 203pp. ISBN 9780979493171, 097949317X.**

Three teenage girls who've got each other's backs form a gang called the Hell Razor Honeys. Vida starts off running with the Come Back Honeys but loses favor when she fights back against queen bee Samara. Tia remembers Vida standing up for her years ago and reaches out after Vida and Samar fall out. The third member of their crew, Ice, is a rich white girl with a street heart. Together the three are unstoppable . . . or are they?

Keywords: Street Code; Teenagers; Washington, DC; Women Hustlers

Similar Reads: *Hell Razor Honeys* is the story of an all-female crew whose members used to be enemies but now stick up for each other. For more about friends who used to be enemies, try Erick S. Gray's *Nasty Girls* or Brandie's *Clique*. For more about all-female hustling crews, try Nisa Santiago's *Cartier Cartel*, K'wan's *Eve*, or Allysha Hamber's *Northside Clit*. Anthony Whyte's <u>Ghetto Girls</u> series is another saga about teen girls who stick up for each other.

Frenemies

Novels in this section focus on the kind of friends who stab each other in the back. Examples include T. Styles's *Black and Ugly*, in which Sky constantly puts down her friend Parade and Parade sleeps with Sky's man, and Black Artemis's *Explicit Content*, in which two former best friends are separated by taking different paths to success in the music industry.

Antoinette, Ashley.

The Prada Plan. **West Babylon, NY: Urban Books, 2009. 264pp. ISBN 978-1601621573, 1601621574.** ☞ ❲❲

The last thing Disaya Morgan's mother tells her before being killed is that every woman needs a Prada Plan—a way to get money. Disaya takes this lesson with her for the rest of her life. In the foster care facility where she is sent after her mother's death, six-year-old Disaya meets Mona, and the two become inseparable when both are abused by the proprietor's seventeen-year-old son. As adults, Disaya and Mona stay close, and together they are recruited by a slick player named Ronnie B, who heads an organization called Elite Management. At first Disaya, Mona, and their Elite mentor Leah enjoy the exclusive parties and opportunities Ronnie B gets them. But when Ronnie B puts pressure on Disaya and Mona to have unsafe, unwanted sex with clients, the two friends grow apart. Meanwhile, Disaya becomes involved with a hustler called Indie. A juicy tale of friendship, betrayal, and the importance of having a Plan.

Keywords: Abuse; New York; Sex Industry

Similar Reads: *The Prada Plan* is a story of abuse, street smarts, and juicy sex. For more children facing abuse together, try Sherrie Walker's *Mistress of the Game*. For more stories of women trapped in a dangerous operation, try Miasha's *Chaser* or C. Stecko's *Brooklyn Brothel*. For more steamy sexuality mixed with a high-stakes plot, try Deja King's <u>Bitch</u> series or Chunichi's <u>Gangster's Girl</u> series.

Core Collection: Adult

Baker, T. N.

Sheisty Series. ᕀᕀ ((

"Sheisty" means dirty, greedy, and underhanded, and that's the perfect word for how things go among three former best friends in Southside Jamaica, Queens.

Keywords: Multiple Perspectives; Queens, NY; Sex Industry

Similar Reads: Sheisty is a high-drama story told from multiple perspectives about three friends who may as well be enemies. For more about drama and competition between friends, try Kendall Banks's *Rich Girls*, E. R. McNair's *Hood Rats*, or T. Styles's *Black and Ugly*, all of which are told from multiple perspectives.

Classic

Core Collection: Adult

Sheisty. Columbus, OH: Triple Crown Publications, 2004. 170 pp. ISBN 9780974789590.

> Stuck up Epiphany relies on her looks and her sex appeal to get ahead. Wholesome Keisha has a new baby and plans to get married and get a master's degree. Shana, tired of Epiphany acting superior, gets a new job as a stripper but keeps it secret. Add in a few men, some drugs, a rape, and some violent scheming, and you've got serious drama. Short chapters with alternating voices keep the story lively.

Still Sheisty. Columbus, OH: Triple Crown Publications, 2004. 248pp. ISBN 0976234904, 9780976234906.

> In this volume, the competition and drama among Keisha, Shana, and Epiphany continue.

Banks, Kendall.

Rich Girls. **Brandywine, MD: Life Changing Books, 2008. 229pp. ISBN 9781934230824, 1934230820.** ᕀᕀ ((

For three young women in Vegas, getting money is harder than it looks. Nadia is broke but pretends to her friends she's getting money, like they are. Tori is shameless and devious and will do whatever it takes to get hers, no matter who gets hurt in the process. Jewell, the leader of their crew, is spoiled and grew up rich: her trick is to pretend to her parents that she needs money to further her career. When money is good, Nadia, Tori, and Jewell are best friends. But when it's tight, tension builds. Which rich girl will end up on top?

Keywords: Las Vegas, NV; Multiple Perspectives

1

2

3

4

5

6

7

8

9

10

11

Similar Reads: *Rich Girls* is a tense, high-drama story of three women whose friendship is mixed with competition and cruelty. For more friends who could just as easily be enemies, try T. N. Baker's *Sheisty*, Mark Anthony's *Queen Bee*, or T. Styles's *Black and Ugly*.

Black Artemis.

Explicit Content. **New York: New American Library, 2004. 332pp. ISBN 045-1212754, 9780451212757.** ☞ ((

Cassandra Rivers and Leila Aponte are old friends trying to make it in the hip-hop music industry. Cassandra is determined not to "sell out," and their friendship takes a turn when Leila signs with Explicit Content, a shady, commercial record label. Hard-hitting and full of unexpected twists, the novel gives an insider's perspective into the hip-hop music industry, friendships, and the particular struggles of women who seek success.

Keywords: Character-Driven; Latino Characters; Music Industry; New York

Similar Reads: *Explicit Content* is a character-driven novel about the music industry and the evolution of a friendship between two independent women. For more about the music industry and its shady dealings, try *Cut Throat* by K. Roland Williams or *Cash Rules* by Thomas Long. For more character-driven novels about women, try Keisha Ervin's *Torn* or Tracy Brown's *White Lines*.

Holmes, Shannon.

B-More Careful. **New York: Teri Woods Publishing, 2001. 288pp. ISBN 978-0967224916.** ☞ ☞ ((

Stylish, scheming Netta always gets her way, with her two best girlfriends and with every man she meets. She sets her sights on Black, an up-and-coming drug dealer with good looks and a whole lot of cash. Black falls in love with Netta, but when he finds out she's been using him, he's set on revenge. Meanwhile, Netta's friend Mimi develops a devastating drug addiction. This first novel by prolific author Shannon Holmes enticingly pulls readers into Netta's fast life and Black's rise on the streets.

Keywords: Baltimore; Drug Addiction; Revenge; Women Hustlers

Similar Reads: *B-More Careful* is a classic contemporary street novel about a queen bee character and her two friends that explores themes of revenge, drug addiction, and material wealth. For more characters like Netta, try Deja King's Bitch series or KaShamba Williams's *Mind Games*. For more characters becoming rich drug dealers like Black, try Gregory Dixon's *Cake Man* or Ed McNair's *My Time to Shine*. For other stories of drug addiction, try Tracy Brown's *White Lines* or Lisa Lennox's *Crack Head*.

Classic

Core Collection: Adult

Long, Thomas.

A Thug's Life. **West Babylon, NY: Urban Books, 2004. 212pp. ISBN 097-4702536, 9780974702537.** ☞☞ ❨❨

Years ago, Dayvon and Ty, friends since they were kids, started the DFL crew—Dogs for Life. They took a vow to be in the drug game together for as long as they lived. Now Ty's in prison, and Dayvon is ready to retire from being a kingpin. But when Dayvon breaks the news to Ty, Ty reminds him of their vow, and that the price of breaking it is death. Life is good for Dayvon now—he's got plenty of cash, and sexy, available women in multiple cities to keep him company—but when Ty starts plotting to bring him down, the game gets a lot more complicated.

Keywords: Baltimore; Prison

Similar Reads: *A Thug's Life* is the story of two friends and one-time hustling partners whose lives have gone in different directions. For more about friendships between hustlers who grew up together, try Anya Nicole's *Corporate Corner Boyz* or Eric Fleming's *Lust, Love, and Lies.*

McNair, E. R.

The Hood Rats. **Columbus, OH: Triple Crown Publications, 2008. 298pp. ISBN 9780979951787, 097995178X.** ☞☞ ❨

LaBrea, better known as Bre, and her three girls call themselves the Hood Rats. CeeCee and Nesha are wild, outspoken "dime pieces." Nikki is jealous of CeeCee but is also secretly sleeping with her man. Bre, the quietest, always ends up the designated driver. The Hood Rats have always been down for each other, but when CeeCee's man gets shot at a party, a chain reaction begins. Who will stay loyal to whom when it all plays out?

Keywords: Drug Addiction; Gary, IN; Multiple Perspectives

Similar Reads: *The Hood Rats* tells a high-drama story of four women friends who sometimes stick up for each other but just as often go behind each other's backs. For more "frenemies," try T. Styles's *Black and Ugly*, T. N Baker's *Sheisty*, or Kendall Banks's *Rich Girls.*

Miller, Mika.

And God Created Woman. **New York: Ghettoheat, 2007. 224pp. ISBN 978-0974298269, 0974298263.** ☞ ❨❨

Four Philadelphia women's lives intersect in this slice of life tale. Mekka is a stripper with two children who makes it a rule to keep business and pleasure strictly separate. Tristan is a successful businesswoman who is all about work, despite her coworkers' suggestions that she needs a man in her life. Melanie, better known as Mel, is a self-identified dyke who is interested in Mekka. Shawn, who works for Tristan, is a pushover who's been known to have one too many drinks when the going gets tough. Throughout the book, we follow each woman through a wild set of circumstances that just might end badly.

Keywords: GLBTQ; Multiple Perspectives; Philadelphia; Sex Industry

Similar Reads: *And God Created Woman* is a slice of life tale featuring a variety of perspectives and a lesbian subplot. *Diamond Playgirls* is another story of several different women with their own personal dramas and how their lives intersect. For more positively portrayed lesbian characters, try *Strapped* by Laurinda D. Brown or *Hush* by Amaleka McCall.

Nicole, Anya.

Corporate Corner Boyz. **Jamaica, NY: Q-Boro Books, 2008. 239pp. ISBN 193-396751X, 9781933967516.** ☞ ((

Brandon and Chris are best friends who co-run a hip-hop label, Indigo Records, in Philadelphia. Brandon is a "corporate cornerboy," a guy with an Ivy League degree who came up in the projects. Chris is 100 percent street and 100 percent ready to jump into bed with any woman—or man—he can get. In their business partnership, tensions run high. And it only gets worse when Brandon starts seeing Mia, a model with expensive tastes. Can their friendship—and their record label—survive?

Keywords: GLBTQ; Music Industry; Philadelphia

Similar Reads: *Corporate Corner Boyz* features a friendship between a die-hard hustler and a college graduate, the music industry, and a bisexual male character. For more friends who grew up together but took separate paths, try Thomas Long's *Thug's Life* or Eric Fleming's *Lust, Love, and Lies*. For more about working in the music industry, try Rahsaan Ali's *Selfish Intentions* or C-Murder's *Death Around the Corner*. For more bisexual male characters, try Clarence Nero's *Three Sides to Every Story* or P. L. Wilson's *Holy Hustler*.

Ridley, Tonya.

Talk of the Town. **Brandywine, MD: Life Changing Books, 252pp. ISBN 1934230928, 9781934230923.** ☞ ☞ ((

Diamond and Mya, two women from Atlanta, work together to set up men and rob them. Mya is in charge, and Diamond follows her lead whether she wants to or not. Diamond wants to make enough money to open her own hair salon one day, and she's willing to put up with taking orders from Mya—and taking advantage of men in vulnerable positions—to do it. But when Mya puts Diamond onto Scottie, a rich and powerful white man, Diamond finds herself in over her head. This wild ride explores the pleasures and dangers of scheming . . . and the consequences.

Keywords: Atlanta; Sex Industry; Street Code; Women Hustlers

Similar Reads: *Talk of the Town* is about scheming women and the pitfalls of robberies gone wrong. For more women who set up men, try J. M. Benjamin's *Down in the Dirty*, JaQuavis Coleman's *Dopeman's Wife*, Anna J's *Get Money Chicks*, or A. J. Rivers's *Cash*

Money. For more about what happens when a robbery goes wrong, try Brandon McCalla's *Spot Rushers* or Allysha Hamber's *Northside Clit.*

Styles, T.

Black and Ugly Series. 🐧🐧 ((

Backstabbing enemies and warm childhood friendships combine in this series about four friends in the Washington, D.C., area.

Keywords: GLBTQ; Hyattsville, MD; Multiple Perspectives; Sex Industry

Similar Reads: *Black and Ugly* contains both warm friendships and backstabbing and features a positively portrayed GLBTQ character. For more about friends who may as well be enemies, try E. R. McNair's *Hood Rats* or T. N. Baker's *Sheisty.* For more positively portrayed GLBTQ characters, try Reginald Hall's *In Love with a Thug* or Treasure E. Blue's *Harlem Girl Lost.*

Black and Ugly. Columbus, OH: Triple Crown Publications, 2006. 241pp. ISBN 9780977880416, 0977880419.

> Parade Knight has dark skin and acne scars, and everyone's been telling her she's ugly for years. Sky has good looks and a bad attitude. Miss Wayne, who considers himself one of the girls, tries to stand up for Parade. Daffany is modest, more of an "Express"-type girl than a designer clothes type. Parade sleeps with Sky's man, figuring she'd better take what she can get. Daffany has sex for money until she gets disturbing news about her health. Drama is everywhere, and then the unthinkable happens: the friends get word of a murder. Could one of them be responsible?

Black and Ugly as Ever. Owings Mills, MD: The Cartel Publications, 2008. 204pp. ISBN 9780979493164, 0979493161.

> In this second volume, Parade, Daffany, and Miss Wayne return and stay strong for each other in the face of HIV, infidelity, and life coming between them.

1

2

3

4

5

6

7

8

9

10

11

Chapter 11

Poetry, Memoir, and Nonfiction

Some works of street lit are nonfiction, including poetry, memoir, and advice. Memoirs of street life published through mainstream publishers are included here, as are works by authors who have written traditional street novels or are involved in street lit publishing. Crystal Lacey Winslow, for example, whose book of autobiographical poetry *Up Close & Personal* appears in this chapter, is the founder of Melodrama Publishing.

Although some of these titles have a different publication history, intended audience, or type of appeal than most street lit, they are included here because the subject matter is relevant to street lit readers. Reymundo Sanchez's *My Bloody Life*, for example, recounts the author's own history with gang life, and Felicia "Snoop" Pearson and David Ritz's *Grace After Midnight* describes Pearson's coming of age on the streets and time spent in prison.

50 Cent.

From Pieces to Weight: Once Upon a Time in Southside Queens. **New York: Pocket Books, 2006 (2005). 223pp. ISBN 0743488040, 9780743488044.** 🐗🐗 (

Before he started G-Unit Books, rapper 50 Cent told his own story. Growing up in Queens with his grandmother, young Curtis Jackson Jr. learned the laws of the streets. Before the age of eighteen, he learned to fight, gamble, and cook up cocaine. After spending time in prison, 50 met Jam Master Jay and entered the music business. But it wasn't until after he famously got shot nine times and survived that the rapper's career took off. A fast-paced, conversational memoir.

Keywords: Memoir; Music Industry; Prison; Queens, NY; Street Code; Teenagers

Similar Reads: *From Pieces to Weight* is a conversational memoir about a boy coming up in the drug game with the help of mentors, then finding success in the entertainment industry. For more about coming of age with a mentor, try Gregory Dixon's *Cake Man* or rapper Dana Dane's novel *Numbers*. Felicia "Snoop" Pearson's *Grace After Midnight* is another memoir about a young person involved in the drug business who became an entertainer.

Core Collection: Young Adult; School Libraries

Carruth, Buffie.

Vixen Icon. Columbus, OH: Triple Crown Publications, 2009. 204pp. ISBN 9780982099636, 0982099630. ☞ (

Now known for her music video appearances, pin-up photos, and connections with celebrities, Buffie Carruth, aka Buffie the Body, describes her roots and her rise to stardom. She spent her childhood among seven brothers and sisters, her adolescence shoplifting and fighting, and her young womanhood as an exotic dancer before achieving fame. Here, Buffie describes her struggles with her body—she was initially considered too skinny to be attractive—some early brushes with drugs and violence, and how her commitment to getting ahead helped her achieve her goals. Sixteen pages of full-color photos are included.

Keywords: Athens, GA; Atlanta; Memoir; Sex Industry

Similar Reads: *Vixen Icon* is a matter of fact, conversational memoir about body image and being a stripper by a woman with a hard childhood who finds fame and success. For more about strippers who enjoy their work, try Shannon Holmes's *Bad Girlz.* Both 50 Cent's *From Pieces to Weight* and Felicia "Snoop" Pearson's *Grace After Midnight* are memoirs that describe the harsh childhood of figures who eventually became famous.

Hickson.

Ghettoheat. New York: Ghettoheat, 2003. 157pp. ISBN 0974298204, 9780974298207. ☞☞ ((

This collection of experimental prose poetry by Hickson, CEO of the publishing company named after the book, evokes images from the down-and-out streets of Harlem, New York. Homelessness, prostitution, desperation, police violence, and sex all emerge as themes, vividly rendered. Hickson's language brings out sounds, smells, spoken words and more. Author and Melodrama Publishing CEO Crystal Lacey Winslow contributes a brief introduction.

Keywords: New York; Poetry

Similar Reads: *Ghettoheat* is a free verse, stream-of-consciousness piece that evokes the streets through imagery. For more imagery that evokes the streets, try Che Parker's *Tragic Flaw.* For another work of poetry by a street lit publisher, try Crystal Lacey Winslow's *Up Close & Personal.*

Core Collection: Adult; Young Adult

LeBlanc, Adrian Nicole.

Random Family: Love, Drugs, Trouble, and Coming of Age in the Bronx. New York: Scribner, 2004 (2003). 408pp. ISBN 0743254430, 9780743254434. ☞ (

Jessica is a Puerto Rican teenager living on Tremont Avenue in the Bronx in the 1980s. She has a way with men and stays out late on the streets, and she drops out of ninth grade to give birth to her first child. Her mother Lourdes is developing a cocaine habit, and her brother Cesar is learning to sell drugs himself. The story follows Jessica and those around her from apartment to apartment, through sex, motherhood, brief fortune, prison, and abuse. Unlike most street literature, this book is written by an outsider. LeBlanc, a journalist, reconstructs years of family drama from observation, interviews, court testimony, and FBI recordings. The narrative voice is neutral, neither passing judgment on the family's actions nor exulting in their gains.

Keywords: Abuse; Bronx, NY; Latino Characters; Prison; Street Code

Similar Reads: *Random Family* is a matter of fact family drama exploring motherhood, addiction, abuse, and the drug trade. Though few works of street lit take as dispassionate a tone as LeBlanc's, many treat similar issues. For more emotional takes on drug addiction, try Tracy Brown's *White Lines* or Y. Blak Moore's *Slipping*. For more about family abuse, try Sapphire's *Push* or Michele A. Fletcher's *Charge It to the Game*.

McCall, Nathan.

Makes Me Wanna Holler: A Young Black Man in America. **New York: Random House, 1994. 404pp. ISBN 0679412689, 9780679412687.** ⲅⲅⲅ ⲅ ((

Now a well-known journalist, Nathan McCall grew up in a rough part of Portsmouth, Virginia. Conversational, unflinching, and righteously angry, his memoir speaks honestly and candidly about the violence and pressures of his childhood and adolescence, his transformation in prison, and the ill effects of racism on the lives of young black men.

Keywords: Memoir; Mentors; Portsmouth, VA; Prison; Social Commentary; Teenagers

Similar Reads: *Makes Me Wanna Holler* is a socially conscious memoir about growing up within a culture of violent dysfunction. For another true story of a teenage boy who fell into violent acts, try *My Bloody Life*, Reymundo Sanchez's memoir of gang membership. For street novels that explore the effects of racism on young black men's choices, try Mark Anthony's *Paper Chasers* or Leo Sullivan's *Life*.

Classic

Core Collection: Adult; Young Adult; School Libraries

Pearson, Felicia "Snoop," and David Ritz.

Grace After Midnight: A Memoir. **New York: Grand Central, 2009 (2007). 217pp. ISBN 9780446195195, 0446195197.** ⲅⲅ (

Best known for her role on HBO's *The Wire*, Felicia "Snoop" Pearson was born in East Baltimore to a crack-addicted mother. Calling herself "a baby born to die," Pearson speaks in plain language of her painful childhood. She was a tomboy attracted to other girls (her first crush was Smurfette), and she quickly found her way to street life. Then, in self-defense, she killed a woman and was sent to a prison known as "the Cut." Snoop's memoir is emotionally intense but ends with hope when actors from *The Wire* invite her to join their cast.

Keywords: Baltimore; GLBTQ; Memoir; Overcoming Adversity; Prison; Teenagers

Similar Reads: *Grace After Midnight* is an uplifting memoir about a harsh childhood, time in prison, and ultimate success and redemption, featuring a female character attracted to women. For another memoir of an entertainer with harsh beginnings, try 50 Cent's *From Pieces to Weight*. To read more about women and the GLBTQ experience in prison, try Amaleka McCall's *Hush* or Damon "Amin" Meadows and Jason Poole's *Convict's Candy*.

Core Collection: Young Adult; School Libraries

Sanchez, Reymundo.

My Bloody Life Series.

Reymundo Sanchez is the pseudonym of a former member of Chicago's Latin Kings. In these grim memoirs, Sanchez describes his life as a gang member and the difficulty of leaving the Latin Kings once he was a part of their violent and destructive operation.

Keywords: Abuse; Chicago; Drug Addiction; Gangs; Latino Characters; Memoir; Street Code; Teenagers

Similar Reads: *My Bloody Life* is a bleak memoir warning readers of the emptiness and cruelty of gang membership. For fiction that is also critical of gang membership, try James Hendricks's *Good Day to Die* or Rochan Morgan's *Crossroads*. For another memoir of a disadvantaged young person involved in activities he now regrets, try Nathan McCall's *Makes Me Wanna Holler*.

Core Collection: Adult; Young Adult; School Libraries

My Bloody Life: The Making of a Latin King. Chicago: Chicago Review Press, 2001. 299pp. ISBN 1556524277, 9781556524271.

> Reymundo Sanchez, a former Latin King, tells the true story of his unhappy childhood and his transformation into a violent Chicago gang member. From his initiation into sex at the hands of an older woman to his vicious initiation into gang life, Sanchez shows how fear, pressure, and the absence of positive alternatives informed his decisions. Told in a matter of fact tone, Sanchez's story reveals the bleakness and meaningless destruction of gang culture.

Once a King, Always a King: The Unmaking of a Latin King. Chicago: Chicago Review Press, 2003. 286pp. ISBN 1556525052, 9781556525056.

> In *My Bloody Life*, Sanchez joined the Latin Kings. In volume 2, Sanchez recounts his difficulties leaving the Latin Kings and moving on after gang life.

Stringer, Vickie M.

How to Succeed in the Publishing Game. Columbus, OH: Triple Crown Publications, 2005. 127pp. ISBN 097678940X, 9780976789406.

Vickie Stringer, wildly successful CEO of Triple Crown Publications, offers a slim, commonsense guide to independent publishing. From startup capital to tax law to distribution and marketing, this guide covers topics relevant to any aspiring publisher.

Keywords: Advice; Street Code

Similar Reads: *How to Succeed in the Publishing Game* is the only widely read guide written specifically for aspiring street authors and entrepreneurs. To read a fictional account of Stringer's street smarts, try her <u>Let That Be the Reason</u> series.

Winslow, Crystal Lacey.

Up Close & Personal. **Bellport, NY: Melodrama Publishing, 2000. 96pp. ISBN 097170211X, 9780971702110.** ☞ ❨❨

Originally published in 2000, this book of poems by Melodrama publisher Winslow documents her first relationships and the street wisdom she acquired at a young age. Some poems are sensual; others begin with the line "I grew up amongst prostitutes and pimps" and describe her difficult childhood. A varied and moving collection.

Keywords: Abuse; Memoir; Poetry; Teenagers

Similar Reads: *Up Close & Personal* is book of autobiographical poetry that evokes a childhood on the streets and the lessons learned there. For more poetry, try Hickson's *Ghettoheat*. For more stories that evoke a childhood "amongst prostitutes and pimps," try Donald Goines's classic *Whoreson* or Tanika Lynch's brutal *Whore*.

Zane.

Dear G-Spot: Straight Talk About Sex and Love. **New York: Atria, 2007. 243pp. ISBN 9780743457057, 0743457056.** ☞ ❨❨❨

In the spirit of her unapologetically explicit fiction, Zane talks pleasure with her readers. Subtitled "Straight Talk About Sex and Love," this volume takes the form of an advice column. Readers ask Zane questions about love, marriage, and the nitty-gritty aspects of sex, and the famous erotica writer responds with matter of fact, candid words.

Keywords: Advice

Similar Reads: Though *Dear G-Spot* is a book of advice, it features Zane's usual frankness and celebration of sexuality. For more of Zane's candid and juicy sex talk, try her *Sex Chronicles* collections or her anthologies *Chocolate Flava, Caramel Flava, Honey Flava,* or *Purple Panties*.

1

2

3

4

5

6

7

8

9

10

11

Appendix A

Core Collection for Adults

These titles constitute a core street lit collection for adults in a large public library. This list includes classic titles, titles with high or enduring popularity, titles representing unique themes or perspectives, and titles by prominent authors.

Anthony, Mark. *Paper Chasers*

Anthony, Mark. *Reasonable Doubt*

Anthony, Mark. *The Take Down*

Antoinette, Ashley. *The Prada Plan*

Around the Way Girls Series

    Around the Way Girls

    Around the Way Girls 2

    Around the Way Girls 3

    Around the Way Girls 4

    Around the Way Girls 5

    Around the Way Girls 6

Ashley and JaQuavis. The Cartel Series

    The Cartel

    The Cartel 2

Ashley and JaQuavis. *Dirty Money*

Ashley and JaQuavis. *Supreme Clientele*

Azárel. Bruised Series

    Bruised

    Bruised 2: The Ultimate Revenge

Azárel. *Carbon Copy*

Azárel. *Daddy's House*

Baker, T. N. Sheisty Series

    Sheisty

    Still Sheisty

Benjamin, J. M. <u>Ride or Die Chick Series</u>

    Ride or Die Chick: The Story of Treacherous and Teflon

    Ride or Die Chick

Blue, Treasure E. *Harlem Girl Lost*

Blue, Treasure E. *Keyshia and Clyde*

Blue, Treasure E. *A Street Girl Named Desire*

Brown, Laurinda D. *Strapped*

Brown, Laurinda D. *Walk Like a Man*

Brown, Tracy. *Black*

Brown, Tracy. *Criminal Minded*

Brown, Tracy. <u>Dime Piece Series</u>

    Dime Piece

    Twisted

Brown, Tracy. *White Lines*

Carter, Quentin. <u>Hoodwinked Series</u>

    Hoodwinked

    In Cahootz

Cash. <u>Trust No Man Series</u>

    Trust No Man

    Trust No Man 2: Disloyalty Is Unforgiveable

Chunichi. <u>A Gangster's Girl Series</u>

    A Gangster's Girl Saga

    The Return of a Gangster's Girl

Clark, Wahida. <u>Payback Is a Mutha Series</u>

    Payback Is a Mutha

    Payback with Ya Life

Clark, Wahida. <u>Thugs Series</u>

    Thugs and the Women Who Love Them

    Every Thug Needs a Lady

    Thug Matrimony

    Thug Lovin'

Endy. <u>In My Hood Series</u>

    In My Hood

    In My Hood II

    In My Hood 3

Ervin, Keisha. *Chyna Black*

Ervin, Keisha. *Gunz and Roses*

Ervin, Keisha. *Torn*

Goines, Donald. *Black Girl Lost*

Goines, Donald. *Dopefiend*

Goines, Donald. *Whoreson*

Hernandez, Treasure. <u>Flint Series</u>

    Choosing Sides: Flint, Book 1

    Working Girls: Flint, Book 2

    Back to the Streets: Flint, Book 3

    Resurrection: Flint, Book 4

    Back in the Hood: Flint, Book 5

    A King Is Born: Flint, Book 6

    Girl from Flint, A: Flint, Book 7

Hickson. *Ghettoheat*

Holmes, Shannon. *B-More Careful*

Holmes, Shannon. <u>Bad Girlz Series</u>

    Bad Girlz

    Bad Girlz 4 Life

Holmes, Shannon. *Dirty Game*

J, Anna. *Snow White*

Jones, Solomon. *Ride or Die*

K'wan. <u>Gangsta Series</u>

    Gangsta: An Urban Tragedy

    Gutter

K'wan. *Street Dreams*

King, Deja. <u>Bitch Series</u>

    Bitch

    Bitch Reloaded

    The Bitch Is Back

    Queen Bitch

    Last Bitch Standing

King, Deja. *Trife Life to Lavish*

King, Joy. <u>Stackin' Paper Series</u>

    Stackin' Paper

    Stackin' Paper II: Genesis' Payback

Lennox, Lisa. <u>Crack Head Series</u>

>*Crack Head*
>
>*Crack Head II: Laci's Revenge*

McCall, Amaleka. *Myra: A Twisted Tale of Karma*

McCall, Nathan. *Makes Me Wanna Holler*

McCaulsky, Marlon. *The Pink Palace*

McNair, Ed. <u>My Time to Shine Series</u>

>*My Time to Shine*
>
>*Black Reign*
>
>*Black Reign 2*

McNeal, Mallori. <u>A Down Chick Series</u>

>*A Down Chick*
>
>*The Set Up*

Meadows, Damon "Amin," and Jason Poole. *Convict's Candy*

Miasha. *Mommy's Angel*

Miasha. <u>Secret Society Series</u>

>*Secret Society*
>
>*Never Enough*

Mink, Meesha, and De'nesha Diamond. <u>Bentley Manor Series</u>

>*Desperate Hoodwives*
>
>*Shameless Hoodwives*
>
>*The Hood Life*

Moore, Shavon. <u>Baby Girl Series</u>

>*Baby Girl*
>
>*Baby Girl II*

Moore. Shavon, *Ecstasy*

Noire. *Candy Licker*

Noire. *Hittin' the Bricks*

Prince, Leondrei. <u>Bloody Money Series</u>

>*Bloody Money*
>
>*Bloody Money 2: The Game Ain't Fair!*
>
>*Bloody Money 3: The City Under Siege*

Prince, Leondrei. <u>Tommy Good Series</u>

>*The Tommy Good Story*
>
>*The Tommy Good Story II: You Reap What You Sow*

Relentless Aaron. *The Last Kingpin*

Relentless Aaron. <u>Push Series</u>

   Push

   To Live and Die in Harlem

Ridley, Tonya. *The Takeover*

Sanchez, Reymundo. <u>My Bloody Life Series</u>

   My Bloody Life: The Making of a Latin King

   Once a King, Always a King: The Unmaking of a Latin King

Santiago, Nisa. *Cartier Cartel*

Sapphire. *Push*

Sidi. <u>Fatou Series</u>

   Fatou, an African Girl in Harlem

   Fatou: Return to Harlem

Slim, Iceberg. *Pimp*

Souljah, Sister. *The Coldest Winter Ever*

Souljah, Sister. *Midnight: A Gangster Love Story*

Stringer, Vickie. <u>Dirty Red Series</u>

   Dirty Red

   Still Dirty

Stringer, Vickie. <u>Let That Be the Reason Series</u>

   Let That Be the Reason

   Imagine This

   The Reason Why

Styles, T. <u>A Hustler's Son Series</u>

   A Hustler's Son

   A Hustler's Son II: Live or Die in New York

Sullivan, Leo. *Innocent*

Sullivan, Leo. *Life*

Swinson, Kiki, *Playing Dirty Series*

   Playing Dirty

   Notorious

Swinson, Kiki. <u>Wifey Series</u>

   Wifey

   I'm Still Wifey

> *Life After Wifey*
>
> *Still Wifey Material*

Thomas, Antoine "Inch." <u>Flower's Bed Series</u>

> *Flower's Bed*
>
> *Black Roses*

Tiphani. <u>Millionaire Mistress Series</u>

> *The Millionaire Mistress*
>
> *Still a Mistress: The Saga Continues*
>
> *Millionaire Mistress: Part 3, Chloe's Revenge*

Turner, Nikki. *Ghetto Superstar*

Turner, Nikki. <u>A Hustler's Wife Series</u>

> *A Hustler's Wife*
>
> *Forever a Hustler's Wife*

Turner, Nikki. *Riding Dirty on I-95*

Tyree, Omar. <u>Flyy Girl Series</u>

> *Flyy Girl*
>
> *For the Love of Money*
>
> *Boss Lady*

Tyree, Omar. *The Last Street Novel*

Warren, Mike. <u>A Private Affair Series</u>

> *A Private Affair*
>
> *Sweet Swagger*

Whitaker, Tu-Shonda L. <u>Flip Side of the Game Series</u>

> *Flip Side of the Game*
>
> *Game Over*

White, Cynthia. <u>Queen Series</u>

> *Queen*
>
> *Always a Queen*

Whyte, Anthony. <u>Ghetto Girls Series</u>

> *Ghetto Girls*
>
> *Ghetto Girls Too*
>
> *Ghetto Girls 3*
>
> *Ghetto Girls IV: Young Luv*

Williams, Brittani. *Daddy's Little Girl*

Williams, Karen, *The People vs. Cashmere*

Woods, Teri. *Alibi*

Woods, Teri. <u>Dutch Series</u>

> *Dutch*
>
> *Dutch II: Angel's Revenge*

Woods, Teri. <u>True to the Game Series</u>
> *True to the Game*
> *True to the Game II*
> *True to the Game III*

Zane. <u>Addicted Series</u>
> *Addicted*
> *Nervous*

Zane. <u>Sex Chronicles Series</u>
> *The Sex Chronicles: Shattering the Myth*
> *Gettin' Buck Wild: Sex Chronicles II*
> *Zane's Sex Chronicles*

Zane, ed. <u>Caramel Flava Series</u>

> *Caramel Flava*
>
> *Sensuality: Caramel Flava II*

Zane, ed. <u>Chocolate Flava Series</u>

> *Chocolate Flava*
>
> *Succulent: Chocolate Flava II*

Appendix B

Core Collection for Young Adults (Public Library)

These titles constitute a core collection for young adults in a public library. Please note that the titles recommended for teens are not "clean" titles but are titles most likely to have meaning for young people. Included here are classics of the genre, titles that are highly popular with teenagers, coming-of-age stories, and stories with prominent teenage characters.

For more information about street lit and young adults, see the section in the introduction called "Street Lit in the Library."

50 Cent. *From Pieces to Weight*

50 Cent and Mark Anthony. *Harlem Heat*

Anthony, Mark. *Lady's Night*

Anthony, Mark. *Paper Chasers*

Anthony, Mark. *Reasonable Doubt*

Ashley and JaQuavis. <u>The Cartel Series</u>

    The Cartel

    The Cartel 2

Baker, T. N. <u>Sheisty Series</u>

    Sheisty

    Still Sheisty

Benjamin, J. M. <u>Ride or Die Chick Series</u>

    Ride or Die Chick: The Story of Treacherous and Teflon

    Ride or Die Chick

Blue, Treasure E. *Harlem Girl Lost*

Britt, A. C. *London Reign*

Brown, Laurinda D. *Strapped*

Brown, Tracy. *Black*

Brown, Tracy. *Criminal Minded*

Brown, Tracy. *White Lines*

C-Murder. *Death Around the Corner*

Dane, Dana. *Numbers*

Desiree, Dawn. *Sunshine & Rain*

DeVaughn, LaShonda. *A Hood Chick's Story*

Dixon, Gregory. *The Cake Man*

Ervin, Keisha. *Chyna Black*

G, Divine. *Baby Doll*

G, Mike. *Young Assassin*

Goines, Donald. *Black Girl Lost*

Gray, Erick S. *Money Power Respect*

Hendricks, James. *A Good Day to Die*

Hickson. *Ghettoheat*

Hilton, Erica. *10 Crack Commandments*

Holmes, Shannon. <u>Bad Girlz Series</u>

    Bad Girlz

    Bad Girlz 4 Life

Holmes, Shannon. *Dirty Game*

Holmes, Shannon. *Never Go Home Again*

J, Anna. *Snow White*

Jihad. *Baby Girl*

Johnson, S. M. *It Can Happen in a Minute*

Jones, Solomon. *Ride or Die*

K'wan. <u>Gangsta Series</u>

    Gangsta: An Urban Tragedy

    Gutter

K'wan. *Street Dreams*

King, Darrell. <u>Dirty South Series</u>

    Dirty South

    Mo Dirty: Still Stuntin'

Lennox, Lisa. <u>Crack Head Series</u>

    Crack Head

    Crack Head II: Laci's Revenge

McCall, Amaleka. *Myra: A Twisted Tale of Karma*

McCall, Nathan. *Makes Me Wanna Holler*

McCaulsky, Marlon. *The Pink Palace*

McNair, Ed. <u>My Time to Shine Series</u>

    My Time to Shine

    Black Reign

    Black Reign 2

McNeal, Mallori. <u>A Down Chick Series</u>

    A Down Chick

    The Set Up

Miasha. *Mommy's Angel*

Miasha. *Sistah for Sale*

Moore, Shavon. <u>Baby Girl Series</u>

    Baby Girl

    Baby Girl II

Moore, Shavon. *Ecstasy*

Moore, Y. Blak. *Slipping*

Morgan, Rochan. *Crossroads*

Pearson, Felicia "Snoop," and David Ritz. *Grace After Midnight*

Prince, Leondrei, <u>Tommy Good Series</u>

    The Tommy Good Story

    The Tommy Good Story II: You Reap What You Sow

Quartay, Nane. *Come Get Some*

Rhodes, Evie. *Street Vengeance*

Ridley, Tonya. *The Takeover*

Sanchez, Reymundo. <u>My Bloody Life Series</u>

    My Bloody Life: The Making of a Latin King

    Once a King, Always a King: The Unmaking of a Latin King

Santiago, Nisa. *Cartier Cartel*

Sapphire. *Push*

Seven. *Gorilla Black*

Sidi. <u>Fatou Series</u>

    Fatou, an African Girl in Harlem

    Fatou: Return to Harlem

Sidi. *The Lesbian's Wife*

Souljah, Sister. *The Coldest Winter Ever*

Souljah, Sister. *Midnight: A Gangster Love Story*

Stacy-Deanne. *Everlasting*

Styles, T. <u>A Hustler's Son Series</u>

    A Hustler's Son

    A Hustler's Son II: Live or Die in New York

Thomas, Antoine "Inch., <u>Flower's Bed Series</u>

    Flower's Bed

    Black Roses

Turner, Nikki. *Ghetto Superstar*

Turner, Nikki. <u>A Hustler's Wife Series</u>

    A Hustler's Wife

    Forever a Hustler's Wife

Tyree, Omar. <u>Flyy Girl Series</u>

    Flyy Girl

    For the Love of Money

    Boss Lady

Tyree, Omar. *The Last Street Novel*

Walker, Sherrie. *Mistress of the Game*

White, Cynthia. <u>Queen Series</u>

    Queen

    Always a Queen

Whyte, Anthony. <u>Ghetto Girls Series</u>

    Ghetto Girls

    Ghetto Girls Too

    Ghetto Girls 3

    Ghetto Girls IV: Young Luv

Williams, Karen. *Harlem on Lock*

Williams, Karen. *The People vs. Cashmere*

Woods, Teri. <u>True to the Game Series</u>

    True to the Game

    True to the Game II

    True to the Game III

Wright, Ana'Gia. *Lil' Sister*

Appendix C

Core Collection for Young Adults (School Library)

The following titles are recommended as a core collection for a high school library. Please note that this is not a list of "clean" titles; nearly all street lit titles contain some amount of sexuality, violence, and profanity. If you plan to collect street lit in a school library, where books are particularly susceptible to challenges, you must be prepared to defend your collection. For more information on the significance of street lit to young people, see the section of this book called "Street Lit in the Library."

Titles included in this collection are classics of the genre, titles that are highly popular with teenagers, coming of age stories, and stories with prominent teenage characters. To support school curricula, emphasis is placed on socially conscious titles, titles with positive messages, and literary titles.

50 Cent. *From Pieces to Weight*

Anthony, Mark. *Paper Chasers*

Anthony, Mark. *Reasonable Doubt*

Blue, Treasure E. *Harlem Girl Lost*

Britt, A. C. *London Reign*

Brown, Laurinda D. *Strapped*

Brown, Tracy. *Black*

Brown, Tracy. *Criminal Minded*

Brown, Tracy. *White Lines*

C-Murder. *Death Around the Corner*

Desiree. *Dawn, Sunshine & Rain*

Ervin, Keisha. *Chyna Black*

Hickson. *Ghettoheat*

Hilton, Erica. *10 Crack Commandments*

Holmes, Shannon. *Never Go Home Again*

Jones, Solomon. *Ride or Die*

Lennox, Lisa. <u>Crack Head Series</u>

   Crack Head

   Crack Head II: Laci's Revenge

McCall, Nathan. *Makes Me Wanna Holler*

McNeal, Mallori. <u>A Down Chick Series</u>

> *A Down Chick*

> *The Set Up*

Miasha, *Sistah for Sale*

Morgan, Rochan. *Crossroads*

Pearson, Felicia "Snoop," and David Ritz. *Grace After Midnight*

Sanchez, Reymundo. <u>My Bloody Life Series</u>

> *My Bloody Life: The Making of a Latin King*

> *Once a King, Always a King: The Unmaking of a Latin King*

Sapphire. *Push*

Seven. *Gorilla Black*

Sidi. <u>Fatou Series</u>

> *Fatou, an African Girl in Harlem*

> *Fatou: Return to Harlem*

Sidi, *The Lesbian's Wife*

Souljah, Sister. *The Coldest Winter Ever*

Souljah, Sister. *Midnight: A Gangster Love Story*

Stacy-Deanne. *Everlasting*

Thomas, Antoine "Inch." <u>Flower's Bed Series</u>

> *Flower's Bed*

> *Black Roses*

Turner, Nikki. *Ghetto Superstar*

Tyree, Omar. <u>Flyy Girl Series</u>

> *Flyy Girl*

> *For the Love of Money*

> *Boss Lady*

Tyree, Omar. *The Last Street Novel*

Williams, Karen. *Harlem on Lock*

Williams, Karen. *The People vs. Cashmere*

Woods, Teri. <u>True to the Game Series</u>

> *True to the Game*

> *True to the Game II*

> *True to the Game III*

Wright, Ana'Gia. *Lil' Sister*

Street Lit Publishers and Imprints

Following are listed significant independent and mainstream publishers of street lit. For large publishing houses, the names of imprints under which street lit is published are also listed.

Amiaya Entertainment
http://www.amiayaentertainment.com/
PO Box 1275
New York, NY 10159
(646) 331-3258

Augustus Publishing
http://www.augustuspublishing.com/
33 Indian Road Suite 3K
New York, NY 10034
(212) 942-9792
info@augustuspublishing.com

The Cartel Publications
http://www.thecartelpublications.com/
5011B Indian Head Highway
Oxon Hill, MD 20745
(240) 724-7225
cartelpublications@yahoo.com

Flowers In Bloom Publishing
http://www.flowersinbloompublishing.com/
PO Box 473106
Brooklyn, NY 11247
(866) 338-4175
flowersinbloom@mail.com

Ghettoheat
http://ghettoheat.com
PO Box 2746
New York, NY 10027
hickson@ghettoheat.com

Hachette Book Group
   http://www.hachettebookgroup.com/
   Street Lit Imprint: Grand Central

Harlem Book Center
   http://www.harlembookcenter.com/
   2355 8th Avenue
   New York, NY 10027
   (212) 316-1213
   Jackie@harlembookcenter.com

Kensington Publishing
   http://www.kensingtonbooks.com/
   119 West 40th Street
   New York, NY 10018
   (800) 221-2647
   Street Lit Imprints: Dafina, Vibe Street Lit

Life Changing Books
http://www.lifechangingbooks.net
   7485 Old Alexander Ferry Road
   Clinton, MD 20735
   (301) 362-6508
   info@lifechangingbooks.net

Melodrama Publishing
   http://www.melodramapublishing.com/
   PO Box 522
   Bellport, NY 11713
   melodramapub@aol.com

Random House
   http://www.randomhouse.com/
   Street Lit Imprints: Ballantine/One World, Striver's Row

Simon & Schuster
   http://www.simonandschuster.com/
   Street Lit Imprints: Pocket Books, Atria

St. Martin's
   http://us.macmillan.com/splash/publishers/st-martins-press.html
   Street Lit Imprints: St. Martin's Griffin, St. Martin's Minotaur

Strebor Books International
   http://www.streborbooks.com/
   PO BOX 6505
   Largo, MD 20792
   (301) 583-0616
   streborbooks@aol.com

Street Knowledge Publishing
http://www.streetknowledgepublishing.com/
205 W. 4th Street
Wilmington, DE 19801-2204
(302) 543-4889

Teri Woods Publishing
http://teriwoodspublishing.com/
PO Box 20069
New York, NY 10001
(201) 840-8660

Triple Crown Publications
http://www.triplecrownpublications.com/
2184 Citygate Drive
Columbus, OH 43219
(614) 478-9402

Urban Books
http://www.urbanbooks.net/
Street Lit Imprints: Q-Boro Books, Urban Books

Wahida Clark Publishing, LLC
http://www.wclarkpublishing.com/
134 Evergreen Place, Suite 305
East Orange, NJ 07018
(973) 678-9982
wahida@wclarkpublishing.com

Resources and Further Reading

For more information about street lit, or to keep up with the latest reviews and release dates, take a look at the resources below.

Articles

Street Lit Today

Barnard, Anne. "Urban Fiction Makes Its Way from Streets to Libraries." *The New York Times,* October 22, 2008. http://www.nytimes.com/2008/10/23/nyregion/23fiction.html

    How Queens Library's embracing street lit has positively affected its patrons.

Broyard, Bliss. "Pulp Princess." *Elle* (July 2009). http://www.elle.com/Pop-Culture/Movies-TV-Music-Books/Pulp-Princess

    Broyard profiles author Miasha and her tireless "hustle."

Koerner, Brendan I. "Candy Licker: A Best-Selling Book About Cunnilingus and Thugs." *Slate*, June 2, 2006. http://www.slate.com/id/2142831/.

    Koerner describes Noire's violent, gritty erotica.

Fialkoff, Francine. "Street Lit Takes a Hit." *Library Journal*, February 1, 2006. http://www.libraryjournal.com/article/CA6299839.html

    A public librarian answers Nick Chiles's editorial criticizing street lit.

Critiques of Street Lit

Chiles, Nick. "Their Eyes Were Reading Smut." *The New York Times*, January 4, 2006. http://www.nytimes.com/2006/01/04/opinion/04chiles.html

    Mainstream African American author Chiles describes his horror at seeing the African American section at his local bookstore expanded to include street lit.

Peterson, Latoya. "The Method, Madness, and Marketing of Street Lit [Response Essay]."

    http://www.racialicious.com/2009/07/29/the-method-madness-and-marketing-of-street-lit-response-essay/.

    Blogger Peterson responds to *Elle*'s profile of Miasha.

Tyree, Omar. "An Urban 'Street Lit' Retirement." *The Daily Voice*, June 19, 2008. http://thedailyvoice.com/voice/2008/06/street-lit-000748.php.

>The noted author of *Flyy Girl* attempts to distance himself from the street lit genre.

Van Kerckhove, Carmen, Tami Winfrey Harris, Latoya Peterson, and Liz Dwyer. "Whitewashed Book Covers, Street Lit, Race and Family." *Addicted to Race Podcast* 113.

>Antiracist activists discuss the social and cultural implications of street lit.

Street Lit and Teens

Corbin, Michael. "The Invisibles: Young Adult Fiction Has Yet to Hear The Voices of Young, Urban, and Black Readers." *Baltimore City Paper*, September 24, 2008. http://citypaper.com/special/story.asp?id=16744.

>A provocative look at YA fiction's shortcomings.

Honig, Megan. "Takin' It to the Street: Teens and Street Lit." *Voice of Youth Advocates* (July/August 2008).

>How to support teen street lit readers in any library.

Jones, Vanessa E. "Urban Fiction Gains Teen Fans and Adult Critics." *Boston Globe*, November 3, 2008. http://www.boston.com/ae/books/articles/2008/11/03/the_real_world/.

>Jones interviews teen urban fiction fans and shares why street lit speaks to them.

Morris, Vanessa. E-Portfolio. www.jahreinaresearch.info/VJMWebsite.

>Vanessa J. Irvin Morris, professor at Drexel University's iSchool, has posted several essays related to street lit and urban teen reading.

Morris, Vanessa, Sandra Hughes-Hassell, Denise E. Agosto, and Darren T. Cottman "Street Lit: Flying Off Teen Fiction Bookshelves in Philadelphia Public Libraries." *Young Adult Library Services* (Fall 2006).

>A group of librarians describe their experience collaborating with Philadelphia teens to create a Teen Street Lit Book Club.

Web Sites and Columns

APOOO Book Club. http://www.apooobooks.com/

>This site for readers of African American fiction of various genres also contains a comprehensive upcoming releases section.

Black Book Releases. http://www.blackbookreleases.com/

> Presented by urban-reviews.com, this Web site lists upcoming African American interest titles in a variety of genres.

Library Journal's "Word on Street Lit."

> Vanessa Morris of Philadelphia and Rollie Welch of Cleveland review new street lit titles in this monthly column.

RAWSISTAZ Literary Group. http://www.rawsistaz.com

> The prolific RAWSISTAZ (RAW is short for "reading and writing") write book reviews for a variety of African American interest genres, including street lit.

Streetfiction.org. http://www.streetfiction.org

> Corrections librarian Daniel Marcou posts short book descriptions, and readers comment with reviews.

Street Literature Review. http://streetlitreview.ning.com/

> Connect with authors and fans on this social network centered around street lit reading and writing.

The Urban Book Source. http://www.theurbanbooksource.com

> This street lit-focused magazine includes book descriptions, author interviews, videos, and a community forum.

Glossary

If you are unfamiliar with street slang, there is no substitute for immersing yourself in street language by reading street lit, listening to hip-hop music, or conversing with people who use street slang in daily conversation. Common terms used in this book, however, are defined below.

B-More. Baltimore

Baby daddy. The father of one's baby.

Baby mama. The mother of one's baby.

Baller. A player who makes large quantities of money, often someone who shows off his wealth.

Boost. To steal or shoplift.

Clique. A crew, usually of women.

Come up. To grow up or rise to power.

Connect. Someone who supplies drug dealers with large quantities of drugs to distribute.

Crew. A group of drug dealers, stick-up artists, or other players or hustlers who work together and have each other's back.

Dime piece. A highly attractive or desirable woman.

Down. In support (of) or committed (to).

Drama. The juicy, voyeuristic "oh no she didn't" factor, including gossip, backstabbing, and betrayals.

The Game. The business of drug dealing.

Ghetto. A poor neighborhood where street culture is prominent, often marked by housing projects, crime, and subpar infrastructure.

Gold digger. A woman looking to be involved with rich men in order to have access to their money.

Government name. A legal or given name.

The Hood. A neighborhood. Often refers to poor neighborhoods where street culture is prominent.

Hood rat. Someone, often a woman, who lives and hangs out in "the hood" with no aspirations of leaving or of working and is often considered sexually promiscuous.

Hustle. A scheme for making money, often but not always illegally.

Hustler. Someone who makes a living from a hustle, such as a drug dealer or con artist.

Mule. Someone who transports drugs or other contraband, often a woman who swallows, inserts, or tapes the contraband to her body to transport it.

O.G. An "original gangster," often someone to be respected because of age, experience level, or status.

Paper. Money.

Paper chaser. Someone whose highest goal is the pursuit of money.

Play. To dupe or trick.

Ride or die chick. A female companion to a male gangster who will support him to the bitter end, often including transporting drugs for him or going to prison for him.

Sheisty. Dirty, greedy, and underhanded.

Snitch. Someone who breaks the code of the streets to give incriminating information to the police.

Street code. The unwritten rules of hustling. Also called the "hustler's code."

Wifey. The number one woman in a man's life.

Author Index

Boldface type indicates the main entry.

Title Index

Boldface type indicates the main entry.

Keyword/Subject Index

About the Author

MEGAN HONIG is a librarian in New York City. She works in young adult service and collection development and frequently speaks to librarians and students about why street lit matters to teens. She is a member of YALSA and an occasional reviewer of young adult fiction.